Directory of Program Grants

Second Edition

A Reference Directory Identifying
Program Grants Available to
Nonprofit Organizations

Research Grant Guides, Inc.
P.O. Box 1214
Loxahatchee, Florida 33470

Richard M. Eckstein
Publisher/Editor

Research and Administrative Staff:
Claire L. Eckstein
Lorraine Moynihan
Debra Reese

Marketing Representative:
CJ Marketing
Cathy J. Tosner
John P. Tosner

Printed in the U.S.A.

ISBN 0-945078-28-5

Table of Contents

Preface

The second edition of the *Directory of Program Grants* will assist fund-raisers seeking grants for program related purposes. The *Directory* identifies foundations which will fund current programs or award grants to start new programs.

To get started, use the *Directory* to research foundations that have previously awarded grants to your type of organization. You should review only the foundations listed within your own state. Be careful to remember that many funders limit grantmaking to their individual geographic areas. Geographic restrictions and grant range are listed when available to our research staff. Next, send a brief letter to the foundation to request a copy of their most recent grant guidelines. Guidelines issued by the funder should always be followed. Before writing a grant proposal, read the suggestions and strategies discussed in the "Introduction" and "Proposal Writing Basics."

Foundations may change their priorities and expenditure levels. Corporate foundations frequently respond to the general economy and may curtail their grantmaking programs until profits reach a satisfactory level. Don't be discouraged if your proposal is not funded on the first try.

Several elements in a successful grant proposal include:

1) Uniqueness of proposal subject matter

2) A clear, well-written application

3) A realistic budget

4) Qualifications of the Project Director

5) Issues of concern to the proposed sponsor

If the proposal warrants, there should be a table of contents to guide the reviewer. A timetable depicting your projected progress may also be helpful. Try to present a readable, professional-looking proposal written in clear language that avoids jargon.

Introduction

Research Grant Guides publishes specialized fund-raising directories. Each directory is an easy to use resource for identifying foundation sources of funding. This Directory, like the others in the series, includes all the information necessary to begin your funding search. This introduction will help you navigate the intricacies of locating just the right foundation sponsors to support your organization. It describes the step-by-step process through which ideas become funded grants. The introduction serves as a guide to the information in the Directory, and together they will help increase your likelihood of being awarded a grant.

What Are Grants?

Although this seems like an obvious question, it is important to understand exactly what a grant is and what it is not before proceeding with a search. It will also be useful to review the nature of foundations as a preface to discussing how to search for grant opportunities.

A grant is a mechanism through which one organization can influence the behavior of another. Grants generally are in the form of money, but they can also be made in the form of technical assistance or equipment. Grants serve as incentives to promote the interests and agenda of the foundation. The foundation awarding the grant is known as the grantor.

Organizations receiving grants are known as grantees. The foundation usually publishes guidelines explaining its interests and procedures for submitting an application or proposal. Any organization wishing to receive a grant should follow the guidelines. The applicant should describe itself and its needs in terms consistent with the foundation's interests.

Foundations generally receive many more applications than they can support. They will choose among them and make decisions based on how well the applicants can promote the foundation's own interests. The successful applicants will be those whose interests are the same or closely aligned with the foundation's and who can demonstrate that their organizations have the necessary experience and competence to carry out the work described in the proposal. Thus, successful applicants always understand the interests of the grantor and present their proposals in those terms. They also always speak with confidence and strength about their programs. Foundations support organizations capable of achieving success in their goals and who have the potential for making a positive impact on the lives of their constituents.

What Are Foundations?

There are several types of organizations calling themselves foundations. We are interested in foundations that award grants, or grantmaking foundations. Unless otherwise specified, when we use the term foundations in this introduction, we mean foundations to which nonprofit organizations may apply for grants.

Foundations can be created by individuals, families or companies interested in setting aside a sum of money to be used for awarding grants. The foundation generally invests the money in an endowment and makes grants from the earnings. In order for foundations to be able to devote as much money as possible for grants, they are not required to pay income taxes on their earnings.

Grants are considered to be in the public interest because they support the activities of tax-exempt nonprofit organizations. The U.S. Internal Revenue Service monitors foundations carefully to ensure that they award grants only to organizations declared tax-exempt. In order to be eligible to receive a grant, applicants must be able to document that their organizations meet all the qualifications listed under Section 501(c)(3) of the IRS Code. That is the section of the Code specifying the characteristics making an organization eligible for nonprofit status. Proper documentation is in the form of a letter from the IRS indicating to the organization that it has been designated tax-exempt under section 501(c)(3). That is the reason nonprofit organizations are also known as 501(c̃)(3) organizations.

The objective of using the directories in the Research Grant Guides' series is to identify the foundations most likely to support your organization. Foundations use grants to promote their own priorities by supporting the activities of nonprofit organizations. Some foundations may have very simple priorities. For example, they might consider any project within a specific community. Some may have extraordinarily specific priorities. An example would be a foundation interested in public or private schools, but not religiously affiliated schools, that provide special educational services to children with a specific disability. Thus, a special education program in a religious school would not be eligible, even though it does provide the type of service specified by the foundation. The possible combinations of priorities are almost endless.

Our research staff analyzes the records of thousands of foundations. We select those that are appropriate for inclusion in the Directory and condense their most important information into compact profiles in an easy to use format. The following is a step-by-step process for using our information to apply for a grant.

Steps for Writing Proposals and Winning Grants

Step 1 - Understand Your Own Organization and its Needs

An absolutely essential part of the grant seeking process is to make sure you have a thorough understanding of your own organization, its priorities and its clients. This may sound obvious, but it is surprising how many staff members working in nonprofit organizations have never even seen the mission statement. Every grant seeker and proposal writer should have available from their organization its annual report, mission statement, accreditation reports and by-laws for reference. These should be reviewed periodically, especially when starting a new grant search.

Step 2 - Develop the Proposal Before Conducting Any Foundation Research

Next, it is equally important to have a clear understanding of the exact nature of the request to be made in the proposal. Planning the proposal/grant application must take place before undertaking any research because your job is to match your proposal with the specific requirements of the foundations you will apply to. The budget is especially important. Foundations vary widely with regard to the size of grants they award. The Directory reports typical grant ranges for most foundations. These ranges are the "comfort zone" for the foundations. Asking for too little money may be as detrimental as asking for too much. There are administrative costs associated with the grantmaking process, and some foundations may feel it is not cost effective to award grants below a certain amount. The "typical grant range" should be interpreted as a guide, not an inflexible standard.

This step is also important when deciding on how many proposals/applications to submit. It may turn out that no single foundation awards grants large enough to cover the entire project. It is perfectly acceptable to apply to several foundations and request grants for part of the budget. That's why it is so important to plan the proposal and determine its scope before doing anything else.

Step 3 - A Geography Lesson

The first thing the reader notices when examining the Directory is that it is subdivided by state. Generally, but not always, foundations tend to award grants close to their home base. They are said to "...give where they live...". Carefully reviewing all the entries for your home state is a good way to start using the Directory. This will provide an overview of foundations in your area.

It is important to make note of any within-state geographic preferences listed for the foundations in your state. This can work for or against you. Note any foundations that list a preference for specific areas. Any that specify your area should be at the top of your list of potential sponsors. Also make note of any within your state whose geographic preferences exclude your organization. Don't throw them out immediately, however. Your organization may be located in one part of the state, but may offer services beyond that immediate area. If that's the case, it is likely that your proposal will be eligible for consideration.

While reviewing the foundations in your state, pay careful attention to their interest areas. Highlight the names or place a check mark next to those whose interests match those of your organization. These will be your best prospects.

Most foundation profiles identify geographic restrictions. Where such information is unavailable, but the foundation is located in your state and specifies interests consistent with your own, send a letter as described in Step 6.

Step 4 - Identifying Specific Foundation Interests

This step presents an alternative method to that described in Step 3. This Directory includes only those foundations interested in the general subject specified in the title of the book. There are many sub-categories of priorities contained within the main subject. When researching foundations our goal is to identify those that are the closest fit. The subject index classifies foundations by interest area. It contains categories that correspond to all the possible priorities of the included foundations.

The foundations are numbered consecutively through the Directory. The first foundation listed under Alabama is number 1, and the last foundation in Wyoming has the highest number. The purpose of these numbers is to facilitate the research process. Make note of the range of foundation entry numbers for your state.

Under each category in the subject index are the entry numbers of all foundations expressing interest in that category. Keep in mind that the activities of your organization may correspond to several categories. Review all that apply to you. Make note of the entries corresponding to foundations that are within your state and that are also under the subject headings appropriate to your search. Eliminate any of these that you identified as having geographic restrictions excluding your region. After completing this step, you may have a lengthy list of entry numbers, which correspond to foundation names.

Step 5 - Narrowing the Search

Just because the foundations on your list match your organization's priorities, however, does not guarantee them to be the very best prospects. You have some more work to do to reduce your list to only the best potential sources. Your next step, therefore, is to review carefully the foundation profile in the Directory for each of the entry numbers on your list. You know from what you have already done that the foundations have an interest in the priority area that concerns you and that they support organizations in your geographic area. What else can you learn about them? A few additional questions will deepen your insight into these sources.

Are they interested in your type of organization? Most of the entries in the Directory list organizations to whom the foundations have made grants. Analyze this information, where available, to determine if any of these grantees are similar in purpose to your own.

1. Is this a community foundation? If so, the grants will be restricted to the geographic area specified in the name.

2. What is the typical grant size? Many of our foundation listings include the typical grant range. This range will tell you if the foundation will be likely to support the entire budget of your application. If not, you will need to apply to several so that your chances of receiving grant funds for the total budget will be greater.

3. Are they interested in the constituents you serve? Are there specific preferences, e.g. children, elderly, people with disabilities? Careful use of the subject index will reveal such preferences.

You must make sure the list includes all possible foundations whose priorities and interests match your own, but who don't exclude you geographically. Once you're satisfied that your list meets these criteria, it's time to start contacting the foundations on your list.

Step 6 - Making Contact with the Foundations

Once you have identified your list of potential foundations, you must next determine the best way to approach each one. Each foundation has its own way of dealing with potential applicants. It will not be productive to approach each in the same way or to develop an all-purpose proposal to send out. This is known as "shotgunning", and rarely results in success. Rather you, as the applicant, must research the procedures of each foundation and follow the instructions exactly.

One of the benefits of the directories from Research Grant Guides is that our staff has already eliminated those foundations that do not accept applications from the grant seeking public. Many small family foundations, for example, prefer to select grant applicants without receiving applications. They tend to support the same group of grantees year after year.

All the foundations listed in the Directory accept applications from nonprofit organizations. Many have specific requirements, while others ask only for a letter from the applicant describing the program for which it seeks support. You now need to contact the foundations themselves to see if they have any additional priorities and any specific procedures to be followed.

The applicant should write to each of the foundations on the list to request an application and any other materials that may be available. This should be in the form of a simple letter requesting their information. A good model would be, "This is to request a copy of your guidelines and any other application information you have available. Please send these to me at the following address." Address the letter, "Dear Foundation Director".

Don't try to describe your organization or the project, even briefly, at this point. The foundation may read such a description and decide to send a rejection letter on that basis alone. It happens frequently and precludes the applicant from submitting a formal proposal.

The scope of information you may receive will vary widely. Some foundations have nothing at all, while others have quite extensive and complex guidelines and procedures. If you do receive materials from the foundations, study the guidelines carefully and follow any instructions to the letter. If you receive nothing, send them a letter based on the outline in *Proposal Writing Basics* beginning on page 10.

What Else Can You Learn?

As noted previously, you will receive specific instructions from many of the foundations to whom you write for information. Some ask only for a letter. This letter, however, needs to include all the components of a typical grant proposal. It must include sections describing the applicant, the need for the grant, specific procedures, how much it will cost, what activities will be conducted, and how the project will be evaluated. Such letter applications should be limited to three single-spaced pages signed by the chief executive officer of the nonprofit organization.

Some foundations will accept common application forms. These grantors have grouped together within specific regions of the country and developed standard proposal formats acceptable to each member of the group. The common application forms are outlines indicating the proposal sections required by the members of the group. New York, Massachusetts, and California among others, have developed common grant application forms. Foundations that accept the common application form will let you know that they do in their response to your inquiry for information. The foundation may also include a copy of the form.

The valuable information contained in this Directory will help applicants prepare the most competitive grant applications. Good luck on your search.

Proposal Writing Basics

Despite the availability of excellent references on the subject, proposal writing still seems an elusive art. Many foundation grant officers despair at the poor quality of proposals they receive.

Proposals that fail to communicate effectively jeopardize the support that might be granted to an otherwise excellent project. Competition for funds is fierce. Many worthwhile projects must be declined because so many organizations pursue the limited dollars available. Poorly written proposals simply make it easy for the foundation to reject the request; there are too many good ones to consider. For the pressured foundation, it is impractical to spend time trying to make sense of unclear proposals.

Some Truths That Should Be Self-Evident

• Research, not writing, is the first step. Foundations have specific interests. These must be researched. Proposals should be submitted only to those sources that have articulated a priority in the type of project to be undertaken by the applicant. To do otherwise is like going shopping for groceries in a hardware store. The response can only be, "You're in the wrong place."

• Proposal writing requires a good writer. Communicating in clear, precise English assumes talent that not everyone possesses. Sometimes a proposal writer is in the wrong job. Although proposal writing is an excellent way to enter the fund-raising profession, it's not for everyone. Skills must be assessed accurately by the employer and job seeker. Writing is only one specialty required in fund-raising. People uncomfortable with writing can find many other rewarding career paths in professional fund-raising.

• Follow directions. Many foundations provide specific instructions on what they want in a submission. If such directions exist, they should be adhered to without deviation. Frequently, however, there are no specific guidelines. For such cases, the following outline provides a model of what should be contained in a proposal. The model is basic and flexible enough to accommodate different writing styles.

Starting: The Most Difficult Part

Questions that are asked frequently are: How should the proposal begin? and What is the best way to introduce the subject? The opening paragraph is of vital importance. It must set the stage and interest the reader enough to make him or her want to know more. All this in two or three sentences.

A most effective way to do this is to begin with a general or global statement of the problem to be addressed. Let's use the example of a project to provide neighborhood transportation for people with disabilities.

For example:

"The absence of accessible transportation constitutes a serious obstacle to people with disabilities in performing the routine tasks of everyday life."

This opening sentence would be followed by two or three other short statements. Their purpose is to focus the general issue to be addressed in the context of the local environment. These statements serve the purpose of describing how this issue manifests itself in the particular situation that is the subject of the proposal. The entire introduction should occupy no more than a half page of a three-page letter or a full page of a five-page formal proposal. Included might be some statistics descriptive of the severity of the problem and the population to be served.

Who Are You? Dealing From Strength

The second paragraph or section should describe the nonprofit organization proposing to conduct the project. The most important thing to remember here is not to assume any knowledge on the part of the reader. It is easy to become too familiar with an issue or organization. The effect on the proposal when this happens is an inadequate description. That's fatal to the case. The applicant must make sure the prospective foundation has a clear idea of precisely who is applying for the grant.

A good way to handle this section is to write several descriptions of the organization in advance. They should be of varying length. Taking time to do this results in a final description that presents the organization in its most favorable light.

That brings up another vital consideration. The nonprofit must convince the foundation that their proposal is the best way to conduct a project dealing with the subject issue. Using our example of a transportation program, the description should touch upon the following items:

- Knowledge of the client population
- Knowledge of the geographic area to be served
- Experience in providing the service proposed
- Familiarity with the issue
- Qualifications of the staff
- Acceptance in the community

If a nonprofit organization cannot present a compelling capability statement without exaggerating, it needs to evaluate its reasons for seeking funds for the project. Foundations strive to invest in organizations that have the ability to put grants to maximum use. This description of capabilities, therefore, is probably the most important information to be covered in a proposal.

How Much Will It Cost?

This is no place to be bashful. The amount of money requested should be indicated as early as possible in the proposal. Ideally it should be included in the first paragraph. The dollar request says a lot about the project. It establishes limits. It tells the foundation the extent of its participation. It says something about cost effectiveness. Finally, if the request is realistic, not too high or low for the foundation to whom it's directed, it tells the foundation that the applicant has done his or her homework.

What Will Be Different?

Until now you have been carefully setting the stage. You have prepared the reader to be interested in the project, which now must be described. What are the goals? How will it work? Who will benefit? Who will do the work? What will be accomplished?

In order for the description to be compelling, the project must have been well thought out. The heart of a good proposal is a good project. When the program has been well planned, this part of the proposal is easy to write. If that's not the case, the project planning must be re-examined. Often, project weaknesses become exposed in the act of attempting a written description that simply won't flow.

Other Considerations

Because writing styles are so individual, proposals will vary even if they are based on a common model. In all cases, the project itself will determine what is appropriate to include and omit. For example, a statement regarding how the organization will measure success is important. The formality and complexity of the evaluation design, however, will vary greatly.

Many foundations like to know whose company they are keeping. It's often useful to indicate what other sources of funding are going to be awarded for this project.

Finally, each organization has ancillary materials that can be appended to a proposal. A certificate of nonprofit status and an audited financial statement are standards. Other attachments should be included only if they make a contribution to the case.

In closing, it bears noting that proposal writing takes practice. It is a skill that requires development. This model provides a guide to the structure of a proposal. Substance and style are very much a function of the individual writer.

FOUNDATIONS

ALABAMA

1
Alabama Power Foundation, Inc.
17N-0011
P.O. Box 2641
Birmingham, AL 35291
(205) 257-2508

Program grants; youth; disabled; social service organizations; environment; community development; education; cultural organizations; Boy Scouts of America (program grant)

Grants awarded to organizations located in Alabama.

Typical grant range: $2,000 to $50,000

2
Calhoun County Community Foundation
1000 Quintard Avenue, Suite 307
P.O. Box 1826
Anniston, AL 36202-1826
(256) 231-5160

Program grants; Calhoun County Board of Education (pregnancy prevention program for teenagers); AIDS Services Center, Inc. (HIV testing program); Alabama Head Injury Foundation, Inc. (program grant); Mental Health Board (treatment program for preschoolers); Interfaith Ministries, Inc. (Meals on Wheels program); YMCA (swimming and safety program); JSU College of Nursing and Health Sciences (program to stop smoking); Calhoun County Sheriff's Office (counseling program for at-risk teens and their parents)

Grants awarded to organizations located in Calhoun County and northeast Alabama.

3
The Community Foundation of Greater Birmingham
2027 First Avenue North, Suite 410
Birmingham, AL 35203
(205) 328-8641

Program grants; youth; disabled; social service organizations; education; cultural organizations; environment; Camp Fire Boys and Girls (program grant); Alabama Head Injury Foundation (recreation program)

Grants awarded to organizations located in the Birmingham vicinity.

Typical grant range: $3,000 to $50,000

4
The Community Foundation of South Alabama
154 St. Louis Street
Mobile, AL 36602
(251) 438-5591

Program grants; cultural organizations; social service organizations; education; community development

Grants awarded to organizations located in the Mobile vicinity.

5
The Hugh Kaul Foundation
c/o AmSouth Bank of Alabama
P.O. Box 11426
Birmingham, AL 35202
(205) 326-4696

Program grants; youth; disabled; education; cultural organizations; community development; Planned Parenthood (education program for teenagers and women); Alabama Shakespeare Festival (program grant)

Grants awarded to organizations located in the Birmingham vicinity.

Typical grant range: $2,000 to $100,000

6
Vulcan Materials Company Foundation
P.O. Box 385014
Birmingham, AL 35238
(205) 298-3229

Program grants; all levels of education;
environment; social service organizations;
youth; disabled; cultural organizations

Grants awarded to organizations located
in areas of company operations (Vulcan
Materials Co.).

Typical grant range: $2,000 to $30,000

7
Susan Mott Webb Charitable Trust
c/o AmSouth Bank of Alabama
P.O. Box 11426
Birmingham, AL 35202
(205) 326-5410

Program grants; social service
organizations; youth; animal welfare;
education; Christian organizations

Most grants awarded to organizations
located in the Birmingham vicinity.

Typical grant range: $2,000 to $25,000

ALASKA

8
Alaska Conservation Foundation
441 W. 5th Avenue, Suite 402
Anchorage, AK 99501
(907) 276-1917

Program grants; Denali Environmental
Crew (recycling program); Alaska Center
for the Environment (project grant);
Alaska Conservation Voters (media
project); Youth Restoration Corps (Susitna
River youth program); Alaska Audubon
(The Kenai Brown Bear Project); Alaska
Natural History Association (project
grant); Sheldon Jackson College (marine
education program)

Most grants awarded to organizations
located in Alaska.

Typical grant range: $1,000 to $20,000

9
The Rasmuson Foundation
301 W. Northern Lights Blvd., Suite 400
Anchorage, AK 99503
(907) 297-2700

Program grants; youth; elderly; women;
social service organizations; education;
health organizations; cultural organizations

Grants awarded to organizations located
in Alaska.

Typical grant range: $500 to $10,000

10
The Skaggs Foundation
P.O. Box 20510
Juneau, AK 99802
(907) 463-4843

Program grants; environment and
environmental education; wildlife;
marine science; children who are disabled

Grants awarded to organizations located
in Alaska.

Typical grant range: $1,000 to $10,000

ARIZONA

11
Arizona Community Foundation
2122 E. Highland Avenue, Suite 400
Phoenix, AZ 85016
(602) 381-1400

Program grants; community development;
youth; social service organizations;
women; disabled; minorities; education;
health organizations; environment;
cultural organizations

Grants awarded to organizations located
in Arizona.

Typical grant range: $2,000 to $40,000

12
Community Foundation for Southern Arizona
2250 E. Broadway Blvd.
Tucson, AZ 85719
(520) 770-0800

Program grants; youth; disabled; social service organizations; education; health organizations; environment; cultural organizations

Grants awarded to organizations located in Cochise, Pima, and Santa Cruz Counties.

Typical grant range: $1,000 to $10,000

13
The Flinn Foundation
1802 N. Central Avenue
Phoenix, AZ 85004-1506
(602) 744-6800

Program grants; health organizations; hospitals; medical research; disabled; cultural organizations; Arizona Opera Company (program grant)

Grants awarded to organizations located in Arizona.

Typical grant range: $5,000 to $150,000

14
The Marshall Fund of Arizona
3295 N. Drinkwater Blvd.
Scottsdale, AZ 85251
(480) 941-5249

Program grants; Sun Cities Area Interfaith Services (counseling program for senior citizens); Southern Arizona AIDS Foundation (program grant); Hospice of the Valley (massage therapy program); Prehab of Arizona (program grant for a homeless shelter); Southwest Wildlife Rehabilitation (educational program); Arizona State University College (Poets in Residence Program)

Grants awarded to organizations located in Arizona.

Typical grant range: $5,000 to $20,000

15
Novis M. Schmitz Foundation, Inc.
c/o Sherman & Howard
1221 East Osborne, Suite 104
Phoenix, AZ 85214
(602) 636-2000

Program grants; youth; homeless; social service organizations; education; cultural organizations; Salvation Army (program grant)

Most grants awarded to organizations located in the Phoenix vicinity.

Typical grant range: $500 to $5,000

16
St. Luke's Health Initiatives
2375 E. Camelback Road, Suite 200
Phoenix, AZ 85016
(602) 385-6500

Program grants; United Methodist Outreach Ministries (domestic violence program); Arizona's Children's Heart Foundation (program grant); Alzheimer's Association (program grant); Arizona Partnership for Infant Immunization (immunization project); EAR Foundation (newborn hearing screening program); Interfaith Services (counseling program for seniors); Alliance to Abolish Homelessness (program grant); Boy Scouts of America (urban program); Heartsprings (violence prevention program); Big Brothers/Big Sisters (volunteer recruitment project); Arizona State University-College of Nursing (health outreach program)

Typical grant range: $5,000 to $50,000

17
Del E. Webb Foundation
P.O. Box 3350
Wickenburg, AZ 85358
(520) 684-7223

Program grants; hospitals; health organizations; youth; social service organizations

Typical grant range: $10,000 to $200,000

ARKANSAS

18
Charles A. Frueauff Foundation, Inc.
Three Financial Centre
900 S. Shakleford, Suite 300
Little Rock, AR 72211
(501) 219-1410

Program grants; disabled; youth; women;
social service organizations; health
organizations; higher education; YWCA
(program grant)

Typical grant range: $5,000 to $60,000

19
**The John G. Leake Charitable
Foundation**
P.O. Box 251414
Little Rock, AR 72225
(501) 666-1885

Program grants; American Amputee
Foundation (Med-Camp Summer
Program); Woodland Hills Community
Church (summer program); YWCA
(program grant); YMCA (summer
program); Pfeifer Kiwanis Camp (summer
camp program); Arkansas School for the
Deaf (Project Play)

Grants awarded to organizations located
in Arkansas.

Typical grant range: $500 to $6,000

20
The Ross Foundation
1039 Henderson Street
Arkadelphia, AR 71923
(870) 246-9881

Program grants; all levels of education;
social service organizations; community
development

Grants awarded to organizations located
in the Arkadelphia vicinity.

Typical grant range: $2,000 to $20,000

21
Windgate Charitable Foundation, Inc.
P.O. Box 826
Siloam Springs, AR 72761
(501) 524-9829

Program grants; First Assembly of God
Church (project grants); Christian Justice
Center (program grant); Funfest/Youth In
Action (summer day camp program); Let
Our Violence End (school program); The
Student Conservation Association, Inc.
(Arkansas Student Conservation project);
Baylor University (Marriage and Family
Emphasis program)

Typical grant range: $3,000 to $50,000

CALIFORNIA

22
AAF
(also known as The Amateur Athletic
Foundation of Los Angeles)
2141 W. Adams Blvd.
Los Angeles, CA 90018
(323) 730-9600

Program grants; Boys and Girls Club
(basketball and football program); Tenth
District Women's Steering Committee
(youth, education and sports program);
Kids in Sports (program grant); Southern
California Cycling Federation (program
for youth); East Los Angeles College
Foundation (diving program for youth)

Grants awarded to organizations located
in southern California.

Typical grant range: $5,000 to $55,000

23
The Thomas C. Ackerman Foundation
600 W. Broadway, Suite 2600
San Diego, CA 92101
(858) 699-5411

Program grants; San Diego Hospice
(bereavement program); The San Diego
Blood Bank Foundation (blood donor
program); Arthritis Foundation (summer
camp program); Burn Institute (fire and
burn prevention program); Boys & Girls
Club (transportation program); YWCA
(teen leadership program); Southeast San
Diego Children/Youth Community Choir
(program grant); Interfaith Shelter
Network (program grant); Senior
Community Centers (program for urban
seniors); I Love A Clean San Diego
(program grant); The Neurosciences
Institute (donor acquisition program);
San Diego Inner City Soccer Foundation
(expand program); Sherman Heights
Community Center (cultural program
for youth)

Grants awarded to organizations located
in the San Diego vicinity.

Typical grant range: $2,000 to $15,000

24
The Ahmanson Foundation
9215 Wilshire Blvd.
Beverly Hills, CA 90210
(310) 278-0770

Program grants; youth; disabled;
minorities; women; social service
organizations; all levels of education;
Hospice Foundation (pediatric hospice
program); American Youth Symphony
(program grant); Big Brothers/Big Sisters
(Bright Futures program); Making the
Right Connections, Inc. (gang prevention
program); Los Angeles Conservation
Corps (Clean & Green Program); National
Council on Alcoholism (Woman to
Woman Domestic Violence Program);
Biola University (honors program)

Grants awarded to organizations located
in southern California, with an emphasis
in the Los Angeles vicinity.

Typical grant range: $5,000 to $50,000

25
American Honda Foundation
P.O. Box 2205
Torrance, CA 90509
(310) 781-4090

Program grants; National Council of
Juvenile and Family Court Judges
(Expedited Adoption Project); Pacific
Science Center (Community Leadership
Project); Autry Museum of Western
Heritage (program grant); College of
Santa Fe (Mobile Science Project)

Typical grant range: $10,000 to $50,000

26
Amgen Foundation, Inc.
One Amgen Center Drive
Thousand Oaks, CA 91320
(805) 447-1000

Program grants; education; environment;
social service organizations; youth;
cultural organizations

Grants awarded to organizations located
in areas of company operations (Amgen,
Inc.), with an emphasis in Ventura County.

27
ARCO Foundation
515 S. Flower Street
Los Angeles, CA 90071
(213) 486-3342

Program grants; National Audubon
Society (nature center program); Boys
and Girls Club (after school program);
Foundation for the Junior Blind (program
grant); River Oak Center for Children
(parenting program); Worksite Wellness
Project (health promotion program); Los
Angeles Chamber Orchestra (program
grant); Buena Vista Museum of Natural
History (education program); Students
Run L.A. (dropout prevention program);
Brentwood School (program grant);
California State University (engineering
program for minorities)

Grants awarded to organizations located
in areas of company operations (Atlantic
Richfield Co.).

28
Atkinson Foundation
1100 Grundy Lane, Suite 140
San Bruno, CA 94066
(650) 876-0222

Program grants; Parkinson's Institute (outreach and education program); Samaritan House (emergency shelter and holiday assistance programs); Bay Area Health Ministries (program for the elderly); Peninsula Network of Mental Health Clients (program grant); Women's Recovery Association (substance abuse program for girls); YMCA (summer and after-school programs); Big Brothers/Big Sisters (program grant); Drawbridge (art program for homeless children); AIDS Community Research Consortium (program grant); San Mateo County Library System (Spanish literacy project); Gilroy United Methodist Church (English as a second language program); Jefferson Union High School District (reading project); College of San Mateo (crime prevention project for youth)

Grants awarded to organizations located in San Mateo County.

Typical grant range: $1,000 to $10,000

29
The Lowell Berry Foundation
Four Orinda Way, Suite 140B
Orinda, CA 94563
(925) 254-1944

Program grants; St. Anthony Foundation (food program); Campus Crusade for Christ (program grant); Girl Scout Council (camp program); Boys and Girls Club (camp program); Regional Parks Foundation (camp program); Cazadero Performing Arts (music program); Regional Parks Foundation (camp program); Women's Initiative for Self Employment (program grant); Chabot Observatory & Science Center (teacher training program); California Association of Student Councils (leadership training program); Jefferson Elementary School (outreach program); Northern Light School (fine arts program); Futures Explored, Inc. (Community College Transition Project)

Grants awarded to organizations located in Contra Costa and Alameda Counties.

Typical grant range: $1,000 to $25,000

30
Blue Oak Foundation
555 Portola Road
Portola Valley, CA 94028

Program grants; youth; women; environment; community development; Hidden Villa (camp program)

Most grants awarded to organizations located in San Mateo and Santa Clara Counties.

Typical grant range: $1,000 to $10,000

31
Bonner Family Foundation
P.O. Box 26327
Fresno, CA 93729

Program grants; performing arts; museums; youth; education; environment

Grants awarded to organizations located in Fresno.

Typical grant range: $1,000 to $10,000

32
California Community Foundation
445 S. Figueroa Street, Suite 3400
Los Angeles, CA 90071
(213) 413-4130

Program grants; social service organizations; disabled; youth; elderly; education; environment; community development; cultural organizations; health organizations; Braille Institute of America (career services program); Girl Scout Council (outreach program); Coeur d'Alene Elementary School (project grant)

Grants awarded to organizations located in Los Angeles County.

Typical grant range: $3,000 to $30,000

33
The California Endowment
21550 Oxnard Street, Suite 600
Woodland Hills, CA 91367
(818) 703-3311

Program grants; Inland Counties Health Systems Agency (violence prevention program for youth); Boys & Girls Club (substance abuse program); Asian Pacific Community Counseling (mental health program); Blind Children's Center (program grant); Colusa Community Hospital Association (radiology efficiency program); St. Joseph Center (welfare to work project); The Wellness Community (cancer program); MotherNet L.A. (program for pregnant women); Del Norte Senior Center, Inc. (nutrition and adult day care programs); Corporation for Supportive Housing (health program for homeless people with substance abuse, mental illness or HIV/AIDS)

Grants awarded to organizations located in California.

34
The California Wellness Foundation
6320 Canoga Avenue, Suite 1700
Woodland Hills, CA 91367
(818) 593-6600

Program grants; health organizations; violence prevention; Los Angeles Commission on Assaults Against Women (violence prevention project); Asian Resources (violence prevention project); Planned Parenthood (reproductive health care program)

Grants awarded to organizations located in California.

Typical grant range: $15,000 to $125,000

35
Callaway Golf Company Foundation
2180 Rutherford Road
Carlsbad, CA 92008
(760) 930-8686

Program grants; hospitals; health organizations; youth; disabled; social service organizations

Most grants awarded to organizations located in San Diego County.

Typical grant range: $5,000 to $15,000

36

The Clorox Company Foundation
c/o The East Bay Community Foundation
200 Frank H. Ogawa Plaza
Oakland, CA 94612
(510) 208-0808

Program grants; Girls Incorporated (teen achievement program); California 4-H Foundation (after school program); Alameda County Community Food Bank (food distribution program); American Red Cross (program grant); Chabot Space & Science Center (education program); Catholic Charities (youth project); The Oakland Museum (natural science and environmental program); Museum of Children's Art (Exhibition Program); Oakland East Bay Symphony (Education and Community Outreach Programs); Berkeley Biotechnology Education, Inc. (Summer Work-Experience program); American Indian Child Resource Center (school-to-work program); The Head Royce School (Heads Up Program)

Grants awarded to organizations located in Oakland and in areas of company operations (Clorox Company).

Typical grant range: $2,000 to $10,000

37

Columbia Foundation
One Lombard Street, Suite 305
San Francisco, CA 94111
(415) 986-5179

Program grants; Northern California Grantmakers AIDS Task Force (HIV prevention program); Gay, Lesbian and Straight Education Network (Western Organizing Project); Center to Prevent Handgun Violence (Legal Action Project); Spectrum (Hate, Violence and Harassment Prevention Program); Environmental Protection Information Center (program grant); Sustainable North Bay (public education project); Independent Press Association (project to promote recycled paper by magazine publishers)

Most grants awarded to organizations located in the San Francisco vicinity.

Typical grant range: $10,000 to $75,000

38

Community Foundation for Monterey County
99 Pacific Street, Suite 155-A
Monterey, CA 93940
(831) 375-9712

Program grants; youth; social service organizations; education; environment; cultural organizations

Grants awarded to organizations located in Monterey County.

39

The Community Foundation of Santa Cruz County
2425 Porter Street, Suite 16
Soquel, CA 95073
(831) 477-0800

Program grants; Diabetes Health Center (education and outreach programs); American Lung Association (education program); Girl Scouts (program grant); Pajaro Valley Arts Council (school outreach programs); Santa Cruz County Symphony Association (program grant); Young at Heart Project (musical program for seniors); O'Neill Sea Odyssey (environmental education program for youth with special needs); Ventana Wilderness Sanctuary (California Condor Recovery Program); Kids and Teens Exploring Nature (summer recreation program); Community Alliance with Family Farmers (program to expand economic opportunities for farmers)

Grants awarded to organizations located in Santa Cruz County.

Typical grant range: $500 to $15,000

40

Community Foundation Silicon Valley
60 S. Market Street, Suite 1000
San Jose, CA 95113
(408) 278-0270

Program grants; cultural organizations; education; youth; women; social service organizations; community development; health organizations; AIDS

Grants awarded to organizations located in Santa Clara County and southern San Mateo County.

41
S.H. Cowell Foundation
120 Montgomery Street, Suite 2570
San Francisco, CA 94104
(415) 397-0285

Program grants; Child Care Resource and Referral Network (Family Resource Center Collaboration Project); Sports 4 Kids (school-based program); Sacramento Area Congregations Together (program to have teachers visit homes); Vertical Slice Cross Age Tutoring Project (program for high school students); West Oakland Community School (literacy program)

Grants awarded to organizations located in northern California.

Typical grant range: $15,000 to $150,000

42
Crail-Johnson Foundation
222 W. Sixth Street, Suite 1010
San Pedro, CA 90731
(310) 519-7413

Program grants; Long Beach Symphony Association (program grant); Hillview Acres Children's Home (reunification program for families); South Central Family Health Center (counseling program for teenagers); Hospice Foundation (Project Heal); Children's Hospital (Kids Count Program); Timeless Educators, Inc. (HIV/AIDS prevention program); Harbor Area Gang Alternatives Program (project grant); Venice Family Clinic (Pediatric Chronic Care Program); The Center for the Partially Sighted (program for infants and children); Community School Parents Association (mentoring program); Crossroads Community Foundation (music program at Beethoven Elementary School)

Grants awarded to organizations located in the Los Angeles vicinity.

Typical grant range: $10,000 to $30,000

43
Carrie Estelle Doheny Foundation
707 Wilshire Boulevard, Suite 4960
Los Angeles, CA 90017-3501
(213) 488-1122

Program grants; Los Angeles Children's Museum (Free Admissions Program); St. Raphael's Church (counseling program); St. Vincent Senior Nutrition (Meals on Wheels program); Retired & Senior Volunteer Program (tutoring program); Boy Scouts of America (Learning for Life program); Boys and Girls Club (after school program); Blind Children's Center (preschool program); Epilepsy Foundation (program grant); Easter Seal Society (day care program for seniors); Salvation Army (program grant); Making the Right Connection (gang prevention program); Women in Recovery, Inc. (program grant); St. John's Well Child Center (health program); St. Mary's School (sports program); Boyle Heights College Institute (mentoring program)

Most grants awarded to organizations located in the Los Angeles vicinity.

Typical grant range: $3,000 to $30,000

44
Joseph Drown Foundation
1999 Avenue of the Stars, Suite 1930
Los Angeles, CA 90067
(310) 277-4488

Program grants; youth; elderly; disabled; social service organizations; education; hospitals; health organizations; cultural organizations; Senior Community Centers (education program); Barbara Sinatra Children's Center (pregnancy prevention program)

Grants awarded to organizations located in California.

Typical grant range: $10,000 to $50,000

45

The East Bay Community Foundation
200 Frank H. Ogawa Plaza
Oakland, CA 94612
(510) 836-3223

Program grants; East Bay Center for the Performing Arts (after school program); California Symphony (educational program); Ann Martin Children's Center (Senior Tutors for Youth project); YMCA (substance abuse treatment project); Camp Fire Boys and Girls (Acorn City Kids Program); Women's Daytime Drop-In Center (Urban Survival Project); Communities for a Better Environment (Petrochemical Pollution Prevention Project); Lindsay Wildlife Museum (environmental science education program); Oakland Public Library (after school tutoring program); Chabot Observatory & Science Center (program grant); Marcus Foster Education Institute (Volunteers in the Public Schools program); University of San Francisco (arts database project)

Grants awarded to organizations located in Alameda and Contra Costa Counties.

46

Fleishhacker Foundation
P.O. Box 29918
San Francisco, CA 94129
(415) 561-5350

Program grants; Z Space Studio (musical theater program); San Jose Institute of Contemporary Art (award program); San Francisco Arts Commission (City Hall Exhibition Program); Community Resources for Science (program support); Bay Area Teachers Center (teacher training program); Park Day School (teacher training workshop program); Families on Track (orientation program for students entering the 6th grade)

Grants awarded to organizations located in the San Francisco Bay area.

Typical grant range: $1,500 to $15,000

47

Flintridge Foundation
1040 Lincoln Avenue, Suite 100
Pasadena, CA 91103
(626) 449-0839

Program grants; National Audubon Society (Landowner Landscape Plans Project); Pacific Forest Trust, Inc. (Land Trust Program); Klamath Forest Alliance (Klamath River Basic Protection Program); Native Fish Society, Inc. (Native Salmon Protection and Recovery Program); The Lands Council (Forest Watch Program); Cornerstone Theater (program grant)

Typical grant range: $5,000 to $25,000

48

Friedman Family Foundation
204 East Second Avenue, PMB 719
San Mateo, CA 94401
(650) 342-8750

Program grants; community development; youth; women; homeless; social service organizations

Most grants awarded to organizations located in the San Francisco vicinity.

49

John Jewett and H. Chandler Garland Foundation
P.O. Box 550
Pasadena, CA 91102

Program grants; disabled; youth; elderly; women; hospitals; education; social service organizations

Most grants awarded to organizations located in Southern California.

Typical grant range: $10,000 to $50,000

50

The Carl Gellert and Celia Berta Gellert Foundation
1169 Market Street, Suite 808
San Francisco, CA 94103
(415) 255-2829

Program grants; all levels of education; disabled; youth; elderly; social service organizations; Roman Catholic organizations

Grants awarded to organizations located in the following counties: Alameda, Contra Costa, Marin, Napa, San Francisco, San Mateo, Santa Clara, Solano and Sonoma.

Typical grant range: $1,500 to $20,000

51

The Fred Gellert Family Foundation
361 3rd Street, Suite A
San Rafael, CA 94901-3580
(415) 256-5420

Program grants; youth; elderly; women; disabled; social service organizations; cultural organizations; environment; health organizations; Marin Abuse Women's Services (program grant); Alzheimer's Association (health program); Catholic Charities (program grant); Bay Area Discovery Museum (program grant)

Grants awarded to organizations located in San Francisco, San Mateo, and Marin Counties.

Typical grant range: $2,000 to $25,000

52

Wallace Alexander Gerbode Foundation
470 Columbus Avenue, Suite 209
San Francisco, CA 94133
(415) 391-0911

Program grants; California Voter Foundation (membership development program); American Civil Liberties Union Foundation (Reproductive Rights Project); California Lawyers for the Arts (project grant); San Francisco Study Center (Performing Arts Assistance Program); National Tropical Botanical Garden (training program for environmental journalists); Planet Drum Foundation (Green City Project); Resource Renewal Institute (San Francisco Bay Area Green Plan Program); San Francisco State University (Journalism's Community Press Consortium Project)

Typical grant range: $5,000 to $50,000

53

William G. Gilmore Foundation
120 Montgomery Street, Suite 1880
San Francisco, CA 94104
(415) 546-1400

Program grants; youth; elderly; social service organizations; education; health organizations; cultural organizations

Typical grant range: $1,500 to $15,000

54
Lisa and Douglas Goldman Fund
1 Daniel Burnham Court, Suite 330C
San Francisco, CA 94109
(415) 771-1717

Program grants; Jewish Community
Center (program for teenagers); Women
Against Rape (project grant); San
Francisco Fire Fighters (toy program);
Yosemite National Institutes
(environmental education program);
Nature Conservancy of California (project
grant); Child Abuse Prevention Center
(Respite Care Program); Kids' Turn
(program to help children and parents
cope with divorce and separation)

Grants awarded to organizations located
in the San Francisco vicinity.

Typical grant range: $500 to $10,000

55
Richard and Rhoda Goldman Fund
One Lombard Street, Suite 303
San Francisco, CA 94111
(415) 788-1090

Program grants; environment; youth;
elderly; minorities; women; social service
organizations

Most grants awarded to organizations
located in the San Francisco vicinity.

Typical grant range: $1,000 to $100,000

56
Josephine S. Gumbiner Foundation
401 E. Ocean Blvd., Suite 503
Long Beach, CA 90802
(562) 437-2882

Program grants; emphasis on women and
children (including grants for health care,
cultural organizations, day care,
education, recreation and shelter for
women)

Grants awarded to organizations located
in Long Beach.

Typical grant range: $2,000 to $50,000

57
Evelyn and Walter Haas, Jr. Fund
One Lombard Street, Suite 305
San Francisco, CA 94111
(415) 398-3744

Program grants; Catholic Charities
(transitional housing program); Shelter for
Women & Children (housing project);
YWCA (mentorship program); Boys and
Girls Club (sports program) Drawbridge
(arts program for homeless children);
Sports 4 Kids (after school sports
program); Alzheimer's Association
(program grant); Goldman Institute on
Aging (health program); Meals on Wheels
(meal delivery program); San Francisco
Child Abuse Prevention Center (family
support and employment program); Jobs
for Homeless Consortium (employment
program); Mission Learning Center
(literacy program); Back on Track (after
school tutoring program)

Grants awarded to organizations located
in San Francisco and Alameda Counties.

Typical grant range: $1,000 to $50,000

58
Walter and Elise Haas Fund
One Lombard Street, Suite 305
San Francisco, CA 94111
(415) 398-4474

Program grants; youth; disabled;
social service organizations; cultural
organizations; education; community
development; Jewish organizations

Grants awarded to organizations located
in the San Francisco Bay vicinity.

Typical grant range: $1,500 to $75,000

59
Haigh-Scatena Foundation
P.O. Box 4399
Davis, CA 95617
(530) 758-5327

Project grants; Northern California Grantmakers (citizenship project); Canal Community Alliance (project grant); Sierra Adoption Services (project grant); Fairfax-San Anselmo Children's Center (project to increase participation of fathers in the lives of their children)

Grants awarded to organizations located in northern California.

Typical grant range: $5,000 to $40,000

60
Harden Foundation
P.O. Box 779
Salinas, CA 93902
(831) 442-3005

Program grants; Meals on Wheels (food delivery program); Prunedale Senior Center, Inc. (arts and crafts program); Salinas Valley Youth Soccer League (program grant); Boys & Girls Club (physical education program); Family Service Association (suicide prevention program); Monterey County Youth Museum (program grant); Monterey Rape Crisis Center (child abuse prevention program); Alliance on Aging (Friendly Visitors Program); American Heart Association (education program); Beacon House (residential program for drug and alcohol abuse); Blind and Visually Impaired Center (program grant); Monterey County AIDS Project, Inc. (Rural Latino Outreach Program); Planned Parenthood (education program); Monterey County Symphony Association (program grant); Hartnell College Foundation (Teaching Excellence Awards program)

Grants awarded to organizations located in Monterey County.

Typical grant range: $5,000 to $40,000

61
Clarence E. Heller Charitable Foundation
One Lombard Street, Suite 305
San Francisco, CA 94111
(415) 989-9839

Program grants; Center for Health and the Global Environment (education program); Environmental Defense (program to educate the public about the human health risks of toxic chemicals); Ecology Action (biointensive farming research project); Center for Eco-Literacy (food project that provides organic meals to public school students); Union of Concerned Scientists (education program about the health problems from gene-altered crops); San Francisco Symphony (training program); Association of California Symphony Orchestras (program grant); The Center for the Future of Teaching and Learning (project to improve classroom teaching); Sonoma State University Foundation (Interactive Mathematics Program)

Most grants awarded to organizations located in California.

Typical grant range: $7,500 to $80,000

62
The William and Flora Hewlett Foundation
525 Middlefield Road, Suite 200
Menlo Park, CA 94025
(650) 329-1070

Program grants; environment; minorities; women; youth; cultural organizations; higher education

Most grants awarded to organizations located in the San Francisco vicinity.

Typical grant range: $25,000 to $100,000

63
The Hofmann Foundation
P.O. Box 907
Concord, CA 94522
(925) 682-4830

Program grants; youth; disabled; social service organizations; environment; education; health organizations; cultural organizations

Most grants awarded to organizations located in the San Francisco Bay Area, with an emphasis in Contra Costa County.

Typical grant range: $500 to $25,000

64
The Humboldt Area Foundation
P.O. Box 99
Bayside, CA 95524
(707) 442-2993

Program grants; Hmong Literacy & Homework Helper (after school literacy and cultural program); Redwood Community Action Agency (children's program in family shelters); Arcata Recreation Division (program for disadvantaged youth); Arcata Endeavor (community gardening project); Chetco Senior Center (program grant); Special Olympics (program grant); Big Brothers/ Big Sisters (program grant); Morris Elementary School (arts program); Mattole Union School District (music program); Eureka High School Project Service (educational projects that connect youth with the community)

Grants awarded to organizations located in Del Norte, Humboldt, Siskiyou, and Trinity Counties.

65
The James Irvine Foundation
One Market Street, Suite 1715
San Francisco, CA 94105
(415) 777-2244

Program grants; women; minorities; youth; environment; education; higher education; cultural organizations; health organizations; The Nature Conservancy (project grant); Japanese American Cultural and Community Center (program grant); Museum of Contemporary Art (program grant); Community Coalition for Substance Abuse Prevention and Treatment (community participation project); First Mexican Baptist Church and Christian Center (leadership development program for immigrants); Reedley Social Services (literacy program for farm workers); Fresno Pacific College (leadership program for youth); Santa Clara University (Peer Educator Program)

Most grants awarded to organizations located in California.

Typical grant range: $5,000 to $250,000

66
George Frederick Jewett Foundation
The Russ Building
235 Montgomery Street, Suite 612
San Francisco, CA 94104
(415) 421-1351

Program grants; youth; disabled; social service organizations; environment; education; cultural organizations; San Francisco Performing Arts Library and Museum (program grant); San Francisco Unified School District (Arts Leadership Project); Meals on Wheels (food program that serves people who are disabled and the elderly)

Typical grant range: $2,000 to $25,000

67
Walter S. Johnson Foundation
525 Middlefield Road, Suite 110
Menlo Park, CA 94025
(650) 326-0485

Program grants; Museum of Children's Art (after-school program); Brava Theater Center (training program); Jamestown Community Center (recreation programs); Bay Area Video Coalition (digital media training program); YMCA (youth development project); Center on Juvenile and Criminal Justice (juvenile offender program); Earth Island Institute (program to make the wilderness more accessible to children from the city); Regents of the University of California (teacher support program); Mills College (professional development program)

Typical grant range: $4,000 to $100,000

68
The Fletcher Jones Foundation
624 S. Grand Avenue, Suite 2920
Los Angeles, CA 90017
(213) 426-6565

Program grants; Kids in Sports (program grant); Boy Scouts of America (program grant); Children's Hospital (Life After Cancer program); Orange County Performing Arts Center (education and children's programs); Woodbury University (student center project); Occidental College (Astronomy program)

Grants awarded to organizations located in California.

Typical grant range: $5,000 to $1,000,000

69
W.M. Keck Foundation
550 S. Hope Street, Suite 2500
Los Angeles, CA 90071
(213) 680-3833

Program grants; Los Angeles County Museum of Natural History (research program); House of Ruth (domestic violence program); Women's Transitional Living Center, Inc. (housing project for abused women and their children); Boys & Girls Club (program grant); Neighborhood Youth Association, Inc. (preschool program); Los Angeles Conservation Corps (clean-up program); Los Angeles Free Clinic (dental program for children); LA's Best (after school literacy program); University of California (seismology program)

Typical grant range: $100,000 to $2,000,000

70
The Karl Kirchgessner Foundation
c/o Greenberg, Glusker, Fields, Claman & Machtinger, L.L.P.
1900 Avenue of the Stars, Suite 2100
Los Angeles, CA 90067
(310) 553-3610

Program grants; visually impaired; blind; eye research

Grants awarded to organizations located in southern California.

Typical grant range: $5,000 to $45,000

71
Koret Foundation
33 New Montgomery Street, Suite 1090
San Francisco, CA 94105
(415) 882-7740

Program grants; youth; elderly; disabled; social service organizations; education; cultural organizations; Jewish organizations

Typical grant range: $5,000 to $250,000

72

Louis R. Lurie Foundation
555 California Street, Suite 5100
San Francisco, CA 94104
(415) 392-2470

Program grants; emphasis on children
from birth through eighteen years old
(culture, education, family support, health
and recreation)

Typical grant range: $10,000 to $50,000

73

Miranda Lux Foundation
57 Post Street, Suite 510
San Francisco, CA 94104
(415) 981-2966

Program grants; Family Service Agency
(teenage pregnancy and parenting
project); Bernal Heights Neighborhood
Center (Youth Employment Skills
Program); Jewish Family & Children's
Services (career futures program); Mount
St. Joseph-St. Elizabeth (program for
abused and single teen mothers); New
Conservatory Theatre Center (youth
vocational training program); Cartoon Art
Museum (computer training program);
Tule Elk Park Children's Center (garden
and environmental education program);
California Culinary Academy Educational
Foundation (training program); California
Poets in the Schools (reading and writing
program); Leadership High School
(technology program); Enterprise for
High School Students (summer gardening
project); Marine Mammal Center (marine
Science Discover Program)

Grants awarded to organizations located
in San Francisco.

Typical grant range: $5,000 to $25,000

74

Margoes Foundation
57 Post Street, Suite 510
San Francisco, CA 94104
(415) 981-2966

Program grants; Easter Seal Society
(program for children); Community Music
Center (after school program of music
instruction); Programs for People with
Mental Disabilities (employment program);
Holy Names College (weekend program
for women); Making Waves Education
Program (Academic Coaching and
Teaching Program); University of
California (academic enrichment program
for minority students in high school)

Grants awarded to organizations located
in the San Francisco vicinity.

Typical grant range: $5,000 to $30,000

75

Marin Community Foundation
17 E. Sir Francis Drake Blvd., Suite 200
Larkspur, CA 94939
(415) 461-3333

Program grants; Canal Youth Soccer
Academy (year-round program); Youth in
Arts, Inc. (education program); County of
Marin Housing Authority (Family Self-
Sufficiency program); Save the Bay
(environmental education program); Bay
Area Discovery Museum (environmental
program); Marin Abused Women's
Services (program grant); Adopt A Family
(program to assist families that are in a
crisis or homeless); Cornerstone
Community Church of God in Christ
(Kindergarten Readiness Program);
Jewish Community Center (program
grant); Marin AIDS Project (education
and prevention programs); Ohlhoff
Recovery Programs (substance abuse
education program); Senior Access (health
care and case management program);
Branson School (summer academic
enrichment program)

Grants awarded to organizations located
in Marin County.

Typical grant range: $1,000 to $100,000

76
McCarthy Family Foundation
P.O. Box 27389
San Diego, CA 92198

Program grants; social service organizations; homeless; environment; AIDS; San Diego Science Alliance (BEWISE Program); Molecular Biology Lab (Seek Out Science Program); Monarch High School Project (homeless project); San Diego City College Foundation (outreach program)

Grants awarded to organizations located in San Diego and Los Angeles Counties.

Typical grant range: $5,000 to $15,000

77
The McConnell Foundation
P.O. Box 492050
Redding, CA 96049
(530) 226-6200

Program grants; Shasta County Women's Refuge (transitional housing program); Mt. Shasta Recreation & Parks District (Senior Nutrition Project); City of Redding, Police Department (Youth Explorers Program); Shasta Union High School District (pregnancy prevention program); College of the Siskiyous (leadership project)

Grants awarded to organizations located in Shasta and Siskiyou Counties.

Typical grant range: $3,000 to $100,000

78
McKesson Foundation, Inc.
One Post Street, 31st Floor
San Francisco, CA 94104
(415) 983-8673

Program grants; health organizations; youth; cultural organizations; education; disabled; social service organizations

Grants awarded to organizations located in the San Francisco vicinity.

Typical grant range: $5,000 to $25,000

79
Mericos Foundation
625 Fair Oaks Avenue, Suite 360
South Pasadena, CA 91030
(626) 441-5188

Program grants; cultural organizations; youth; elderly; education

Grants awarded to organizations located in southern California.

80
Monterey Peninsula Foundation
P.O. Box 869
Monterey, CA 93942
(831) 649-1533

Program grants; recreation; youth; social service organizations; health organizations; education; environment

Grants awarded to organizations located in Monterey County.

Typical grant range: $5,000 to $30,000

81
The Kenneth T. and Eileen L. Norris Foundation
11 Golden Shore, Suite 450
Long Beach, CA 90802
(562) 435-8444

Program grants; youth; women; disabled; social service organizations; health organizations; education; cultural organizations; community development

Grants awarded to organizations located in southern California.

Typical grant range: $5,000 to $80,000

82

Peter Norton Family Foundation
225 Arizona Avenue, Suite 350
Santa Monica, CA 90401
(310) 576-7700

Program grants; Coalition for Humane Immigrant Rights (domestic violence program for immigrants); Los Angeles Women's Foundation (program to reduce violence against women and children); El Rescate (literacy program); Five Acres (school based counseling program); Clare Foundation (after school program for at-risk youth)

Typical grant range: $1,000 to $50,000

83

Orange County Community Foundation
2081 Business Center Drive, Suite 100
Irvine, CA 92612
(949) 553-4202

Program grants; youth, including education; cultural organizations; minorities; disabled; social service organizations; Boys and Girls Club (after-school program); YMCA (program grants); Fullerton Interfaith Emergency Services, Inc. (Life Skills/Job Development Program)

Grants awarded to organizations located in Orange County.

Typical grant range: $5,000 to $30,000

84

Pacific Life Foundation
700 Newport Center Drive
Newport Beach, CA 92660
(949) 640-3787

Program grants; health organizations; social service organizations; disabled; community development; cultural organizations; education; environment

Typical grant range: $1,000 to $45,000

85

The David and Lucile Packard Foundation
300 Second Street, Suite 200
Los Altos, CA 94022
(650) 948-7658

Program grants; Family Violence Prevention Fund (prevention project); Natural Resources Defense Council (river restoration project); Nature Conservancy (land conservation project); Women and Their Children's Housing (project grant); Samaritan House (shelter program); Second Harvest Food Bank (program grant); Boys and Girls Clubs (program grant); San Jose Children's Discovery Museum (program grant); Lucile Salter Packard Children's Hospital (Reach Out and Read Program); Monterey Jazz Festival (education program); Santa Clara Valley Youth for Christ (employment program); American Lung Association (Open Airways for Schools Program); Jefferson School District (child care program); All Saints' Episcopal Day School (Orchestra in the Schools Program)

Most grants awarded to organizations located in Monterey, San Mateo, Santa Clara, and Santa Cruz Counties.

Typical grant range: $10,000 to $200,000

86

The Parker Foundation
4365 Executive Drive, Suite 1600
San Diego, CA 92121
(858) 677-1431

Program grants; youth; elderly; disabled; social service organizations; cultural organizations; health organizations; Girl Scouts (after school program); Blood Bank Foundation (blood donation program); YMCA (literacy program); Community Resource Center (Children's Domestic Violence Counseling Program)

Grants awarded to organizations located in San Diego County.

Typical grant range: $5,000 to $25,000

87
The Ralph M. Parsons Foundation
1055 Wilshire Blvd., Suite 1701
Los Angeles, CA 90017
(213) 482-3185

Program grants; Pasadena Symphony Association (education program); Los Angeles Children's Museum (literacy project); Bienvenidos Children's Center, Inc. (emergency shelter program); Meals on Wheels (meal program for the elderly); Bishop Gooden Home (alcohol and drug treatment program); Fuller Theological Seminary (mental health program); House of Ruth, Inc. (domestic violence program for women and children); Making the Right Connections, Inc. (gang prevention program); Boys and Girls Club (program grant); Cancer Detection Center (cancer screening program); Aid for AIDS (Housing and Utilities Assistance program); Heart of Los Angeles Youth (after school program); Remedial Reading and Learning Center (tutoring program); Pasadena City College (biotechnology program)

Most grants awarded to organizations located in Los Angeles County.

Typical grant range: $20,000 to $150,000

88
Peninsula Community Foundation
1700 S. El Camino Real, Suite 300
San Mateo, CA 94402
(650) 358-9369

Program grants; disabled; youth; elderly; minorities; social service organizations; women; education; cultural organizations; health organizations

Typical grant range: $2,000 to $40,000

89
The Ralphs-Food 4 Less Foundation
1100 W. Artesia Boulevard
Compton, CA 90220
(310) 884-6250

Program grants; youth; education; health organizations; minorities; disabled; social service organizations; cultural organizations

Most grants awarded to organizations located in southern California.

Typical grant range: $500 to $25,000

90
The Riordan Foundation
300 S. Grand Avenue, 29th Floor
Los Angeles, CA 90071
(213) 229-8402

Program grants; Music Center Opera Association (In-School Opera Program); Boys and Girls Club (educational program); Big Sisters (mentoring program for young women); Helen Keller International (ChildSight Program); United Way (Volunteer Leadership Development Program); Rx for Reading (technology-assisted literacy program); Pasadena Educational Foundation (Early Childhood Education Program)

Most grants awarded to organizations located in California.

Typical grant range: $2,000 to $10,000

91
The Roberts Foundation
P.O. Box 29906
San Francisco, CA 94129
(415) 561-6677

Program grants; education; health organizations; animal welfare; youth; social service organizations; Northern California Cancer Center (education program); California Academy of Sciences (Intern Program)

Typical grant range: $5,000 to $150,000

92
Rosenberg Foundation
47 Kearny Street, Suite 804
San Francisco, CA 94108
(415) 421-6105

Project grants; California Budget Project (living wage project); ACLU Foundation (Language Rights Project); Farmworker Justice Fund (Guestworker Project); Rural California Housing Corporation (project grant); Association for Children for Enforcement of Support (California Child Support Enforcement Project)

Most grants awarded to organizations located in California.

Typical grant range: $5,000 to $90,000

93
The San Francisco Foundation
225 Bush Street, Suite 500
San Francisco, CA 94104
(415) 733-8500

Program grants; Children's Hospital of Oakland (asthma education program); AIDS Community Research Consortium (project grant); American Cancer Society of San Francisco (educational program); California Child Care Health Program (Family Child Care Health Advocate Project); East Bay Center for Performing Arts (program for youth); Oceanview Recreation Center (after school arts program); Meals on Wheels (program for seniors); Girls After School Academy (program for girls who live in public housing); Prevent Blindness Northern California (screening program); Women in Community Service (employment training and job placement program); Camp Fire Boys and Girls (project grant); Refugee Transitions (family literacy project)

Grants awarded in Alameda, Contra Costa, Marin, San Francisco, and San Mateo Counties.

Typical grant range: $2,000 to $60,000

94
Santa Barbara Foundation
15 E. Carrillo Street
Santa Barbara, CA 93101
(805) 963-1873

Program grants; Women's Economic Ventures (Career and Personal Development Program); Sousson Foundation (Youth Environmental Leadership Program); Land Trust for Santa Barbara County (Sea Nature Center Educational Program); Santa Barbara Grand Opera Association (program grant); County of Santa Barbara Arts Fund (High School Arts Mentorship Program)

Grants awarded to organizations located in Santa Barbara County.

Typical grant range: $2,000 to $30,000

95
Sierra Health Foundation
1321 Garden Highway
Sacramento, CA 95833
(916) 922-4755

Program grants; health organizations; hospitals; youth; women; elderly; social service organizations; AIDS

Typical grant range: $5,000 to $55,000

96
The May and Stanley Smith Trust
720 Market Street, Suite 250
San Francisco, CA 94102
(415) 391-0292

Program grants; elderly; youth; blind; social service organizations; health organizations

Most grants awarded to organizations located in the San Francisco vicinity.

97
Sobrato Family Foundation
10600 N. De Anza Boulevard, Suite 200
Cupertino, CA 95014
(408) 446-0700

Program grants; youth; disabled; women; social service organizations; education; community development

Typical grant range: $5,000 to $20,000

98
Y. & H. Soda Foundation
Two Theatre Square, Suite 211
Orinda, CA 94563
(925) 253-2630

Program grants; social service organizations; homeless; women; youth; job training; all levels of education; health organizations; Catholic organizations

Grants awarded to organizations located in Alameda and Contra Costa Counties.

Typical grant range: $1,000 to $25,000

99
Community Foundation Sonoma County
250 D Street, Suite 205
Santa Rosa, CA 95404
(707) 579-4073

Program grants; Catholic Charities (food program); Church of the Incarnation (program for homeless women); Petaluma People Services Center (dining program for the elderly); Committee on the Shelterless (housing program); EVOLVE Institute for Violence Prevention (rape and violence prevention program); Friends of Shotokan Karate (leadership development program); South Park and Comstock Middle Schools (after school program); Sonoma State University (Support Our Students Program)

Grants awarded to organizations located in Sonoma County.

Typical grant range: $500 to $10,000

100
John Stauffer Charitable Trust
301 N. Lake Avenue, 10th Floor
Pasadena, CA 91101
(626) 793-9400

Program grants; hospitals; colleges and universities

Grants awarded to organizations located in California.

Typical grant range: $50,000 to $250,000

101
Glen and Dorothy Stillwell Charitable Trust
301 N. Lake Avenue, 10th Floor
Pasadena, CA 91101
(626) 793-9400

Program grants; Girls Incorporated (pregnancy prevention program); Big Brothers/Big Sisters (program grant); Graceworks Ministries (program for the elderly who have limited mobility); Blind Children's Learning Center (mentoring program for preschool students who are blind)

Grants awarded to organizations located in Orange County.

Typical grant range: $3,000 to $10,000

102
The Stuart Foundation
50 California Street, Suite 3350
San Francisco, CA 94111
(415) 393-1551

Program grants; Home Connection, Inc. (foster home program); Fred Finch Youth Center (program for children who are emotionally disturbed;) Children's Hospital (prevention program for child abuse); The Tides Center (recreation program); National Center for Family Literacy (program grant); Center for the Future of Teaching and Learning (preparation program for teachers); California State University (teacher education program)

Typical grant range: $25,000 to $200,000

103
The Morris Stulsaft Foundation
100 Bush Street, Suite 825
San Francisco, CA 94104
(415) 986-7117

Program grants; Community Music Center (Inner City Young Musicians Program); San Francisco Museum of Modern Art (program for youth); First United Methodist Church (Music Instruction Program); George Mark Children's House (Pediatric Hospice & Respite Program); San Francisco Zoological Society (educational program); Wildcare: Terwilliger Nature Education and Wildlife Rehabilitation (educational program); San Leandro Shelter for Women and Children (project grant); New Connections (Substance Abuse Prevention Program); Saint Mary's Center (preschool program serving low income and homeless families); Berkeley Public Library Foundation (project grant); San Francisco School Volunteers (literacy program); Stege Elementary School (Educational Study Trips Program)

Grants awarded to organizations located in the San Francisco vicinity.

Typical grant range: $2,500 to $25,000

104
Swift Memorial Health Care Foundation
1317 Del Norte Road, Suite 150
Camarillo, CA 93010
(805) 988-0196

Program grants; health organizations; hospices; disabled; youth; social service organizations; AIDS

Grants awarded to organizations located in Ventura County.

Typical grant range: $1,000 to $5,000

105
Transamerica Foundation
600 Montgomery Street
San Francisco, CA 94111

Program grants; youth; education; minorities; social service organizations; cultural organizations

Most grants awarded to organizations located in the San Francisco vicinity.

Typical grant range: $1,000 to $25,000

106
Alice Tweed Tuohy Foundation
205 E. Carrillo Street, Room 219
Santa Barbara, CA 93101
(805) 962-6430

Program grants; Santa Barbara Zoological Foundation (Nature Pavilion project); YMCA (summer camp program); Girls Incorporated (after school program); United Boys & Girls Clubs of Santa Barbara County (High Sierra Challenge program)

Grants awarded to organizations located in the Santa Barbara vicinity.

Typical grant range: $1,000 to $40,000

107
The Upjohn California Fund
P.O. Box 90
Carmel Valley, CA 93924

Program grants; youth; disabled; social service organizations; animal welfare; environment; education; secondary education; cultural organizations; Carmel Bach Festival (educational program); Maritime Museum (educational program); North Monterey County High School (dance program)

Typical grant range: $1,000 to $3,000

108
The Valley Foundation
16450 Los Gatos Blvd., Suite 210
Los Gatos, CA 95032
(408) 358-4545

Program grants; Northside Theater Company (Community Outreach Ticket Program); San Jose Cleveland Ballet (program grant); American Heart Association (research project); American Red Cross (lifesaving program); Boy Scouts of America (Learning for Life program); Camp Fire Boys and Girls (program grant); San Jose Family Shelter (Family Services Program); Homeless Care Force (program grant); First United Methodist Church (employment program); Junior Achievement (Elementary School Program); Franklin McKinley School District (Pre-K Program); San Jose Unified School District (Parent Liaison Program); Alta Vista High School (Community Consortium Project)

Grants awarded to organizations located in Santa Clara County.

Typical grant range: $10,000 to $100,000

109
Wayne and Gladys Valley Foundation
1939 Harrison Street, Suite 510
Oakland, CA 94612
(510) 466-6060

Program grants; Classical Philharmonic (Concerts for Kids program); Berkeley Symphony Orchestra (education program); Ace Foundation (youth golf program); Alameda County Community Food Bank (program grant); Special Olympics (program grant); San Francisco Bay Wildlife Society (National Wildlife Refuge Complex Interpretive Program); John Wayne Institute for Cancer Treatment and Research (cancer vaccine program); Samaritan Neighborhood Center (Student Tutorial Endeavor Program); California Society for Biomedical Research (science education program for youth); Fremont Children's Education Foundation (after school band program); Julia Morgan School for Girls (after school programs); Roman Catholic Diocese of Oakland (Schools in Need program); St. Elizabeth Elementary School (special needs program); Northern Light School (Performing and Fine Arts program)

Typical grant range: $5,000 to $125,000

110
J.B. and Emily Van Nuys Charities
P.O. Box 2946
Palos Verdes Peninsula, CA 90274
(310) 544-8045

Program grants; disabled; youth; elderly; women; social service organizations; health organizations; hospitals; Big Sisters (program grant)

Grants awarded to organizations located in the Los Angeles vicinity.

Typical grant range: $2,000 to $10,000

111
Ventura County Community Foundation
1317 Del Norte Road, Suite 150
Camarillo, CA 93010
(805) 988-0196

Program grants; youth; disabled; social service organizations; environment; education; cultural organizations; health organizations

Grants awarded to organizations located in Ventura County.

112
Vodafone-US Foundation
One California Street, 17th Floor
San Francisco, CA 94111
(415) 658-2300

Program grants; San Francisco Ballet (dance program at schools); San Francisco Opera Association (residency program); Zoological Society (Arctic Encounter School Assembly Program); Asian Neighborhood Design (employment training program); Hamilton Family Center (program grant); American Red Cross (CPR training program); Big Brothers/Big Sisters (mentoring program); YMCA (program grant); Women's Economic Agency Project (computer training program); The Mothers' Living Stories Project (volunteer listener project for mothers with cancer)

Grants awarded to organizations located in areas of company operations, with an emphasis in San Francisco.

Typical grant range: $5,000 to $25,000

113
Weingart Foundation
1055 W. Seventh Street, Suite 3050
Los Angeles, CA 90017
(213) 688-7799

Program grants; Southwest Chamber Music Society (educational program); Young Musicians Foundation (mentor program); Santa Monica Museum of Art (educational program); Boys & Girls Club (educational program); Girl Scouts (Outdoor Adventure Project); Boy Scouts (Learning for Life program); Community Day Nursery (child care program); Greater Los Angeles Zoo Association (exhibit project); Gay and Lesbian Adolescent Social Services (program grant); Los Angeles Metropolitan Churches (rehabilitation project for juvenile youth offenders); St. Raphael Catholic Church (program for at-risk youth); Harbor Interfaith Shelter, Inc. (project for homeless families)

Grants awarded to organizations located in southern California.

Typical grant range: $5,000 to $200,000

114
Wood-Claeyssens Foundation
P.O. Box 30586
Santa Barbara, CA 93130
(805) 966-0543

Program grants; Santa Barbara Grand Opera Association (program grant); Park and Recreation Community Foundation (program grant); Goleta Valley Community Center (program for seniors); Scleroderma Research Foundation (program grant); Goleta Valley Library (lighting project); Santa Barbara County Sheriff's Council (DARE program-drug prevention program for teenagers)

Most grants awarded to organizations located in Santa Barbara and Ventura Counties.

Typical grant range: $5,000 to $50,000

115
WWW Foundation
625 Fair Oaks Avenue, Suite 360
South Pasadena, CA 91030
(626) 441-5188

Program grants; animal welfare; cultural organizations; social service organizations

Grants awarded to organizations located in the Los Angeles vicinity.

Typical grant range: $1,000 to $50,000

COLORADO

116
The Anschutz Family Foundation
555 17th Street, Suite 2400
Denver, CO 80202
(303) 293-2338

Program grants; Catholic Charities (program for seniors); Boys & Girls Clubs (program grant); Big Brothers/Big Sisters (mentoring program); Cortez Cultural Center (program grant); Crisis Support Services (domestic violence program); Neighborhood Partners (job training program for women); Advocates for Children (programs for victims of abuse); Community Resources, Inc. (educational program for at-risk youth); Creative Expressions Center, Inc. (after-school arts program); Meals on Wheels (breakfast program); Project Angel Heart (food program for people who have HIV/AIDS); Interfaith Hospitality Network of Greater Denver, Inc. (program for the homeless); Shannon's Hope (teen pregnancy program); Denver Public Schools (drop-out prevention program); Mesa County Public Library District (literacy program); Highland Middle School (Outdoor Adventure Program for children who are disabled); Creative Recreation in Special Populations (recreation program for people with special needs)

Grants awarded to organizations located in Colorado.

Typical grant range: $3,000 to $7,500

117
The Aspen Valley Community Foundation
110 East Hallam Street, Suite 126
Aspen, CO 81611
(970) 925-9300

Program grants; social service organizations; disabled; elderly; youth; education; cultural organizations; Miles for Smiles (dental program for low-income children); Advocate Safehouse Project (program to eliminate sexual assault and domestic violence); CMC Senior Programs (transportation and meal program for the elderly); The Environment Foundation (program grant); Latino Youth Camp (program grant); Valley Libraries (reading program for children); Children's Rocky Mountain School (Spanish language program); Aspen Elementary School (summer program for at-risk students); Aspen High School (adult mentoring program)

Grants awarded to organizations located in Pitkin, Garfield and West Eagle Counties.

Typical grant range: $1,000 to $35,000

118
The Sam S. Bloom Foundation
P.O. Box 2413
Littleton, CO 80161-2413
(303) 771-2266

Program grants; Big Brothers/Big Sisters (mentoring program); Foster Parent Association (education program); Child Nursery Centers, Inc. (learning program for low-income children); Curtis Park Community Center (day care program); Denver Botanic Gardens (program for at-risk youth); Denver Kids, Inc. (teen mother education project); Victims Service Center (program grant); Anchor Center for Blind Children (preschool program); Goodwill Industries (school to work program); Mi Casa Resource Center for Women (business development program); Westside Christian Community Buildings (summer education program); Jefferson Hall (transitional housing program); Metropolitan State College (literacy program)

Grants awarded to organizations located in Colorado.

Typical grant range: $1,000 to $5,000

119
Boettcher Foundation
600 17th Street, Suite 2210 South
Denver, CO 80202
(303) 534-1937

Program grants; disabled; youth; environment; cultural organizations; community development; health organizations; Boys and Girls Club (program grant); Planned Parenthood (project grant); Colorado Easter Seal Society (camp program for children who are disabled); Prowers County Department of Social Services (project grant)

Grants awarded to organizations located in Colorado.

Typical grant range: $5,000 to $125,000

120
Bonfils-Stanton Foundation
Daniels and Fisher Tower
1601 Arapahoe Street, Suite 500
Denver, CO 80202
(303) 825-3774

Program grants; Prospect Home Care-Hospice, Inc. (program grant); The Association of Senior Citizens, Inc. (Friendly Visitor Volunteer Program); Alzheimer's Disease and Related Disorders Association (program grant); American National Red Cross (transportation program); Colorado Children's Chorale (program grant); Colorado Ballet Company (apprentice program); Big Brothers/Big Sisters (mentoring program); Bonfils Blood Center Foundation (program grant); Boy Scouts of America (program grant); Central City Opera House Association (training program); Cherry Creek School District Parent Teacher Community Council, Inc. (Thanksgiving SHARE Basket Project); The Colorado Coalition for the Homeless (program grant); The Colorado Springs Child Nursery Centers, Inc. (health program); Colorado Women's Employment and Education, Inc. (welfare-to-work program); Colorado Youth Symphony Orchestra (education program); The Denver Dumb Friends League (Pets for People program); Domestic Violence Prevention Center, Inc. (Family Violence Training Program); Eleanor Roosevelt Institute for Cancer Research (research program); Goodwill Industries (school to work programs); National Multiple Sclerosis Society (Independent Living Program)

Grants awarded to organizations located in Colorado.

121
Temple Hoyne Buell Foundation
1666 S. University Blvd., Suite B
Denver, CO 80210
(303) 744-1688

Program grants; Colorado Youth
Symphony (after school program);
Colorado Ballet (program for girls); Brush
Area Museum and Cultural Center (youth
program); Mesa County Public Library
District (Family Literacy program); Girl
Scouts (program grant); Jefferson Center
for Mental Health (Early Intervention
Opportunity program); Golden Plains
Recreation Center (youth program);
Mountain States Children's Home (Foster
Care program); National Sports Center for
the Disabled (program grant); The Center
for the Prevention of Domestic Violence
(program for children); Denison
Montessori Elementary School (after
school program); Family Learning Center
(early childhood program); The Denver
Street School (child care program for
single teenage parents)

Most grants awarded to organizations
located in Colorado.

Typical grant range: $3,000 to $50,000

122
The Chamberlain Foundation
501 N. Main Street, Suite 222
Pueblo, CO 81003
(719) 543-8596

Program grants; cultural organizations;
museums; youth; education; reduce
poverty

Grants awarded to organizations located
in Pueblo County.

123
The Christian Foundation
P.O. Box 457
Louisville, CO 80027

Program grants; Christian organizations;
Churches; youth; disabled; education;
social service organizations; Wilson
Methodist Church (Christian education
program); Therapeutic Riding Center
(horse riding program for people who are
disabled)

Most grants awarded to organizations
located in Colorado.

Typical grant range: $2,000 to $15,000

124
Collins Foundation
c/o Wells Fargo Bank, Trust Department
P.O. Box 299
Boulder, CO 80306
(303) 441-0309

Program grants; social service
organizations; cultural organizations;
youth; health organizations

Grants awarded to organizations located
in Boulder County.

Typical grant range: $1,000 to $5,000

125

Colorado Springs Community Trust Fund

P.O. Box 1443
Colorado Springs, CO 80901
(719) 389-1251

Program grants; Center for the Prevention of Domestic Violence (Safehouse Program); American Cancer Society (educational program); American Heart Association (Slim for Life program); Colorado Springs Symphony (program grant); Children's Chorale (program grant); Trails and Open Space Coalition (educational program); Newborn Hope (prematurity prevention program); Pikes Peak Mental Health (expand housing program); YMCA (program for people who are developmentally disabled)

Most grants awarded to organizations located in Colorado, with an emphasis in El Paso County.

Typical grant range: $500 to $4,000

126

The Community Foundation Serving Northern Colorado

420 S. Howes Street, Suite 101
Fort Collins, CO 80521
(970) 224-3462

Program grants; elderly; disabled; social service organizations; education; community development; health organizations; cultural organizations; Poudre Valley Hospital Foundation (Learn to Care program); Literacy, Education and Arts for Families (program grant)

Grants awarded to organizations located in northern Colorado.

127

Comprecare Foundation, Inc.

1145 Bannock Street
Denver, CO 80204
(303) 629-8661

Program grants; Northwest Colorado Visiting Nurse Association, Inc. (Senior Wellness Program); Colorado Action for Healthy People (projects for the elderly); Kids in Need of Dentistry (dental program for children); Damen House (transitional housing program); Planned Parenthood (program to prevent adolescent pregnancy); Montrose County Public Health Nursing Service (injury prevention program); Colorado Academy of Family Physicians Foundation (tobacco education program)

Grants awarded to organizations located in Colorado.

Typical grant range: $3,000 to $10,000

128

Adolph Coors Foundation

4100 E. Mississippi Ave., Suite 1850
Denver, CO 80246
(303) 388-1636

Program grants; Girl Scouts (educational program); Boys & Girls Club (program grant); Family and Community Education and Support (program to prevent family violence and child abuse); Health SET (computer training program for the elderly); Mesa County Partners (mentoring, recreation and educational program for at-risk youth); Mizel Museum of Judaica (educational program); Mount Evans Hospice, Inc. (bereavement program); Family Learning Center (educational program for low-income families); The Children's Literacy Center (Parents as Tutors program); Frontiers of Science Institute/University of Northern Colorado (science and mathematics program for high school students)

Grants awarded to organizations located in Colorado.

Typical grant range: $3,000 to $125,000

129
The Denver Foundation
950 S. Cherry Street, Suite 220
Denver, CO 80246
(303) 300-1790

Program grants; The Friends of Bluff Lake (environmental education program); Colorado Wildlife Federation (conservation education program); Foundation for the Denver Performing Arts Complex (program grant); Opera Colorado (educational program); United Black Women (African American Leadership Program); Arvada United Methodist Church (literacy program); Big Brothers/Big Sisters (mentoring program); Denver Museum of Natural History (educational program); Aurora Mental Health Center (Women's Empowerment Program); National Jewish Medical and Research Center (Community Outreach program); United Cerebral Palsy (Early Education program); American Humane Association (project grant); Community Housing Services, Inc. (elder abuse prevention program); Stein Elementary School (Early Start Summer Program)

Typical grant range: $5,000 to $20,000

130
El Pomar Foundation
Ten Lake Circle
Colorado Springs, CO 80906
(719) 633-7733

Program grants; health organizations; youth; disabled; recreation; all levels of education; cultural organizations

Grants awarded to organizations located in Colorado.

Typical grant range: $2,500 to $100,000

131
Gates Family Foundation
3200 Cherry Creek South Drive, Suite 630
Denver, CO 80209
(303) 722-1881

Program grants; Boys and Girls Club (summer camp program); United Way (program grant); South Park Seniors (project grant); Volunteers for Outdoor Colorado (public land improvement project); Colorado Minority Engineering (MESA program); University of Colorado (Senior Executive Program)

Most grants awarded to organizations located in Colorado, with an emphasis in the Denver vicinity.

Typical grant range: $10,000 to $100,000

132
A.V. Hunter Trust, Inc.
650 S. Cherry Street, Suite 535
Denver, CO 80246
(303) 399-5450

Program grants; youth; elderly; disabled; women; social service organizations; Catholic Charities and Community Services (transitional housing program); Center for Women's Employment and Education (program grant); Community Housing Services, Inc. (Elder Abuse Prevention Program); Boy Scouts of America (Inner City and In-School Scouting Program)

Most grants awarded to organizations located in Denver.

Typical grant range: $2,000 to $30,000

133
JJJ Foundation, Inc.
287 Century Circle, Suite 100
Louisville, CO 80027
(303) 926-1111

Program grants; Big Brothers/Big Sisters
(mentoring program); Boys and Girls
Club (after school program); Children's
Outreach Project (child care program for
disadvantaged children); Friends of Bluff
Lake (environmental education program);
The Adoption Exchange (program to
facilitate adoption process); Colorado
RUSH (soccer program for children who
are disabled); Tiny Tim Developmental
Preschool (specialized learning program
for children with special needs)

Grants awarded to organizations located
in Colorado.

Typical grant range: $1,000 to $5,000

134
**Helen K. and Arthur E. Johnson
Foundation**
1700 Broadway, Suite 1100
Denver, CO 80290
(303) 861-4127

Program grants; Colorado AIDS Project
(education program); Denver Museum of
Natural History (program grant); COMPA
Food Ministry (project grant); Disabled
Resource Services (Youth Employment
Program); Center for Hearing, Speech and
Language, Inc. (Kidscreen Program);
Curtis Park Community Center (Junior
High Helper Program); Grand Valley
Hospice (program for youth); Kids in
Need of Dentistry (program grant);
Seniors! Inc. (respite care program);
St. Mary's Hospital Foundation (nurse
training program); Denver Public Library
(reading project); Laradon Hall Society
for Exceptional Children (safety project);
Eagle Lodge, Inc. (after-school homework
program); Graland Country Day School
(summer program)

Grants awarded to organizations located
in Colorado.

Typical grant range: $5,000 to $75,000

135
**The Carl W. and Carrie Mae Joslyn
Charitable Trust**
Trust Department
P.O. Box 1699
Colorado Springs, CO 80942
(719) 227-6439

Program grants; health organizations;
education; disabled; youth; elderly

Most grants awarded to organizations
located in El Paso County.

Typical grant range: $1,000 to $10,000

136
Kenneth Kendal King Foundation
900 Pennsylvania Street
Denver, CO 80203
(303) 832-3200

Program grants; youth; disabled; social
service organizations; higher education;
cultural organizations; Christian
organizations; Aurora Teen Pregnancy
Prevention Project

Grants awarded to organizations located
in Colorado, with an emphasis in Denver.

Typical grant range: $500 to $20,000

137
The J.K. Mullen Foundation
333 Logan Street, Suite 100
Denver, CO 80203
(303) 722-3557

Program grants; disabled; youth; women;
social service organizations; education;
Roman Catholic organizations

Most grants awarded to organizations
located in the Denver vicinity.

Typical grant range: $500 to $15,000

138
The Aksel Nielsen Foundation
13115 N. Melody Lane
Parker, CO 80138
(303) 841-3581

Program grants; disabled; social service
organizations; cultural organizations

Most grants awarded to organizations
located in Colorado.

139
H. Chase Stone Trust
c/o Bank One, Colorado Springs, N.A.
P.O. Box 1699
Colorado Springs, CO 80942
(719) 227-6441

Program grants; social service
organizations; youth; education; cultural
organizations; health organizations

Grants awarded to organizations located
in El Paso County.

Typical grant range: $1,000 to $20,000

140
The Summit Foundation
P.O. Box 4000
Breckenridge, CO 80424
(970) 453-5970

Program grants; environment; youth;
disabled; social service organizations;
education; health organizations; cultural
organizations; recreation; Bristlecone
Home Care and Hospice (program grant);
Summit Historical Society (program
grant); League for Animals and People of
the Summit (spay and neuter program)

Grants awarded to organizations located
in Summit County.

CONNECTICUT

141
The Barnes Foundation, Inc.
P.O. Box 315
East Hartland, CT 06027-0315
(860) 653-0462

Program grants; New Canaan Nature
Center (environmental education
program); Connecticut Audubon Society
(Schoolyard Area Nature Program);
ConnectKids (after school and summer
tutoring program); Center City Churches
(after-school and summer programs);
4-H Farm Resource Center, Inc.
(environmental education program);
Hartford Stage Company (education
program); Young Writers Institute
(mentoring program); Lake Champlain
Maritime Museum (Discovery Program);
Long Wharf Theatre (educational touring
company program); Music & Arts for
Humanity (after school arts program);
Science Museum of Connecticut, Inc.
(Math/Science/Technology Program);
Children's Community School
(mathematics program); East Lyme Public
Schools (literacy program); Hartford
Consortium for Higher Education
(mentoring program); University of
Hartford (program using college
education majors as tutors)

Grants awarded to organizations located
in Connecticut.

Typical grant range: $2,500 to $10,000

142
**Fred R. & Hazel W. Carstensen
Memorial Foundation, Inc.**
c/o Tellalian & Tellalian
211 State Street
Bridgeport, CT 06604
(203) 333-5566

Program grants; youth; education; cultural
organizations; Protestant organizations;
Boy Scouts (program grant)

Most grants awarded to organizations
located in the Bridgeport vicinity.

Typical grant range: $1,000 to $9,000

143

The Community Foundation for Greater New Haven
70 Audubon Street
New Haven, CT 06510
(203) 777-2386

Program grants; community development; education; cultural organizations; youth; elderly; social service organizations; health organizations; AIDS

Grants awarded to organizations located in the New Haven vicinity.

144

The Community Foundation of Southeastern Connecticut
P.O. Box 769
New London, CT 06320
(860) 442-3572

Program grants; East Lyme Youth Service Association (drug abuse prevention program); Children's Museum (after school program); Connecticut Teen Peace (teen conflict resolution program); Opportunities Industrialization Center (job training program); Thames River Family Program (transitional housing program); Connecticut Storytelling Center (program at New London schools); Interdistrict School for Arts and Communication (literacy program); Mohegan Elementary School (after school program); Connecticut College Office of Volunteers for Community Service (tutoring program)

Grants awarded to organizations located in southeastern Connecticut.

Typical grant range: $1,000 to $15,000

145

The Educational Foundation of America
35 Church Lane
Westport, CT 06880
(203) 226-6498

Program grants; environment; reproductive freedom; overpopulation; youth; education; cultural organizations; Native Americans

Typical grant range: $10,000 to $100,000

146

Fairfield Community Foundation
523 Danbury Road, Route 7
Wilton, CT 06897
(203) 834-9393

Program grants; youth; elderly; disabled; social service organizations; education; environment; cultural organizations; community development; Girl Scouts Council (Read to G.R.O.W. Program); Nature Center for Environmental Activities (educational program); Child Guidance Center (sexual abuse treatment program); American Classical Orchestra (program for children); Catholic Charities of Fairfield (program grant); Alzheimer's Association (Hispanic Outreach Project); American Red Cross (HIV/AIDS educational program); Visiting Nurse Care Network (program grant); Caroline House (preschool program); Fairfield University, Connecticut Writing Project (academic and creative writing program)

Grants awarded to organizations located in Fairfield County.

Typical grant range: $1,000 to $20,000

147

The Greater Bridgeport Area Foundation, Inc.
940 Broad Street
Bridgeport, CT 06604
(203) 334-7511

Program grants; Girl Scouts Council (after school program); YMCA (Youth Alternative to Violence project); Center for Creative Youth (summer program); Connecticut Council for Philanthropy (educational program on the environment); Audubon Center (program grant); United Visiting Nurse Association (program grant); Interfaith Housing Association (employment program); Bridgeport Hospital (Lead Safe Program); Child Guidance Center (sexual abuse treatment program); Saving Lives from Drugs and Alcohol (program for women and children); Caroline House (literacy program); Sacred Heart University (Science Ambassador Program); Hartford College for Women at University of Hartford, The Entrepreneurial Center (business development program)

Grants awarded in the following communities: Bridgeport, Easton, Fairfield, Milford, Monroe, Shelton, Stratford, Trumbull, and Westport.

Typical grant range: $1,000 to $15,000

148

Hartford Foundation for Public Giving
85 Gillett Street
Hartford, CT 06105
(860) 548-1888

Program grants; Hartford Symphony Orchestra, Inc. (education program); Hartford Children's Theatre, Inc. (training program); West Hartford Public Library (project for teenagers); Catholic Family Services (after school program); Jewish Federation (education program); Boys and Girls Club (training program); Hartford Food System, Inc. (Agency Automation Project); Hartford Interval House, Inc. (Domestic Violence Intervention Service Program); South Park Inn (program for the homeless); Hartford Hospital-Institute of Living (Grow Program); Literacy Volunteers (Agency Automation Project); American School for the Deaf (Mobile Hearing Project); Watkinson School (summer program); West Middle School Committee, Inc. (after school program); Hartford Public Schools (after school program); Manchester Community-Technical College (child development associate certificate program)

Grants awarded to organizations located in the Hartford vicinity.

Typical grant range: $1,000 to $75,000

149

The Cyrus W. & Amy F. Jones & Bessie D. Phelps Foundation, Inc.
c/o Tellalian & Tellalian
211 State Street
Bridgeport, CT 06604
(203) 333-5566

Program grants; hospitals; youth; disabled; social service organizations; community development; cultural organizations; Christian organizations; Bridgeport Area Youth Ministry (program grant)

Grants awarded to organizations located in Connecticut, with an emphasis in Bridgeport.

Typical grant range: $500 to $10,000

150

The John G. Martin Foundation
2 Batterson Park Road
Farmington, CT 06032
(860) 677-4574

Program grants; elderly; youth; social
service organizations; all levels of
education; health organizations; cultural
organizations

Grants awarded to organizations located
in the Hartford vicinity.

Typical grant range: $500 to $20,000

151

**New Britain Foundation for Public
Giving**
29 Russell Street
New Britain, CT 06052
(860) 229-6018

Program grants; youth; women; disabled;
social service organizations; education;
cultural organizations; Wheeler Clinic
(program to reduce domestic violence);
New Britain Police Athletic League
(recreation and education program);
YMCA (literacy program for adults who
are learning disabled); New Britain High
School Student Athletes Tutoring Program
(tutoring program)

Typical grant range: $1,000 to $25,000

152

Olin Corporation Charitable Trust
501 Merritt Seven
P.O. Box 4500
Norwalk, CT 06856
(203) 750-3000

Program grants; environment; minorities;
social service organizations

Grants awarded to organizations located
in areas of company operations (Olin
Corporation).

Typical grant range: $500 to $20,000

153

Emily Hall Tremaine Foundation, Inc.
290 Pratt Street
Meriden, CT 06450
(203) 639-5544

Program grants; learning disabled;
environment; youth; education; cultural
organizations

Typical grant range: $5,000 to $50,000

154

Union Carbide Foundation, Inc.
39 Old Ridgebury Road
Danbury, CT 06817
(203) 794-6945

Program grants; all levels of education;
engineering; science; mathematics;
environment; minorities

Grants awarded to organizations located
in areas of company operations (Union
Carbide Corporation).

Typical grant range: $2,000 to $20,000

155

Robert C. Vance Charitable Foundation
21 Winesap Road
Kensington, CT 06037
(860) 828-6037

Program grants; youth; social service
organizations; cultural organizations;
education; Friendship Center (emergency
needs program); Children in Placement
(program grant)

Grants awarded to organizations located
in the New Britain vicinity.

Typical grant range: $1,500 to $75,000

156

The Waterbury Foundation
81 W. Main Street
Waterbury, CT 06702
(203) 753-1315

Program grants; social service
organizations; youth; education; cultural
organizations; health organizations;
community development

Grants awarded to organizations located
in the Waterbury vicinity.

DELAWARE

157
Chichester duPont Foundation, Inc.
3120 Kennett Pike
Wilmington, DE 19807
(302) 658-5244

Program grants; environment; education; youth; disabled; health organizations

Typical grant range: $10,000 to $150,000

158
Delaware Community Foundation
P.O. Box 1636
Wilmington, DE 19899
(302) 571-8004

Program grants; social service organizations; disabled; youth; elderly; recreation; community development; cultural organizations; health organizations; Rehoboth Beach Public Library (program grant); YWCA (program grant); Delawareans United to Prevent Child Abuse (violence prevention program)

Grants awarded to organizations located in Delaware.

Typical grant range: $2,000 to $20,000

159
Milton and Hattie Kutz Foundation
100 W. 10th Street, Suite 301
Wilmington, DE 19801
(302) 427-2100

Program grants; youth; social service organizations

Grants awarded to organizations located in Delaware.

160
Laffey-McHugh Foundation
1220 Market Building
P.O. Box 2207
Wilmington, DE 19899
(302) 654-1680

Program grants; youth; elderly; disabled; social service organizations; all levels of education; Roman Catholic organizations

Most grants awarded to organizations located in Delaware, with an emphasis in Wilmington.

Typical grant range: $5,000 to $50,000

161
Longwood Foundation, Inc.
100 W. 10th Street, Suite 1109
Wilmington, DE 19801
(302) 654-2477

Program grants; youth; elderly; disabled; social service organizations; education; cultural organizations

Most grants awarded to organizations located in Delaware, with an emphasis in Wilmington.

Typical grant range: $50,000 to $300,000

162
The Raskob Foundation for Catholic Activities, Inc.
P.O. Box 4019
Wilmington, DE 19807
(302) 655-4440

Program grants; health organizations; education; youth; social service organizations; Roman Catholic organizations; Casa San Francisco (food program for migrants and the poor); Corpus Christi Parish (science program); St. Francis Hospital (program for the poor, homeless and uninsured); St. Catherine of Siena Parish (Hispanic Ministry Program)

Most grants awarded to Roman Catholic organizations.

Typical grant range: $500 to $20,000

163
Welfare Foundation, Inc.
100 W. 10th Street, Suite 1109
Wilmington, DE 19801
(302) 654-2489

Program grants; disabled; youth; elderly; social service organizations; education; environment; cultural organizations

Most grants awarded to organizations located in Delaware, with an emphasis in Wilmington.

Typical grant range: $5,000 to $75,000

DISTRICT OF COLUMBIA

164
Walter A. Bloedorn Foundation
888 17th Street, N.W., Suite 1075
Washington, DC 20006
(202) 452-8553

Program grants; youth; social service organizations; education; health organizations

Grants awarded to organizations located in the Washington, DC vicinity.

Typical grant range: $1,000 to $20,000

165
The Morris and Gwendolyn Cafritz Foundation
1825 K Street, N.W., 14th Floor
Washington, DC 20006
(202) 223-3100

Program grants; youth; elderly; disabled; women; minorities; social service organizations; environment; cultural organizations; health organizations; AIDS

Grants awarded to organizations located in the Washington, DC vicinity.

Typical grant range: $10,000 to $150,000

166
The Community Foundation for the National Capital Region
1112 16th Street, N.W., Suite 340
Washington, DC 20036
(202) 955-5890

Program grants; homeless; youth; social service organizations; cultural organizations

Grants awarded to organizations located in the Washington, DC vicinity.

167
The Lois & Richard England Family Foundation, Inc.
P.O. Box 11582
Washington, DC 20008
(202) 244-4636

Program grants; cultural organizations; youth; disabled; education; social service organizations; community development; Jewish organizations

Most grants awarded to organizations located in the Washington, DC vicinity.

Typical grant range: $2,000 to $10,000

168
Fannie Mae Foundation
North Tower, Suite One
4000 Wisconsin Avenue, N.W.
Washington, DC 20016
(202) 274-8000

Program grants; youth; minorities; women; homeless; social service organizations; community development; Foggy Bottom Food Pantry of the United Church (program to feed the homeless); Covenant House (emergency housing program for homeless youth)

Typical grant range: $5,000 to $50,000

169

John Edward Fowler Memorial Foundation
1725 K Street, N.W., Suite 1201
Washington, DC 20006
(202) 728-9080

Program grants; St. Aloysius Church (program for homeless men); Catholic Charities (social service programs); The Christ Child Society, Inc. (School Counseling Program); Anacostia Community Outreach Center (youth programs); Capital Area Food Bank (program grant); Center for Artistry in Teaching (Student and Teacher Enrichment Project); Community Family Life Services (employment program); The Company, Inc. (Writing Workshop program); Girl Scout Council (Summer Day Program); Midtown Youth Academy (after school and summer programs); Multiple Sclerosis Society (program grant); Perry School Community Services Center (program grant); Round House Theatre (Outreach Touring Program); United Community Ministries (housing program for homeless families); The Washington Ballet (outreach program); Friends of Marie Reed School and Recreation Center (after school and summer programs); Dinner Program for Homeless Women (program grant); Archbishop Carroll High School (social service program)

Most grants awarded to organizations located in the Washington, DC vicinity.

Typical grant range: $5,000 to $25,000

170

The Freed Foundation
1025 Thomas Jefferson St., Suite 308 East
Washington, DC 20007
(202) 337-5487

Program grants; Hospice Care of the District of Columbia (education program); Healthy Babies Project (teen pregnancy program); American Kidney Fund (summer camp program); Ford's Theatre Society (education and outreach program for children); Byte Back (computer education program for children); Crohn's & Colitis Foundation of America (summer camp program for children); National Wildlife Federation (Schoolyard Habitats Programs); Reading is Fundamental (reading program); Recording for the Blind & Dyslexic (project grant); Accokeek Foundation (environmental education program); For Love of Children (tutoring program); National Crime Prevention Council (program grant); Spanish Education Development Center (after school program); Gallaudet University (Response Team and Parent Education Programs)

Grants awarded to organizations located in the Washington, DC vicinity.

Typical grant range: $10,000 to $50,000

171
The Philip L. Graham Fund
c/o The Washington Post Co.
1150 15th Street, N.W.
Washington, DC 20071
(202) 334-6640

Program grants; education; disabled; women; youth; social service organizations; cultural organizations; Discovery Creek Children's Museum (educational program); Young Playwrights Theater (program grant); Black Student Fund (program grant); Children's National Medical Center (program grant); Alzheimer's Association (project grant); Dinner Program for Homeless Women (program grant); Kids Computer Workshop (computer training program); Church Association for Community Services (after-school program); New Hope Ministries (program for homeless who are mentally ill)

Grants awarded to organizations located in the Washington, DC vicinity.

Typical grant range: $5,000 to $50,000

172
Jovid Foundation
5335 Wisconsin Avenue, N.W., Suite 440
Washington, DC 20015
(202) 686-2621

Program grants; Dinner Program for Homeless Women (food preparation and service training program); Calvary Bilingual Multicultural Learning Center (early childhood training certification program); The Children's Foundation (training program for in-home childcare providers); Latin American Youth Center (job readiness and placement program for young adults); Washington Performing Arts Society (education program); The Family Place (literacy program); Southeast Ministry (GED preparation and job readiness program)

Most grants awarded to organizations located in Washington, DC.

Typical grant range: $1,000 to $25,000

173
Anthony Francis Lucas-Spindletop Foundation
c/o Sun Trust Bank
1445 New York Avenue, N.W.
Washington, DC 20005
(202) 661-0605

Program grants; youth (including education and social service organizations)

Grants awarded to organizations located in Washington, DC.

Typical grant range: $250 to $3,000

174
Gilbert and Jaylee Mead Family Foundation
2700 Virginia Avenue, N.W., No. 701
Washington, DC 20037
(202) 338-0398

Program grants; Capital Area Community Food Bank (program grant); Asian American LEAD (mentoring program); Baptist Home for Children and Families (employment readiness program); Florence Crittenton Services (teen pregnancy prevention program); For Love of Children (tutoring program); Musical Theater Center (program grant); Washington Opera (program grant); United Methodist Church (mentoring program for suspended teenagers); Western Presbyterian Church Project Create (arts program); St. Johns Episcopal School (programs for mathematics and Latin); DC Scores (after-school writing and mentoring program)

Typical grant range: $1,000 to $10,000

175

Eugene and Agnes E. Meyer Foundation
1400 16th Street, N.W., Suite 360
Washington, DC 20036
(202) 483-8294

Program grants; Food & Friends, Inc. (meal delivery program); Computer Community OutReach and Education (employment training program); IONA Senior Services (program grant); National Law Center on Homelessness and Poverty (self-sufficiency project); Eastern Choral Society (program grant); National Symphony Orchestra (community outreach program); YWCA (program grant); Women Empowered Against Violence (program for legal services); Discovery Creek Children's Museum (educational program)

Grants awarded to organizations located in the Washington, DC vicinity.

Typical grant range: $5,000 to $50,000

176

Public Welfare Foundation, Inc.
1200 U Street, N.W.
Washington, DC 20009
(202) 965-1800

Program grants; Congress Heights United Methodist Church (education program); Southeast Ministry (Men's Employment Network Program); National Minority AIDS Council (Women of Color and Their Families Project); Concerned Black Men (program grant); Clean and Sober Streets (substance abuse program); Inner Thoughts (programs for youth to enhance their artistic, academic, recreational and social skills); Parklands Community Center (Road to Success/Summer Camp program); Center to Prevent Handgun Violence (Legal Action Project); Recording for the Blind and Dyslexic (project grant); City Lights School (food service training program); Perry School Community Services Center (youth development and education program)

Typical grant range: $25,000 to $75,000

177

Hattie M. Strong Foundation
1620 I Street, N.W., Suite 700
Washington, DC 20006
(202) 331-1619

Program grants; Family Place (literacy program); Center for Artistry in Teaching (teacher mentoring program); Community Preservation and Development Corporation (Teen Assistant Internship Program); The Garden Family and Child Care Center (Language Education Acceleration Program); Washington Architectural Foundation (program introducing students to architecture); National Building Museum (program grant); Discovery Creek Children's Museum of Washington (environmental education program); Boys and Girls Club (summer school program); Levine School of Music (program grant); Wider Opportunities for Women (Work Skills Program); Institute for Advanced Studies in Immunology and Aging (mentoring program for minority students)

Most grants awarded to organizations located in the Washington, DC vicinity.

Typical grant range: $2,000 to $7,500

FLORIDA

178

Ruth Anderson Foundation
2511 Ponce De Leon Blvd., Suite 320
Coral Gables, FL 33134
(305) 444-6121

Program grants; social service organizations; youth; elderly; homeless; public education; environment; health organizations; cultural organizations

Grants awarded to organizations located in Dade County.

Typical grant range: $1,000 to $8,000

179
Cordelia Lee Beattie Foundation
1800 Second Street, Suite 750
Sarasota, FL 34236
(941) 957-0442

Program grants; cultural organizations, with an emphasis on performing arts

Grants awarded to organizations located in Sarasota County.

180
Edyth Bush Charitable Foundation, Inc.
199 E. Welbourne Avenue
P.O. Box 1967
Winter Park, FL 32790
(407) 647-4322

Program grants; youth; disabled; women; social service organizations; education; hospitals; health organizations; animal welfare; cultural organizations; National Charities Information Bureau (program grant); Boys and Girls Club (program grant); Jewish Family Services (Family Life Education Program)

Grants awarded in the following counties: Orange, Seminole, Osceola and Lake.

Typical grant range: $1,000 to $125,000

181
The Chatlos Foundation, Inc.
P.O. Box 915048
Longwood, FL 32791
(407) 862-5077

Program grants; youth; elderly; disabled; social service organizations; higher education; health organizations; Christian organizations

Typical grant range: $2,500 to $25,000

182
Community Foundation for Palm Beach and Martin Counties, Inc.
700 S. Dixie Highway, Suite 200
West Palm Beach, FL 33401
(561) 659-6800

Program grants; cultural organizations; youth; elderly; disabled; education; social service organizations; environment; The Women's Studies Institute (Group and Peer Counselor Project); Palm Beach County Literacy Coalition, Inc. (Family Literacy Education Program); Jupiter Elementary School (mentoring program)

Grants awarded to organizations located in Palm Beach and Martin Counties.

Typical grant range: $1,000 to $25,000

183
Community Foundation of Broward
1401 E. Broward Blvd., Suite 100
Ft. Lauderdale, FL 33301
(954) 761-9503

Program grants; animal welfare; youth; social service organizations; health organizations; cultural organizations

Grants awarded to organizations located in Broward County.

184

Community Foundation of Central Florida, Inc.
P.O. Box 2071
Orlando, FL 32802
(407) 872-3050

Program grants; Junior Achievement (Your Child Plus One program); YMCA (Hispanic Achievers Program); Edgewood Children's Ranch (group therapy program); Center for Drug Free Living (program for adolescents); Crealde Arts, Inc. (painting and drawing program); Jewish Family Services (The Women's Forum program); Mental Health Association of Central Florida (program grant); Second Harvest Food Bank (program grant); Adult Literacy League (Literacy for the Deaf program); A Gift for Teaching (Kids for Kids program); Seminole County Victims' Rights/ Safehouse (Middle School Prevention Project)

Grants awarded to organizations located in central Florida, with an emphasis in Orange, Osceola, and Seminole Counties.

Typical grant range: $2,000 to $10,000

185

Community Foundation of Collier County
2400 Tamiami Trail North, Suite 300
Naples, FL 34103
(941) 649-5000

Program grants; youth; disabled; environment; cultural organizations; health organizations; social service organizations; Immokalee Child Care Center (Parent Involvement Program); Guadalupe Center (literacy program); N.A.A.C.P. (after-school program); Redlands Christian Migrant Association (program grant); Boys and Girls Club (drug and alcohol prevention program)

Grants awarded to organizations located in Collier County.

Typical grant range: $2,000 to $11,000

186

The Community Foundation of Sarasota County, Inc.
P.O. Box 49587
Sarasota, FL 34230
(941) 955-3000

Program grants; social service organizations; youth; education; cultural organizations; health organizations; School Board of Sarasota County (Model Classroom Program); Sarasota Ballet of Florida (Dance the Next Generation Program)

Grants awarded to organizations located in Sarasota County.

Typical grant range: $1,000 to $20,000

187

The Community Foundation of Tampa Bay
4950 W. Kennedy Blvd., Suite 250
Tampa, FL 33609
(813) 282-1975

Program grants; disabled; youth; elderly; social service organizations; education; cultural organizations; health organizations

Grants awarded to organizations located in the Tampa vicinity.

188

Dade Community Foundation, Inc.
200 S. Biscayne Blvd., Suite 505
Miami, FL 33131
(305) 371-2711

Program grants; social service organizations; youth; community development; cultural organizations; African Americans

Grants awarded to organizations located in Dade County.

189

Jessie Ball duPont Fund
225 Water Street, Suite 1200
Jacksonville, FL 32202
(904) 353-0890

Program grants; Saint Vincent's Medical
Center, Inc. (outreach program); Arthritis
Foundation (program grant); Clara White
Mission (food program); Children's Home
Society (program for abused children);
YWCA (program grant); YMCA (child
care program for low income families);
City of Jacksonville (racial reconciliation
project); Florida Orchestra Guild
(program grant); Saint James Episcopal
Church (summer day camp project);
Episcopal Diocese of Florida (reading and
tutoring program for children); Florida
State University (Florida Arts Community
Enrichment Program); Stetson University
(environmental studies program)

Only previous recipients of funding from
this foundation are eligible to apply for
another grant.

Typical grant range: $5,000 to $150,000

190

**The Lucy Gooding Charitable
Foundation Trust**
10287 Shady Crest Lane
Jacksonville, FL 32221
(904) 737-8735

Program grants; disabled; youth; social
service organizations; education; animal
welfare

Grants awarded to organizations located
in the Jacksonville vicinity.

Typical grant range: $5,000 to $25,000

191

**The Community Foundation
in Jacksonville**
121 W. Forsyth Street, Suite 900
Jacksonville, FL 32202
(904) 356-4483

Program grants; I.M. Sulzbacher Center
for the Homeless (pediatric care program);
YMCA (program grant); Friends of the
Carpenter (transitional housing program
for recovering addicts); St. John's
Evangelical Lutheran Church (program
for the elderly); Youth Leadership
Jacksonville (leadership training
program); The Amelia Arts Academy
(cultural program for people who are
mentally disabled); The Cathedral Arts
Project (dance program); Moncrief
Missionary Baptist Church (tutoring
program); The Jericho School (outreach
program); The City of Jacksonville Beach
(after school tutoring program)

Most grants awarded to organizations
located in the Jacksonville vicinity.

Typical grant range: $2,000 to $20,000

192

**John S. and James L. Knight
Foundation**
One Biscayne Tower, Suite 3800
Two S. Biscayne Blvd.
Miami, FL 33131
(305) 908-2600

Program grants; Girl Scout Council (gang
prevention program); Catholic Charities
(adult education and literacy program);
The Salvation Army (housing program);
Miami Art Museum (education program);
Magic of Music Symphony Orchestra
Initiative (program grant); Institute for
Change in Higher Education (evaluation
program); Association of Schools of
Journalism and Mass Communication
(Newspapers-in-Residence Program)

Typical grant range: $15,000 to $200,000

193
The Charles N. & Eleanor Knight Leigh Foundation, Inc.
2511 Ponce De Leon Blvd., Suite 320
Coral Gables, FL 33134
(305) 444-6121

Program grants; youth; elderly; homeless; social service organizations; environment; cultural organizations

Grants awarded to organizations located in Dade County.

Typical grant range: $2,500 to $10,000

194
The Lost Tree Village Charitable Foundation, Inc.
11555 Lost Tree Way
North Palm Beach, FL 33408
(561) 622-3780

Program grants; Hispanic Human Resource Council (preschool and child care programs); Hospice of Palm Beach County (counseling program for parents); Cafe Joshua (lunch program for the homeless); New Hope Anger Management (counseling program); The Lord's Place (Project Family CARE); Ballet Florida (Inner-City Outreach Dance Program); DePorres P.L.A.C.E. (literacy program); Norton Museum of Art (after-school program); Vision Teen Parent Foundation (tutoring program for children on suspension from school); Autism Society of America (arts program); Palm Beach Habilitation Center (program grant); Rebekah's House (counseling program for homeless women); Dress for Success (program providing low-income women with a business suit)

Grants awarded to organizations located in Palm Beach County and southern Martin County.

Typical grant range: $3,000 to $30,000

195
Alex & Agnes O. McIntosh Foundation
2511 Ponce De Leon Blvd., Suite 320
Coral Gables, FL 33134
(305) 444-6121

Program grants; environment; youth; elderly; homeless; social service organizations; education; cultural organizations

Most grants awarded to organizations located in Dade County.

Typical grant range: $1,000 to $10,000

196
The Dr. P. Phillips Foundation
P.O. Box 3753
Orlando, FL 32802
(407) 422-6105

Program grants; youth; social service organizations; education; health organizations; cultural organizations

Grants awarded to organizations located in Orange and Osceola Counties.

Typical grant range: $1,000 to $40,000

197
The John E. & Aliese Price Foundation, Inc.
1279 Lavin Lane
North Fort Myers, FL 33917
(941) 656-0196

Program grants; youth; disabled; education; health organizations; Christian organizations

Most grants awarded to organizations located in the Fort Myers vicinity.

198
Publix Super Markets Charities
P.O. Box 407
Lakeland, FL 33802
(863) 688-1188

Program grants; youth; disabled; social service organizations; higher education; cultural organizations

Grants awarded to organizations located in Florida.

Typical grant range: $1,000 to $50,000

199

Paul E. & Klare N. Reinhold Foundation, Inc.
c/o Reinhold Corporation
320 Corporate Way, Suite 200
Orange Park, FL 32073
(904) 269-5857

Program grants; youth; social service organizations; cultural organizations; health organizations; YMCA (before and after school care program); Lutheran Social Services (Crisis Relief and Food Recovery Program)

Typical grant range: $1,000 to $20,000

200

William J. and Tina Rosenberg Foundation
2511 Ponce De Leon Blvd., Suite 320
Coral Gables, FL 33134
(305) 444-6121

Program grants; social service organizations; youth; elderly; homeless; environment; education; cultural organizations; health organizations

Most grants awarded to organizations located in Dade County.

Typical grant range: $500 to $15,000

201

The Saunders Foundation
P.O. Box 31813
Tampa, FL 33631
(813) 225-8364

Program grants; education; youth; social service organizations

Most grants awarded to organizations located in the Tampa Bay vicinity.

Typical grant range: $5,000 to $25,000

202

The Southwest Florida Community Foundation, Inc.
8260 College Parkway, Suite 101
Fort Myers, FL 33919
(941) 274-5900

Program grants; social service organizations; youth; education; health organizations

Grants awarded to organizations located in Lee County and surrounding Counties.

203

The Wahlstrom Foundation, Inc.
3055 Cardinal Drive, Suite 106
P.O. Box 3276
Vero Beach, FL 32964
(561) 231-7513

Program grants; Riverside Children's Theatre (program grant); Phone Friend (program to assist latchkey children); Adult Literacy (reading program for at-risk children); Space Coast Early Intervention (Project Autism); Exchange Club C.A.S.T.L.E. (program to help children cope with the divorce of their parents); Volunteer Action Center (summer volunteer program); Girl Scout Council (program grant); Junior Achievement (program to teach business operations to fifth graders)

Most grants awarded to organizations located in Indian River County.

204
Wilson-Wood Foundation, Inc.
3665 Bee Ridge Road, Suite 302
Sarasota, FL 34233
(941) 921-2856

Program grants; Epilepsy Foundation (employment program); Women's Resource Center (employment program); Child Development Center (program grant); Consumer Credit Counseling Service (program grant); Girl Scouts (program for people who are disabled); Easter Seals (program for children); Mana-Sota Lighthouse for the Blind (Independent Living Adult Program); Volunteer Center of Sarasota (teen volunteer program); Gulf Coast Marine Institute (program grant); Literacy Council (program grant); Sarasota Kiwanis Foundation (literacy program)

Grants awarded to organizations located in Sarasota and Manatee Counties.

Typical grant range: $3,000 to $20,000

GEORGIA

205
The Peyton Anderson Foundation, Inc.
577 Mulberry Street, Suite 1015
Macon, GA 31201
(478) 743-5359

Program grants; youth; disabled; minorities; women; social service organizations; cultural organizations; Aunt Maggie's Kitchen Table (program grant); Museum of Aviation at Robins AFB (education program)

Grants awarded to organizations located in Bibb County.

206
Callaway Foundation, Inc.
209 Broome Street
P.O. Box 790
LaGrange, GA 30241
(706) 884-7348

Program grants; Troup Family Connection Authority (program to reduce teen pregnancy); West Georgia Christian Academy, Inc. (media center project); City of LaGrange (recreation project); Troup County Board of Education (technology pilot program); LaGrange College (baseball facility and park project)

Grants awarded to organizations located in Georgia, with an emphasis in LaGrange.

Typical grant range: $1,000 to $100,000

207
The Coca-Cola Foundation, Inc.
One Coca-Cola Plaza, N.W.
Atlanta, GA 30313
(404) 676-2568

Program grants; all levels of education; minorities; cultural organizations

Typical grant range: $20,000 to $150,000

208
The Community Foundation for Greater Atlanta, Inc.
The Hurt Building, Suite 449
Atlanta, GA 30303
(404) 688-5525

Program grants; social service organizations; youth; community development; health organizations; education; cultural organizations

Grants awarded to organizations located in the Atlanta vicinity.

209
Philip and Irene Toll Gage Foundation
3414 Peachtree Road, Suite 722
Atlanta, GA 30326
(404) 842-1870

Program grants; youth; education; health organizations; cultural organizations; Protestant organizations

Grants awarded to organizations located in the Atlanta vicinity.

Typical grant range: $1,000 to $10,000

210
Georgia Health Foundation
57 Executive Park South, N.E., Suite 315
Atlanta, GA 30329
(404) 636-2525

Program grants; Grant Park Family Health Center, Inc. (program grant); Hillside Hospital, Inc. (Community Intervention Program); Spina Bifida Association (education program); Easter Seal Society (program for young adults with head and spinal cord injuries)

Grants awarded to organizations located in Georgia.

211
John H. and Wilhelmina D. Harland Charitable Foundation, Inc.
Two Piedmont Center, Suite 106
Atlanta, GA 30305
(404) 264-9912

Program grants; Spruill Center for the Arts (program grant); Academy Theatre (training program); Georgia Council on Child Abuse, Inc. (child abuse prevention program); Quality Care for Children (program grant); Resource Service Ministries, Inc. (home repair project); Hemophilia of Georgia, Inc. (camping program); The Howard School, Inc. (facilities planning project); Project Read, Inc. (tutor training and academic consulting program); Morehouse School of Medicine (head start program)

Grants awarded to organizations located in Georgia, with an emphasis in Atlanta.

Typical grant range: $5,000 to $25,000

212
The Ray M. and Mary Elizabeth Lee Foundation, Inc.
3414 Peachtree Road, Suite 722
Atlanta, GA 30326
(404) 842-1870

Program grants; youth; education; health organizations; cultural organizations; social service organizations

Most grants awarded to organizations located in the Atlanta vicinity.

Typical grant range: $1,000 to $15,000

213
The Newland Family Foundation, Inc.
230 Hampton Court
Athens, GA 30605
(706) 543-3938

Program grants; youth; elderly; social service organizations; education; environment

Grants awarded to organizations located in Georgia, with an emphasis in Athens-Clarke County.

Typical grant range: $2,000 to $10,000

214
The Rich Foundation, Inc.
11 Piedmont Center, Suite 204
Atlanta, GA 30305
(404) 262-2266

Program grants; cultural organizations; social service organizations; youth; higher education; health organizations

Grants awarded to organizations located in the Atlanta vicinity.

Typical grant range: $5,000 to $115,000

215
The Sapelo Foundation
308 Mallory Street, Suite C
St. Simons Island, GA 31522
(912) 638-6265

Program grants; environment; minorities; education; community development

Grants awarded to organizations located in Georgia.

Typical grant range: $500 to $30,000

216

The Frances Wood Wilson Foundation, Inc.
250 E. Ponce De Leon Avenue, Suite 702
Decatur, GA 30030
(404) 370-0035

Program grants; youth; education; disabled; health organizations; Protestant organizations

Most grants awarded to organizations located in Georgia.

Typical grant range: $2,000 to $50,000

217

Robert W. Woodruff Foundation, Inc.
50 Hurt Plaza, Suite 1200
Atlanta, GA 30303
(404) 522-6755

Program grants; New Town Macon (downtown redevelopment program); Upper Chattahoochee Riverkeeper Fund, Inc. (watershed education program); Georgia Partnership for Excellence in Education (program grant); Georgia Council on Economic Education (program grant); Robert W. Woodruff Health Sciences Fund, Inc. (program grant); Atlanta Baptist Association (program grant); Side by Side Clubhouse (rehabilitation program for people with a disability caused by brain injury)

Grants awarded to organizations located in Georgia, with an emphasis in Atlanta.

Typical grant range: $50,000 to $1,000,000

HAWAII

218

Alexander & Baldwin Foundation
P.O. Box 3440
Honolulu, HI 96801
(808) 525-6642

Program grants; St. Francis Healthcare Foundation (hospice program); Kauai Senior Centers (oral history project); Agricultural Leadership Foundation of Hawaii (leadership training program); Junior Achievement (economics/business education program); Kauai Junior Golf Association (program grant); Hawaii 4-H (program grant); Domestic Violence Clearinghouse (program grant); Hawaii Family Support Center (Healthy Start program)

Typical grant range: $500 to $25,000

219

Atherton Family Foundation
c/o Hawaii Community Foundation
900 Fort Street Mall, Suite 1300
Honolulu, HI 96813
(808) 537-6333

Program grants; youth; disabled; women; social service organizations; education; environment; health organizations; cultural organizations

Grants awarded to organizations located in Hawaii.

Typical grant range: $5,000 to $50,000

220

James & Abigail Campbell Foundation
1001 Kamokila Blvd.
Kapolei, HI 96707
(808) 674-3122

Program grants; education; youth; disabled; social service organizations; Nanaikapono Elementary School (reading program); Hawaii Nature Center (wetland education program); Junior Achievement of Hawaii (business education program)

Grants awarded to organizations located in Hawaii.

Typical grant range: $2,000 to $50,000

221

Harold K.L. Castle Foundation
146 Hekili Street, Suite 203A
Kailua, HI 96734
(808) 262-9413

Program grants; youth; women; education; health organizations; social service organizations; cultural organizations; Hawaii Opera Theater (program grant); Maui Economic Development Board (literacy program); Friends of Kailua High School (AIDS prevention project)

Grants awarded to organizations located in Hawaii.

Typical grant range: $5,000 to $200,000

222

Samuel N. and Mary Castle Foundation
733 Bishop Street, Suite 1275
Honolulu, HI 96813
(808) 522-1101

Program grants; Mothers Against Drunk Driving (education program); Horizons Academy (mental health program); Hawaii Opera Theater (program grant); Honolulu Symphony (education program for youth); Kauai Independent Daycare Services (special needs program for children); The Salvation Army (program grant); Big Island Substance Abuse Council (program for children); Pacific and Asian Affairs Council (high school education program); Hawaii Alliance for Arts Education (education program); Hui Malama Learning Center (education program); Star of the Sea Early Learning Center (traveling preschool project); Hawaii Association for the Education of Young Children (project grant); Chaminade University of Honolulu (Montessori Teacher Education Program)

Grants awarded to organizations located in Hawaii.

Typical grant range: $2,000 to $100,000

223

Cooke Foundation, Limited
Hawaii Community Foundation
900 Fort Street Mall, Suite 1300
Honolulu, HI 96813
(808) 537-6333

Program grants; Honolulu Symphony (youth education program); Hawaii State Dance Council (Dance Feast 2000 project); Hawaiian Music Hall of Fame and Museum, Inc. (Let's All Sing Together project); Honolulu Theatre for Youth (education program); Kauai Children's Discovery Museum (youth intern program); Hawaii Literacy, Inc. (literacy program); Hui Malama Learning Center (education program); National Tropical Botanical Garden (program grant); Women in Need (program grant); Friends of Youth for Environmental Service, Inc. (Kaneohe Bay Watershed Improvement project); Big Brothers/Big Sisters (after-school mentoring program)

Grants awarded to organizations located in Hawaii.

Typical grant range: $2,000 to $50,000

IDAHO

224

The Leland D. Beckman Foundation
c/o Stephen E. Martin
P.O. Box 3189
Idaho Falls, ID 83403

Program grants; youth; disabled; education; social service organizations; cultural organizations; South Bannock Free Library District (Read to Me project)

Grants awarded to organizations located in Idaho Falls.

Typical grant range: $1,000 to $11,000

225
Idaho Community Foundation
P.O. Box 8143
Boise, ID 83707
(208) 342-3535

Program grants; Priest River Public Library (program for children); Clearwater Valley Schools (latchkey program); Idaho Shakespeare Festival (program grant); Community Assistance League (art education program); Coeur d'Alene School District (Outdoor Education Program); Spirit Lake Elementary School (reading program); Bryan Elementary School (parent involvement program); University of Idaho Cooperative Extension System (after school program)

Grants awarded to organizations located in Idaho.

226
The John F. Nagel Foundation, Inc.
P.O. Box 1157
Boise, ID 83701
(208) 344-2666

Program grants; Nature Conservancy for Idaho (Middle Snake Water Awareness Program); Family Advocate Program (Family Outreach Program); Big Brothers/ Big Sisters (mentoring program); World Sports Humanitarian (sports program for youth); L. Cabin Literary Center (Writer Residency Program); Boise State University (nursing program)

Grants awarded to organizations located in southwestern Idaho.

Typical grant range: $5,000 to $35,000

227
The Whittenberger Foundation
P.O. Box 1073
Caldwell, ID 83606
(208) 459-3402

Program grants; youth; education; cultural organizations

Grants awarded to organizations located in southwestern Idaho.

Typical grant range: $1,000 to $8,000

ILLINOIS

228
Aon Foundation
123 N. Wacker Drive
Chicago, IL 60606
(312) 701-3000

Program grants; youth; disabled; social service organizations; hospitals; education; cultural organizations

Typical grant range: $5,000 to $100,000

229
The Baxter Allegiance Foundation
One Baxter Parkway
Deerfield, IL 60015
(847) 948-4604

Program grants; Infant Welfare Society (health project); Central Baptist Children's Home (foster grandparent program); YMCA (program grant); MENDAC Institute on Early Childhood (program for babies who are deaf); Daisy's Resource and Development Center (certified nursing assistant program); Waukegan Schools Foundation (program to train science education teachers); College of Lake County Foundation (Access to Success program); Barat College (program to train science education teachers)

Typical grant range: $3,000 to $60,000

230
The Blowitz-Ridgeway Foundation
1 Northfield Plaza, Suite 230
Northfield, IL 60093
(847) 446-1010

Program grants; Lake County Council Against Sexual Assault (children's program); Polish American Association (Women's Counseling Program); Fox Valley Hospice (volunteer training program); Housing Options for the Mentally Ill (program grant); Howard Brown Health Center (HIV/AIDS program); Jayne Shover Easter Seal (educational program); Snow City Arts Foundation (program grant); Big Brothers/Big Sisters (mentoring program); Howard Area Community Center (social service program); Information Technology Resource Center (project grant); Restoration Ministries (gang prevention and youth development program); Lakeview Shelter (Homeless Health Care program); Rush-Presbyterian-St. Luke's Medical Center (Nurse Practitioner Program)

Grants awarded to organizations located in Illinois.

Typical grant range: $2,500 to $30,000

231
Helen Brach Foundation
55 W. Wacker Drive, Suite 701
Chicago, IL 60601
(312) 372-4417

Program grants; House of the Good Shepherd (domestic violence program); Catholic Charities (program grant); Boys and Girls Clubs (program for girls); Chicago Youth Centers (after-school program); Chicago Institute of Neurosurgery (brain tumor diagnostic program); Children's Home and Aid (child abuse prevention program); Cradle Society (adoption service program); Holy Family Medical Center (prenatal program); Lake County Haven (program for homeless women and children); Performing Animal Welfare Society (program grant); Chicago Lighthouse for the Blind (Family Intervention Program); Rainbow Riders Horseback (program for people who are mentally and physically disabled); Roseland Training Center (Child Educational Tutoring Program); Trinity High School (science program); Cristo Rey Jesuit High School (reading program); Kenyon College (Summer Seminars Program)

Typical grant range: $3,000 to $30,000

232
Fred J. Brunner Foundation
9300 King Avenue
Franklin Park, IL 60131
(847) 678-3232

Program grants; health organizations; education; youth; social service organizations

Grants awarded to organizations located in Illinois, with an emphasis in the Chicago vicinity.

Typical grant range: $1,000 to $5,000

233
Elizabeth F. Cheney Foundation
120 S. LaSalle Street, Suite 1740
Chicago, IL 60603
(312) 782-1234

Program grants; performing arts; theatre and dance organizations; museums

Most grants awarded to organizations located in the Chicago vicinity.

Typical grant range: $1,000 to $40,000

234
The Chicago Community Trust
222 N. LaSalle Street, Suite 1400
Chicago, IL 60601
(312) 372-3356

Program grants; youth; elderly; disabled; education; community development; health organizations; social service organizations; cultural organizations

Grants awarded to organizations located in Cook County, with an emphasis in Chicago.

235
Chicago Tribune Foundation
435 N. Michigan Avenue
Chicago, IL 60611
(312) 222-4300

Program grants; cultural organizations; youth; minorities; education; social service organizations

Most grants awarded to organizations located in the Chicago vicinity.

Typical grant range: $3,000 to $30,000

236
Arie and Ida Crown Memorial
222 N. LaSalle Street, Suite 2000
Chicago, IL 60601
(312) 236-6300

Program grants; youth; women; social service organizations; cultural organizations; environment; health organizations; Jewish organizations

Most grants awarded to organizations located in the Chicago vicinity.

Typical grant range: $1,000 to $30,000

237
Doris and Victor Day Foundation, Inc.
1705 Second Avenue, Suite 424
Rock Island, IL 61201
(309) 788-2300

Program grants; minorities; youth; social service organizations; recreation; education; Martin Luther King Center (job training program); YMCA (mentoring program); Black Hawk College Foundation (Family Literacy Program)

Grants awarded to organizations located in the Illinois/Iowa Quad Cities vicinity.

238
DeKalb County Community Foundation
2225 Gateway Drive
Sycamore, IL 60178
(815) 748-5383

Program grants; DeKalb Area Women's Center (Art Gallery Program); St. Mary Church (adult education program); Ben Gordon Center (Volunteer Services Program); Kishwaukee Education Consortium (Student Philanthropic Project)

Grants awarded to organizations located in DeKalb County.

Typical grant range: $500 to $15,000

239
Gaylord and Dorothy Donnelley Foundation
35 E. Wacker Drive, Suite 2600
Chicago, IL 60601
(312) 977-2700

Program grants; minorities; youth; social service organizations; education; cultural organizations; Lowcountry Food Bank (nutrition education program); Ballet Chicago (classical ballet training program); University of Chicago (environmental studies program)

Typical grant range: $3,000 to $20,000

240
Evanston Community Foundation
828 Davis Street, Suite 301
Evanston, IL 60201
(847) 492-0990

Program grants; Family Focus Violence-Prevention Project (African American youth program); The Lighthouse Partnership (school project to improve scholastic achievement of lower performing students); Leadership Evanston (community leadership development program); The Institute for Art Resource for Teachers and Students (program to integrate arts into public school classes); Oakton School Books & Breakfast Program (project to serve breakfast to students)

Grants awarded to organizations located in Evanston.

Typical grant range: $5,000 to $10,000

241
The Field Foundation of Illinois, Inc.
200 S. Wacker Drive, Suite 2080
Chicago, IL 60606
(312) 831-0910

Program grants; Blocks Together (Women's Organizing Project); Women Employed Institute (GED project); Bethany Hospital (Senior Resident Outreach program); AIDS Foundation (HIV prevention program); Chicago Shakespeare Theater (Team Shakespeare program); Joffrey Ballet of Chicago (Middle School Dance Club program); Chicago Metro History Education Center (Bilingual History Fair program); Family Matters (Latchkey Learning programs); Openlands Project (Urban Greening program); Open Hand Chicago (nutrition program); Friends of the Chicago River (project grant); Chicago Youth Programs (Adolescent Health Outreach program); Governors State University (Learning in Context project); James Otis Elementary School (teaching program)

Grants awarded to organizations located in the Chicago vicinity.

Typical grant range: $5,000 to $35,000

242
Lloyd A. Fry Foundation
120 S. LaSalle Street, Suite 1950
Chicago, IL 60603
(312) 580-0310

Program grants; Horizon Hospice (bereavement program); Cook County Hospital (art therapy program); AIDS Foundation of Chicago (HIV Prevention Research Project); Chicago Abused Women Coalition (Hospital Crisis Intervention Project); Chicago Youth Programs, Inc. (education and recreation programs for teenagers); Asian Human Services, Inc. (mentoring program); Catholic Charities (job preparation and placement program); Chicago Legal Clinic (domestic violence program); Friends of the Parks (program grant); Museum of Contemporary Art (program grant); Girl Scouts (Homeless Shelter Troops program); Housing Opportunities & Maintenance for the Elderly (Volunteer Services Program); YWCA (Primary Pregnancy Prevention program); Dominican University (early childhood certification program); Parents United for Responsible Education (project to monitor early childhood education); Teachers' Task Force (literacy program); Lawndale Community School (after school program); North Park University (community development program)

Grants awarded to organizations located in the Chicago vicinity.

Typical grant range: $2,000 to $40,000

243

The Joyce Foundation
70 W. Madison Street, Suite 2750
Chicago, IL 60602
(312) 782-2464

Program grants; education; minorities;
women; employment; environment;
Women Employed Institute (job training
program); League of Women Voters
(Campaign for Political Reform Project);
Orchestral Association (Musicians
Residency Program); Illinois Coalition for
Immigrant and Refugee Rights (Don't
Count Me Out Project); African American
Arts Alliance (Black Arts Week Program);
Boys and Girls Club (program grant);
Chicago Academy of Sciences (program
grant); Community Media Workshop
(Chicago Successful Schools Project);
Chicago State University (preparation
program for teachers); University of
Illinois (educational program for teachers)

Typical grant range: $10,000 to $250,000

244

James S. Kemper Foundation
c/o Kemper Insurance Companies
1 Kemper Drive
Long Grove, IL 60049
(847) 320-2847

Program grants; Joffrey Ballet of Chicago
(educational program); Goodman Theater
(support the matinee program); Chicago
Symphony Orchestra (education and
community programs); Boys and Girls
Club (management program); Northern
Illinois Council on Alcoholism and
Substance Abuse (Women's and
Children's Educational Program); Ravinia
Festival (Young Singers Program);
Association of Governing Boards (higher
education program); Augustana College
(computer lab project); College of
Insurance (enhance the quality of the
MBA program); Bradley University
(International Insurance Scholars
Program)

Typical grant range: $2,500 to $35,000

245

Sara Lee Foundation
3 First National Plaza
Chicago, IL 60602
(312) 558-8448

Program grants; women; youth;
minorities; social service organizations;
employment programs; cultural
organizations

Most grants awarded to organizations
located in the Chicago vicinity.

Typical grant range: $2,500 to $40,000

246

**John D. and Catherine T. MacArthur
Foundation**
140 S. Dearborn Street
Chicago, IL 60603
(312) 726-8000

Program grants; cultural organizations;
minorities; youth; women; disabled;
education; community development

Typical grant range: $50,000 to $500,000

247

The Nalco Foundation
One Nalco Center
Naperville, IL 60563
(630) 305-1556

Program grants; women; youth; elderly;
disabled; social service organizations;
education; health organizations; hospitals;
cultural organizations

Grants awarded to organizations located
in areas of company operations (Nalco
Chemical Co.).

248

The Northern Trust Company Charitable Trust

c/o The Northern Trust Company
Community Affairs Division
50 South LaSalle Street
Chicago, IL 60675
(312) 444-4059

Program grants; Catholic Charities (job preparation program); Girl Scouts (program grant); Big Brothers/Big Sisters (mentoring program); Chicago Youth Centers (program grant); Infant Welfare Society (pediatric dental program); Rush Hospice Partners (program grant); Suburban Primary Health Care Council (Access to Care program); The Core Foundation (AIDS/HIV Health Center Project); The Family Institute (Bilingual Community Outreach Program); Greater Chicago Food Depository (program grant); Housing Opportunities & Maintenance for the Elderly (program grant); Urban Solutions (summer youth employment program); Jewish Council on Urban Affairs (program grant); Chicago Symphony Orchestra (education and community programs); Suzuki-Orff School for Young Musicians (community outreach program); One-To-One Learning Center (Read-to-Win program); University of Illinois (Urban Developers Certificate Program)

Most grants awarded to organizations located in the Chicago vicinity.

Typical grant range: $1,500 to $15,000

249

Peoria Area Community Foundation

331 Fulton Street, Suite 310
Peoria, IL 61602
(309) 674-8730

Program grants; West Bluff Neighborhood Housing Services (program grant); WTVP 47 Literacy Fund (First Book Program); I. Bluffs Community School (substance abuse training program); Elmwood Elementary School (after-school program)

Grants awarded to organizations located in the Peoria vicinity.

Typical grant range: $1,000 to $10,000

250

Polk Bros. Foundation, Inc.

420 N. Wabash Avenue, Suite 204
Chicago, IL 60611
(312) 527-4684

Program grants; youth; women; minorities; disabled; social service organizations; cultural organizations; education; health organizations; Jewish organizations

Grants awarded to organizations located in the Chicago vicinity.

Typical grant range: $5,000 to $100,000

251

The Quaker Oats Foundation
Quaker Tower, Suite 27-5
P.O. Box 049001
Chicago, IL 60604
(312) 222-7377

Program grants; Junior Achievement
(program grant); Boys and Girls Club
(homework and tutoring program); Byrd
Community Academy (School Partners
Program); YMCA (educational and youth
development programs); Westside
Community Services (youth mentoring
program); Cabrini-Green Tutoring
Program (tutoring program for elementary
school students); Center for Excellence in
Education (leaders project for minority
high school students); Wells Community
Academy High School (School Partners
Program providing tutoring); Arthur A.
Libby Elementary School (School
Partners Program); Northwestern
University (summer scholars program for
teachers and students)

Grants awarded to organizations located
in areas of company operations (Quaker
Oats Co.).

Typical grant range: $1,000 to $30,000

252

Rauch Family Foundation I, Inc.
1705 2nd Avenue, Suite 424
Rock Island, IL 61201
(309) 788-2300

Program grants; Floreciente
Neighborhood Association (program
grant); Quad Cities Youth Conference
(program grant); Girl Scout Council
(project grant); Rock Island Clean &
Beautiful, Inc. (project grant)

Grants awarded to organizations located
in Rock Island.

Typical grant range: $500 to $5,000

253

The Retirement Research Foundation
8765 W. Higgins Road, Suite 430
Chicago, IL 60631
(773) 714-8080

Program grants; Suicide Prevention
Services (program to prevent suicide
among the elderly); Catholic Charities
(Nutrition Service Program); Alzheimer's
Association (program grant); Arbor
Hospice, Inc. (volunteer program); Mercy
Hospital and Medical Center (volunteer
program); Ravenswood Hospital Medical
Center (mobile dental program); Central
Institute for the Deaf (audiology
program); Little Brothers Friends of the
Elderly (program grant); Famous Door
Theatre Co. (program grant for
performing for the elderly); Jewish
Children's Bureau of Chicago (program
grant); Lutheran Home and Services
(child day care program); Archbishop
Thomas J. Murphy High School (program
grant); Northwestern University School of
Speech (research project)

Most grants awarded to organizations
helping the elderly.

Typical grant range: $10,000 to $150,000

254

Irvin Stern Foundation
116 W. Illinois Street, Suite 2 East
Chicago, IL 60610
(312) 321-9402

Program grants; social service
organizations; vocational training; health
organizations; community development;
Jewish organizations

Most grants awarded to organizations
located in the Chicago vicinity.

Typical grant range: $2,000 to $30,000

255
W.P. and H.B. White Foundation
540 Frontage Road, Suite 3240
Northfield, IL 60093
(847) 446-1441

Program grants; education; community
development; health organizations;
cultural organizations; youth; social
service organizations

Grants awarded to organizations located
in the Chicago vicinity.

Typical grant range: $5,000 to $20,000

256
Woods Fund of Chicago
360 N. Michigan Ave., Suite 1600
Chicago, IL 60601
(312) 782-2698

Program grants; minorities; youth;
cultural organizations; education;
community development

Most grants awarded to organizations
located in the Chicago vicinity.

Typical grant range: $5,000 to $45,000

INDIANA

257
Ball Brothers Foundation
222 S. Mulberry Street
P.O. Box 1408
Muncie, IN 47308
(765) 741-5500

Program grants; all levels of education;
youth; social service organizations;
recreation; community development;
cultural organizations; health
organizations

Grants awarded to organizations located
in Indiana, with an emphasis in Muncie
and East Central Indiana.

Typical grant range: $3,000 to $100,000

258
George and Frances Ball Foundation
P.O. Box 1408
Muncie, IN 47308
(765) 741-5500

Program grants; higher education;
environment; youth; social service
organizations; hospitals; community
development; cultural organizations

Most grants awarded to organizations
located in central Indiana and Delaware
County, with an emphasis in Muncie.

Typical grant range: $1,500 to $75,000

259
Florence V. Carroll Charitable Trust
c/o Wells Fargo Bank
112 West Jefferson Blvd.
South Bend, IN 46601
(219) 237-3475

Program grants; youth; cultural
organizations; education; social service
organizations

Grants awarded to organizations located
in the South Bend vicinity.

Typical grant range: $5,000 to $40,000

260
The Clowes Fund, Inc.
320 N. Meridian Street, Suite 316
Indianapolis, IN 46204-1722
(800) 943-7209

Program grants; all levels of education;
disabled; women; youth; social service
organizations; cultural organizations;
Crawfordsville Community School
Corporation (GED program)

Typical grant range: $5,000 to $50,000

261

Community Foundation of St. Joseph County
P.O. Box 837
South Bend, IN 46624
(219) 232-0041

Program grants; community development; youth; education; cultural organizations; health organizations; South Bend Regional Museum of Art (program for children); City of South Bend Parks and Recreation Department (after school program for computer training)

Grants awarded to organizations located in St. Joseph County.

262

Dearborn County Community Foundation
406 2nd Street
Aurora, IN 47001
(812) 926-9300

Program grants; Indiana Theatre (summer musical project); Lawrenceburg Lions Club (program for youth); YMCA (summer program); Bright Volunteer Fire Company (radio communication project); Southeast Regional Community Corrections (juvenile home detention program); Dearborn County Juvenile Center (education program); Salvation Army (Tools for School program); Mores Hill Elementary School (after school care program)

Grants awarded to organizations located in Dearborn County.

Typical grant range: $1,000 to $5,000

263

The Dekko Foundation, Inc.
1208 E. Lakeside Drive
P.O. Box 548
Kendallville, IN 46755
(219) 347-1278

Program grants; YWCA (domestic violence education prevention program); County Public Health Nursing Agency (Parents as Teachers program); Athens City Schools (technology training program); Central Decatur Community School District (summer reading and science program)

Typical grant range: $5,000 to $50,000

264

Elkhart County Community Foundation, Inc.
P.O. Box 2932
Elkhart, IN 46515
(219) 295-8761

Program grants; Oaklawn Community Mental Health Center (family support program); Elkhart County Council on Aging (Senior Advocate Program); Boys and Girls Club of Goshen (program grant); Elkhart County Special Education Cooperative (education program); Elkhart County Symphony Association (program grant); Pyramid Productions (musical program for people with special needs); Woodlawn Nature Center (Hands on Bugs project)

Grants awarded to organizations located in Elkhart County.

Typical grant range: $1,500 to $8,000

265

Fort Wayne Community Foundation, Inc.
701 S. Clinton Street, Suite 210
Fort Wayne, IN 46802
(219) 426-4083

Program grants; youth; cultural organizations; education; social service organizations; health organizations

Grants awarded to organizations located in the Fort Wayne vicinity.

266
Greater Lafayette Community Foundation
1114 State Street
P.O. Box 225
Lafayette, IN 47902
(765) 742-9078

Program grants; social service organizations; youth; cultural organizations

Grants awarded to organizations located in the Lafayette vicinity.

267
The Health Foundation of Greater Indianapolis
Marott Center, First Floor
342 Massachusetts Avenue
Indianapolis, IN 46204
(317) 630-1805

Program grants; health organizations; youth; women; minorities; social service organizations; Martin Luther King Multi-Service Center (program grant); Ruth Lilly Center for Health Education (mentoring program); Indiana Coalition on Housing & Homeless Issues, Inc. (Children's Health Insurance Program)

Grants awarded to organizations located in Marion County and seven contiguous counties in central Indiana.

Typical grant range: $1,000 to $25,000

268
The Indianapolis Foundation
615 N. Alabama Street, Room 119
Indianapolis, IN 46204
(317) 634-2423

Program grants; youth; disabled; social service organizations; community development; cultural organizations

Grants awarded to organizations located in Marion County.

Typical grant range: $2,000 to $55,000

269
Irwin-Sweeney-Miller Foundation
P.O. Box 808
Columbus, IN 47202
(812) 372-0251

Program grants; community development; cultural organizations; youth; education

Grants awarded to organizations located in the Columbus vicinity.

Typical grant range: $500 to $20,000

270
Johnson County Community Foundation
18 W. Jefferson
P.O. Box 217
Franklin, IN 46131
(317) 738-2213

Program grants; Johnson County Senior Services (transportation program); Reach for Youth (project grant); Girls, Inc. (Growing Girls program); Town of Prince's Lake (bike and hike trail project); Humane Society (program grant); Mother/Baby Wellness Center (program grant); Sugar Grove Elementary School (sculpture project); Clark Pleasant School Corporation (parenting skills education program)

Most grants awarded to organizations located in Johnson County.

Typical grant range: $500 to $4,000

271
Lilly Endowment Inc.
2801 N. Meridian Street
Indianapolis, IN 46208
(317) 924-5471

Program grants; women; youth; minorities; disabled; animal welfare; cultural organizations; all levels of education; Indianapolis Children's Choir (project grant); Boy Scouts of America (urban scouting programs)

Grants awarded to organizations located in Indiana, with an emphasis in Indianapolis.

Typical grant range: $20,000 to $200,000

272
The Lincoln Financial Group Foundation, Inc.
1300 S. Clinton Street
P.O. Box 7863
Fort Wayne, IN 46801
(219) 455-3868

Program grants; cultural organizations; youth; disabled; education; social service organizations; The Lost Puzzle of Gondwana (music education project for children)

Grants awarded to organizations located in areas of company operations.

Typical grant range: $3,000 to $75,000

273
Madison County Community Foundation
P.O. Box 1056
Anderson, IN 46015
(765) 644-0002

Program grants; community development; minorities; youth; social service organizations; education; cultural organizations; Dr. Martin Luther King Memorial Commission (transit program for the elderly); Anderson Public Library (summer reading program)

Grants awarded to organizations located in Madison County.

Typical grant range: $500 to $5,000

274
The Martin Foundation, Inc.
500 Simpson Avenue
Elkhart, IN 46515
(219) 295-3343

Program grants; youth; women; social service organizations; environment; health organizations; cultural organizations

Grants awarded to organizations located in Indiana.

Typical grant range: $1,000 to $20,000

275
Noble County Community Foundation
1599 Lincolnway S.
Ligonier, IN 46767-9731
(219) 894-3335

Program grants; recreation; youth; social service organizations; education; cultural organizations; health organizations; community development

Grants awarded to organizations located in Noble County.

276
Nicholas H. Noyes, Jr. Memorial Foundation, Inc.
PMB 356
1950 E. Greyhound Pass #18
Carmel, IN 46033
(317) 844-8009

Program grants; social service organizations; youth; education; health organizations; cultural organizations

Grants awarded to organizations located in the Indianapolis vicinity.

277
Portland Foundation
112 E. Main Street
Portland, IN 47371
(219) 726-4260

Program grants; youth; cultural organizations; community development; Pregnancy Care Center (abstinence program); Community and Family Services (program grant)

Grants awarded to organizations located in Jay County.

Typical grant range: $1,000 to $20,000

IOWA

278
Marie H. Bechtel Charitable Remainder Uni-Trust
1000 Firstar Center
201 W. Second Street
Davenport, IA 52801
(563) 328-3333

Program grants; at-risk children; social service organizations; higher education; health organizations

Grants awarded to organizations located in Scott County.

Typical grant range: $5,000 to $100,000

279
Roy J. Carver Charitable Trust
202 Iowa Avenue
Muscatine, IA 52761
(319) 263-4010

Program grants; Muscatine County Emergency Medical Services Association (child safety program); Lutheran Social Service (project grant); YMCA (Leadership Week program for at-risk youth); Iowa Natural Heritage Foundation (program to acquaint Iowa youth with public and private natural lands); Reading Recovery Center (program grant); Central College (library automation project); Chickasaw County Extension (after school science education program); University of Northern Iowa Foundation (summer research program for undergraduates)

Grants awarded to organizations located in Iowa.

Typical grant range: $5,000 to $200,000

280
Community Foundation of the Great River Bend
111 East 3rd Street, Suite 710
Davenport, IA 52801
(563) 326-2840

Program grants; Mississippi Valley Girl Scouts (Discovery Program); Alzheimer's Association (program grant); Child Abuse Council (Sexual Abuse Treatment Program); Moline Soccer Club (Green Valley Capital Improvement Project); Safer Foundation (Juvenile Delinquency Disruption Program); Center for Alcohol and Drug Services, Inc. (after school art project); Clinton Public Library (summer reading program); Villa Montessori School (Infant and Toddler Program); Iowa State University (after-school program)

Typical grant range: $1,000 to $5,000

281
The Gazette Foundation
500 3rd Avenue, S.E.
Cedar Rapids, IA 52401
(319) 398-8207

Program grants; environment; social service organizations; youth; higher education; cultural organizations

Grants awarded to organizations located in the Cedar Rapids vicinity.

282
The Greater Cedar Rapids Community Foundation
200 First Street, S.W.
Cedar Rapids, IA 52404
(319) 366-2862

Program grants; youth; social service organizations; health organizations; environment; education; community development; cultural organizations

Grants awarded to organizations located in Linn County.

283
The Fred Maytag Family Foundation
P.O. Box 366
Newton, IA 50208
(641) 791-0395

Program grants; environment; education; youth; disabled; social service organizations; cultural organizations; health organizations

Most grants awarded to organizations located in Newton and Des Moines.

284
R.J. McElroy Trust
KWWL Building, Suite 318
500 E. Fourth Street
Waterloo, IA 50703
(319) 287-9102

Program grants; Nature Conservancy (college internship program); Family Service League (child advocacy and family service programs); Waterloo/Cedar Falls Symphony (educational program); Waterloo Swimming Association (expand swimming program); Junior Achievement (educational program); Boy Scouts Council (program grant); Cedar Valley Hospice (youth program); Veterans Hospital (education programs); Waterloo Community Schools (cultural project); St. Mary's Preschool (project grant); Iowa College Foundation (faculty research program); University of Northern Iowa (early childhood education program)

Grants awarded to organizations located in northeastern Iowa.

Typical grant range: $2,000 to $100,000

285
Mid-Iowa Health Foundation
550 39th Street, Suite 104
Des Moines, IA 50312
(515) 277-6411

Program grants; disabled; youth; social service organizations; health organizations; AIDS

Grants awarded to organizations located in the Polk County vicinity.

Typical grant range: $5,000 to $25,000

286
Pella Rolscreen Foundation
c/o Pella Corporation
102 Main Street
Pella, IA 50219
(641) 628-1000

Program grants; higher education; cultural organizations; youth; community development

Grants awarded to organizations located in areas of company operations (Pella Corp.).

Typical grant range: $250 to $25,000

287
The Principal Financial Group Foundation, Inc.
711 High Street
Des Moines, IA 50392
(515) 247-5091

Program grants; youth; disabled; social service organizations; community development; education; cultural organizations

Grants awarded to organizations located in areas of company operations, with an emphasis in Des Moines.

Typical grant range: $1,000 to $40,000

288

Siouxland Community Foundation
P.O. Box 2014
Sioux City, IA 51104
(712) 239-3303

Program grants; minorities; women; youth; social service organizations; cultural organizations

Grants awarded to organizations located in the Sioux City vicinity.

Typical grant range: $500 to $2,500

289

John H. Witte, Jr. Foundation
c/o Firstar Bank Iowa, N.A.
P.O. Box 1088
Burlington, IA 52623
(319) 752-2761

Program grants; social service organizations; youth; education; cultural organizations

Grants awarded to organizations located in the Burlington vicinity.

Typical grant range: $1,000 to $20,000

KANSAS

290

Dane G. Hansen Foundation
P.O. Box 187
Logan, KS 67646
(785) 689-4832

Program grants; disabled; hospitals; youth; education

Typical grant range: $5,000 to $45,000

291

Frank and Betty Hedrick Foundation
8150 E. Douglas, Suite 40
Wichita, KS 67206
(316) 683-2354

Program grants; youth; elderly; education; health organizations; Protestant organizations

Most grants awarded to organizations located in Wichita.

Typical grant range: $100 to $3,000

292

Hutchinson Community Foundation
P.O. Box 298
Hutchinson, KS 67504
(316) 663-5293

Program grants; education; disabled; youth; social service organizations; community development; health organizations; Break the Molds Schools (mathematics and reading project)

Grants awarded to organizations located in Reno County.

Typical grant range: $2,000 to $12,000

293

Kansas Health Foundation
309 East Douglas
Wichita, KS 67202
(316) 262-7676

Program grants; health organizations; Healthy Steps (project to improve the health of children); Douglas County Community Health Improvement Project (project grant); Drug-Free Healthy People (program to educate children about the effects of tobacco and alcohol on their health)

Grants awarded to organizations located in Kansas.

Typical grant range: $30,000 to $400,000

294

Ethel and Raymond F. Rice Foundation
700 Massachusetts Street
Lawrence, KS 66044
(785) 841-9961

Program grants; cultural organizations; historical societies; youth; health organizations; animal welfare; social service organizations; Plymouth Congregational Church (Christian youth education program); Spencer Museum of Art (public education programs)

Grants awarded to organizations located in the Lawrence vicinity.

Typical grant range: $1,000 to $30,000

295
Topeka Community Foundation
P.O. Box 4525
Topeka, KS 66604
(785) 272-4804

Program grants; youth; social service organizations; cultural organizations

Most grants awarded to organizations located in the Topeka vicinity.

296
Wichita Community Foundation
151 North Main, Suite 140
Wichita, KS 67202
(316) 264-4880

Program grants; social service organizations; health organizations; environment; education; cultural organizations

Most grants awarded to organizations located in the Wichita vicinity.

KENTUCKY

297
C.E. and S. Foundation, Inc.
3300 First National Tower
Louisville, KY 40202

Program grants; social service organizations; youth; education; cultural organizations; Public Libraries

Most grants awarded to organizations located in Louisville.

Typical grant range: $5,000 to $75,000

298
The Community Foundation of Louisville, Inc.
Waterfront Plaza
325 W. Main Street, Suite 1110
Louisville, KY 40202
(502) 585-4649

Program grants; youth; disabled; social service organizations; education; cultural organizations; Boy Scouts of America (Sports Club Education Program); Lincoln Elementary School (Kids and Family Summer Learning Project)

Grants awarded to organizations located in Louisville.

Typical grant range: $3,000 to $25,000

299
Foundation for the Tri-State Community, Inc.
P.O. Box 2096
1401 Winchester Avenue
Ashland, KY 41105
(606) 324-3888

Program grants; Huntington Museum of Art (children's program); Fairview Independent Schools (fitness program); Big Brothers/Big Sisters (school based mentoring program); American Red Cross (Automated External Defibrillator Training Program); Boyd County Youth Services Center (Challenge Leadership Program); J.W. Scott Community Center (after-school computer awareness program)

Typical grant range: $650 to $2,500

300
The Gheens Foundation, Inc.
One Riverfront Plaza, Suite 705
Louisville, KY 40202
(502) 584-4650

Program grants; social service organizations; youth; disabled; education; higher education; cultural organizations

Most grants awarded to organizations located in Kentucky, with an emphasis in Louisville.

Typical grant range: $5,000 to $75,000

301
Haywood Foundation, Inc.
One West McDonald Parkway
Maysville, KY 41056
(606) 563-9333

Program grants; education; health
organizations; youth; social service
organizations; Adult Literacy Council (job
skills program); YMCA (program grant);
Boys and Girls Club (program grant);
Buffalo Trace ADD (adult day care and
home health care program)

Typical grant range: $2,000 to $25,000

302
Margaret Hall Foundation, Inc.
291 S. Ashland Avenue
Lexington, KY 40502
(859) 269-2236

Program grants; St. Francis High School
(program to reduce prejudice); Sayre
School (program for visiting authors);
High Rocks Academy (history project);
Maryhurst School (cultural education
program); The June Buchanan School
(academic enrichment program); The
David School (science education
program); St. Andrew's (summer program
for at-risk students)

Typical grant range: $3,000 to $13,000

303
Lester E. Yeager Charitable Trust B
P.O. Box 964
Owensboro, KY 42302

Program grants; Owensboro Symphony
(education program); Theatre Workshop
(youth program); Girls, Inc. (program
grant); Dream Factory (projects for
terminally ill children); Free Clinic of
Owensboro (prescription drug program);
Junior Achievement (economics program
at elementary schools); Diocese of
Owensboro (school projects); Volunteer
Center (elementary school reading
program); Daviess County Board of
Education (projects at various schools)

Typical grant range: $1,000 to $10,000

LOUISIANA

304
Charles T. Beaird Foundation
Transcontinental Tower
330 Marshall Street, Suite 1112
Shreveport, LA 71101
(318) 221-8276

Program grants; youth; disabled; social
service organizations; Christian
organizations; YMCA (summer literacy
program)

Grants awarded to organizations located
in the Shreveport vicinity.

Typical grant range: $500 to $15,000

305
The Booth-Bricker Fund
826 Union Street, Suite 300
New Orleans, LA 70112
(504) 581-2430

Program grants; all levels of education;
youth; social service organizations;
cultural organizations

Most grants awarded to organizations
located in New Orleans.

306
**The Community Foundation of
Shreveport-Bossier**
401 Edwards Street, Suite 1111
Shreveport, LA 71101
(318) 221-0582

Program grants; women; youth; elderly;
disabled; social service organizations;
education; cultural organizations

Grants awarded to organizations located
in Caddo and Bossier Parishes.

Typical grant range: $2,000 to $25,000

307
Coughlin-Saunders Foundation, Inc.
P.O. Box 1910
Alexandria, LA 71309
(318) 487-4332

Program grants; education; cultural organizations; youth; social service organizations

Grants awarded to organizations located in central Louisiana, with an emphasis in Alexandria.

Typical grant range: $500 to $20,000

308
The Ella West Freeman Foundation
P.O. Box 13218
New Orleans, LA 70185-3218
(504) 895-1984

Program grants; social service organizations; community development; education; cultural organizations

Grants awarded to organizations located in the New Orleans vicinity.

309
German Protestant Orphan Asylum Association
P.O. Box 158
Mandeville, LA 70470
(504) 674-5328

Program grants; Girl Scouts of America (camping program); Boy Scouts of America (program grant); YWCA (after school care program); Straight Street Home for Girls (family counseling program); Family and Youth Counseling Agency (child abuse prevention program); Greater Mt. Carmel Tutorial Program (program grant); St. John the Baptist Church (academic program); St. Mark's Community Center (youth program); Volunteers of America (literacy program); Family Resources of New Orleans (youth employment program); Tulane University (after school program)

Grants awarded to organizations located in Louisiana.

Typical grant range: $3,000 to $30,000

310
The Greater New Orleans Foundation
1055 Saint Charles Avenue, #100
New Orleans, LA 70130
(504) 598-4663

Program grants; youth; disabled; social service organizations; education; health organizations; cultural organizations

Grants awarded to organizations located in the New Orleans vicinity.

311
The Lupin Foundation
3715 Prytania Street, Suite 304
New Orleans, LA 70115
(504) 849-0518

Program grants; social service organizations; youth; disabled; cultural organizations

Grants awarded to organizations located in Louisiana.

MAINE

312
The Harold Alfond Foundation
c/o Dexter Enterprises
Two Monument Square
Portland, ME 04101
(207) 828-7999

Program grants; health organizations; hospitals; disabled; youth; recreation; private secondary education; higher education

Most grants awarded to organizations located in Maine, with an emphasis in central Maine.

313
Edward H. Daveis Benevolent Fund
P.O. Box 586
Portland, ME 04112
(207) 774-4000

Program grants; Wayside Evening Soup Kitchen (food program); Youth and Family Outreach (Teen Adventure Program)

Grants awarded to organizations located in the Portland vicinity.

Typical grant range: $1,000 to $5,000

314
Libra Foundation
Box 17516
Portland, ME 04112
(207) 879-6280

Program grants; social service organizations; youth; education; recreation; cultural organizations; Big Brothers/Big Sisters (mentoring project); Miller After School Program (after school program for elementary school students)

Grants awarded to organizations located in Maine.

315
The Maine Community Foundation, Inc.
245 Main Street
P.O. Box 148
Ellsworth, ME 04605
(207) 667-9735

Program grants; education; youth; community development; environment; cultural organizations

Grants awarded to organizations located in Maine.

316
The Morton-Kelly Charitable Trust
c/o Jensen Baird Gardner & Henry
Ten Free Street, Box 4510
Portland, ME 04112
(207) 775-7271

Program grants; Dyer Library Association (youth program); Ferry Beach Ecology (program grant); Center for Environmental Enterprise (program grant); Maine Volunteer Lake Monitoring Program (educational project); Bangor Symphony Orchestra (school outreach program); Portland Harbor Museum (Bug Light Park Project); Portland Stage Company (educational program); Winslow Junior High (research program on wars); Saint Joseph's College of Maine (community leaders program)

Grants awarded to organizations located in Maine.

Typical grant range: $2,000 to $20,000

317
The Simmons Foundation, Inc.
c/o Perkins, Thompson, Hinckley & Keddy
One Canal Plaza
P.O. Box 426
Portland, ME 04112
(207) 774-2635

Program grants; cultural organizations; youth; women; social service organizations; health organizations

Grants awarded to organizations located in Maine.

Typical grant range: $1,000 to $8,000

MARYLAND

318
Charles S. Abell Foundation, Inc.
8401 Connecticut Avenue, Suite 1111
Chevy Chase, MD 20815
(301) 652-2224

Program grants; Luther Place Memorial
Church (program to assist the homeless);
Anacostia Community Outreach Ministry,
Inc. (food program); Red Wiggler
Foundation, Inc. (program for people who
are developmentally disabled); St. Ann's
Infant & Maternity Home (program for
pregnant teenagers); Community Family
Life Services, Inc. (employment program
for the homeless); St. Columba's
Episcopal Church (program for women);
Hannah House (program to provide
housing, employment and services to
homeless and low-income women)

Typical grant range: $5,000 to $40,000

319
The Abell Foundation, Inc.
111 S. Calvert Street, Suite 2300
Baltimore, MD 21202
(410) 547-1300

Program grants; Helping Up Mission
(program to assist the homeless who have
a substance abuse problem); Baltimore
Opera Company (educational program);
Patterson Park Community Development
Corporation (Home Value Guarantee
Program); Baltimore Partnership for
Vocational Education, Inc. (job training
program); Baltimore City Health
Department (pregnancy prevention
program); Boy Scouts of America
(program grant); People Lacking Ample
Shelter and Employment (Housing
Development Project); Enoch Pratt Free
Library (Team Read program); Baltimore
City Public School System (speech and
debate program); Johns Hopkins
University (Live Near Your Work
program)

Most grants awarded to organizations
located in Maryland, with an emphasis in
Baltimore.

Typical grant range: $2,000 to $100,000

320
**The William G. Baker, Jr. Memorial
Fund**
The Latrobe Building
Two E. Read Street, 9th Floor
Baltimore, MD 21202
(410) 332-4171

Program grants; education; youth; elderly;
social service organizations

Grants awarded to organizations located
in the Baltimore vicinity.

321

The Baltimore Community Foundation
The Latrobe Building
Two E. Read Street, 9th Floor
Baltimore, MD 21202
(410) 332-4171

Program grants; youth; disabled; social
service organizations; education;
elementary and secondary education;
environment; community development;
YMCA (intervention program for at-risk
students); Advocates for Children and
Youth (after school program); Irvine
Natural Science Center (outdoor
educational program); Maryland Center
for Community Development (economic
literacy training program)

Grants awarded to organizations located
in the Baltimore vicinity.

Typical grant range: $1,000 to $20,000

322

**Community Foundation of the Eastern
Shore, Inc.**
200 W. Main Street
Salisbury, MD 21801
(410) 742-9911

Program grants; community development;
social service organizations; youth;
education; environment; health
organizations; cultural organizations

Grants awarded to organizations located
in Somerset, Wicomico and Worcester
Counties.

323

**Morris Goldseker Foundation of
Maryland, Inc.**
The Latrobe Building
Two E. Read Street, 9th Floor
Baltimore, MD 21202
(410) 837-5100

Program grants; Eden Jobs (employment
placement and training program); Big
Brothers/Big Sisters (mentoring program);
Coalition for Low-Income Community
Development (community mapping
project); Comprehensive Housing
Association, Inc. (program grant); Morgan
State University (magnet program at high
school to prepare students for a career in
finance)

Grants awarded to organizations located
in the Baltimore vicinity.

Typical grant range: $3,000 to $200,000

324

The Hobbs Foundation, Inc.
c/o Friedman & Friedman
409 Washington Ave., Suite 900
Towson, MD 21204
(410) 494-0100

Program grants; disabled; youth;
homeless; social service organizations;
hospitals; health organizations

Grants awarded to organizations located
in the Baltimore vicinity.

Typical grant range: $2,000 to $20,000

325

Grayce B. Kerr Fund, Inc.
117 Bay Street
Easton, MD 21601
(410) 822-6652

Program grants; Mental Health
Association (project grant); Penobscot
Marine Museum (Watercraft Education
Project); Mystic Seaport (American
Maritime Education and Research Center
Project); Eastern Shore Athletic
Organization (athletic and academic
programs); Kent School (Horizons
Student Enrichment Program)

Most grants awarded to organizations
located in Maryland.

Typical grant range: $5,000 to $200,000

326

**The Marion I. and Henry J. Knott
Foundation, Inc.**
3904 Hickory Avenue
Baltimore, MD 21211
(410) 235-7068

Program grants; youth; disabled; social
service organizations; elementary and
secondary education; community
development; cultural organizations;
Roman Catholic organizations; Handel
Choir (program grant); South Baltimore
Homeless Shelter (program grant); South
East Community Organization (Head Start
program); B&O Railroad Museum
(program grant); Neighborhood Design
Center (Playing Safe Program)

Typical grant range: $1,000 to $75,000

327

George Preston Marshall Foundation
4300 Montgomery Avenue, Suite 104
Bethesda, MD 20814
(301) 654-7774

Program grants; Fellowship of Christian
Athletes (program grant); Friends of Fort
DuPont Ice Rink (inner city skating
program); Foundation for Exceptional
Children (mentoring program for children
who are disabled); The Children's Guild
(theater program for children who are
emotionally disturbed); Civic Ventures
(program matching senior citizen mentors
with children); The Family Place (healthy
babies program); Friends of Jug Bay
(wetlands education program); One
Ministries Unique Learning Center
(summer program); Higher Achievement
Program (tutoring program); Multicultural
Career Learning Center (child care
program); The Campagna Center
(program for children suspended from
public schools)

Typical grant range: $1,000 to $15,000

328

**T. Rowe Price Associates Foundation,
Inc.**
100 E. Pratt Street
Baltimore, MD 21202
(410) 345-2000

Program grants; social service
organizations; youth; community
development; secondary and higher
education; cultural organizations;
Baltimore City Foundation (Youth Works
Summer Jobs Program)

Most grants awarded to organizations
located in the Baltimore vicinity.

Typical grant range: $5,000 to $30,000

MASSACHUSETTS

329
The Paul and Edith Babson Foundation
c/o Nichols & Pratt
50 Congress Street
Boston, MA 02109
(617) 523-6800

Program grants; Boston Area Rape Crisis Center (Peer Leadership Program); Asian Task Force Against Domestic Violence (children's program); Center for Women and Enterprise (Community Entrepreneurs Program); Museum of Fine Arts (program for youth); Metropolitan Opera Association (program grant); Roca, Inc. (wetland restoration project); South End Lower Roxbury Open Space Land Trust (Urban Nature Program); Women's Educational and Industrial Union (Horizons Transitional Housing Program); Boston Public Library Foundation (homework program); B.E.L.L. Foundation, Inc. (after-school tutoring program); Boston Partners in Education (training program for volunteers); Massachusetts Pre-Engineering Program (mathematics and science program for inner-city youth)

Most grants awarded to organizations located in the Boston vicinity.

Typical grant range: $1,000 to $15,000

330
The Blossom Fund
c/o Loring Wolcott & Coolidge
230 Congress Street
Boston, MA 02110
(617) 523-6531

Program grants; Fourth Presbyterian Church (music and art program); Brookline Public Library (summer program for children); Hull Lifesaving Museum (program grant); Bird Street Community Center (Sports and Fitness Program); YMCA (program grant); Codman Square Library (summer writing program); Boston Education Development Foundation (School Parent Council Multicultural Arts Enrichment Program)

Typical grant range: $2,000 to $15,000

331
The Boston Foundation, Inc.
75 Arlington Street
Boston, MA 02116
(617) 723-7415

Program grants; Community Art Center, Inc. (teen media program); Boston Urban Youth Foundation, Inc. (program grant); Boston Justice Ministries (Safe Havens program); Deaf Blind Video Project (documentary project); Massachusetts Coalition for the Homeless, Inc. (The Motel Program); Partners for Youth with Disabilities (youth independence program); Family Nuturing Center (parent education and training program); Massachusetts School Age Coalition, Inc. (improve out of school programs)

Grants awarded to organizations located in the Boston vicinity.

Typical grant range: $20,000 to $55,000

332

The Boston Globe Foundation II, Inc.
P.O. Box 2378
135 Morrissey Blvd.
Boston, MA 02107
(617) 929-3160

Program grants; environment; women;
disabled; youth; hospitals; cultural
organizations; education; social service
organizations

Grants awarded to organizations located
in the Boston vicinity.

Typical grant range: $1,000 to $20,000

333

Cabot Corporation Foundation, Inc.
2 Seaport Lane, Suite 1300
Boston, MA 02210
(617) 342-6105

Program grants; STRIVE Boston
Employment Service (job training
program); Our Lady Queen of All Saints
Church (Care and Share program);
Commonwealth Shakespeare Company
(program grant); Boys and Girls Clubs
(program grant); Junior Achievement of
Eastern Massachusetts (public school
program); Board of Education (local
school science program); Friends and
Fellows of Harvard College (after-school
tutorial program)

Grants awarded to organizations located
in areas of company operations (Cabot
Corp.).

Typical grant range: $2,000 to $15,000

334

Cabot Family Charitable Trust
c/o Cabot-Wellington LLC
70 Federal Street
Boston, MA 02110-1906
(617) 451-1744

Program grants; environment; education;
higher education; women; youth

Typical grant range: $5,000 to $50,000

335

Clipper Ship Foundation, Inc.
c/o Grants Management Associates
77 Summer Street, 8th Floor
Boston, MA 02110
(617) 426-7172

Program grants; Help for Abused Women
and Their Children (program at a shelter);
Global Habitat Project (environmental
education project); Saint Elizabeth's
Hospital (Healthy Boston Program);
Boston Asian Youth Essential Service
(project grant); Boston Symphony
Orchestra (program at public schools);
YWCA (program grant); YMCA (summer
day camp program); Notre Dame
Education Center (literacy program);
Shelter, Inc. (transitional housing
program); Partners for Youth with
Disabilities (program grant)

Grants awarded to organizations located
in the Boston vicinity.

Typical grant range: $2,000 to $20,000

336
Community Foundation of Western Massachusetts
1500 Main Street, Suite 622
P.O. Box 15769
Springfield, MA 01115
(413) 732-2858

Program grants; Noble Hospital (heart attack prevention program); Tapestry Health Systems, Inc. (needle exchange project); Enchanted Circle Theater (literacy project); The Fund for Women Artists (teacher training program); Girl Scouts (Outdoor Education Discovery Program); Boys Club (youth mural project); Housing Discrimination Project, Inc. (mortgage lending counseling program); The Food Bank (program grant); Dunbar Community Center (summer youth program); North End Community Center (recreation program); Holyoke Neighborhood Networks Center (computer training program); Northern Educational Service (after school leadership program); Willie Ross School for the Deaf (early intervention program)

Grants awarded to organizations located in western Massachusetts.

Typical grant range: $1,000 to $15,000

337
Irene E. and George A. Davis Foundation
1 Monarch Place, 14th Floor
Springfield, MA 01144
(413) 734-8336

Program grants; youth; elderly; women; social service organizations; education; cultural organizations; health organizations

Grants awarded to organizations located in Hampden County.

Typical grant range: $2,500 to $25,000

338
Eastman Charitable Foundation
31 Milk Street, Room 501
Boston, MA 02109
(617) 423-5599

Program grants; disabled; youth; education; cultural organizations; Worldwise, Inc. (educational program); Community Minority Cultural Center (extra curricular projects for public school students)

Most grants awarded to organizations located in Massachusetts.

Typical grant range: $300 to $5,000

339
GenRad Foundation
P.O. Box 444
West Groton, MA 01472
(978) 448-8942

Program grants; youth; elderly; social service organizations; education; cultural organizations; health organizations

Most grants awarded to organizations located in the Concord vicinity.

Typical grant range: $1,000 to $15,000

340
Greater Worcester Community Foundation, Inc.
44 Front Street, Suite 530
Worcester, MA 01608
(508) 755-0980

Program grants; Catholic Charities (literacy and citizenship program for Hmong residents); Centro Las Americas (mentoring program for Latino youth); Massachusetts Audubon Society (educational program); Rape Crisis Center (program grant); AIDS Project Worcester (educational program); Very Special Arts (program grant); Central Massachusetts Agency on Aging (program grant); Friends of the Milford Youth Center (after school program); YMCA (after school program); Girls Incorporated (after school program); Bancroft School (summer program)

Grants awarded to organizations located in the Worcester vicinity.

Typical grant range: $1,500 to $20,000

341
The Health Foundation of Central Massachusetts, Inc.
446 Main Street
Worcester, MA 01608
(508) 438-0009

Program grants; Worcester Youth Center (Teen Action Group and Peer Leaders Program); Children's Aid and Family Service, Inc. (mentoring program at a high school); Massachusetts College of Pharmacy and Health Sciences (Pharmacy Development Program)

Grants awarded to organizations located in Central Massachusetts.

Typical grant range: $1,000 to $80,000

342
The Hyams Foundation, Inc.
175 Federal Street, 14th Floor
Boston, MA 02110
(617) 426-5600

Program grants; Health Care for All (Boston Health Access Project); St. Elizabeth's Medical Center (Healthy Boston Project); AIDS Action Committee, Inc. (Women in Action Project); Goodwill Industries, Inc. (project grant); Boys and Girls Club (Family Learning Program); St. Mary's Womens and Infants Center (Welfare to Work Program); Boston Center for the Arts, Inc. (program for teenagers); Spanish Dance Theatre, Inc. (after school program); Massachusetts Coalition for the Homeless (project grant); Catholic Charitable Bureau of the Archdiocese of Boston, Inc. (Latino Pride Project)

Most grants awarded to organizations located in Boston and Chelsea.

Typical grant range: $5,000 to $40,000

343
Island Foundation, Inc.
589 Mill Street
Marion, MA 02738
(508) 748-2809

Program grants; Massachusetts Audubon (coastal waterbird program); Charles River Watershed Association (project grant); New England Aquarium (whale research program); Buttonwood Park Zoological Society (education program); United Interfaith Action (after school program); Catholic Social Services (Safety Net Program); YWCA (anti-racism project); Boys and Girls Club (Teen Achievement Program)

Typical grant range: $2,000 to $35,000

344
Edward Bangs Kelley and Elza Kelley Foundation, Inc.
243 South Street
P.O. Drawer M
Hyannis, MA 02601
(508) 775-3117

Program grants; social service organizations; youth; environment; health organizations; cultural organizations

Grants awarded to organizations located in Barnstable County.

Typical grant range: $500 to $5,000

345
Amelia Peabody Charitable Fund
10 Post Office Square North, Suite 995
Boston, MA 02109
(617) 451-6178

Program grants; Student Conservation Association (summer program); Perkins School for the Blind (program for toddlers); Cambridge Art Association (program for students with special needs); Pro Arte Chamber Orchestra (program grant); Dana-Farber Cancer Institute (program for cancer survivors); Big Sisters Association (mentoring program); Paraprofessional Healthcare Institute (training program)

Most grants awarded to organizations located in the Boston vicinity.

Typical grant range: $5,000 to $200,000

346
Amelia Peabody Foundation
One Hollis Street, Suite 215
Wellesley, MA 02482
(781) 237-6468

Program grants; social service organizations; women; minorities; youth; education; health organizations

Grants awarded to organizations located in Massachusetts.

Typical grant range: $5,000 to $75,000

347
Perpetual Trust for Charitable Giving
c/o Fleet Asset Management
NFP Grantmaking
100 Federal Street, MC MADE 10020B
Boston, MA 02110
(617) 434-4846

Program grants; youth; social service organizations; education; women; hospitals; health organizations

Grants awarded to organizations located in Massachusetts.

Typical grant range: $1,000 to $25,000

348
Last minute update: The foundation originally listed here has terminated.

349
The Harold Whitworth Pierce Charitable Trust
c/o Nichols and Pratt, LLP
50 Congress Street
Boston, MA 02109
(617) 523-8368

Program grants; Boys and Girls Club (children's garden project); YWCA (education program); Emerald Necklace Conservancy (project grant); The Food Project (youth program); Isabella Steward Gardner Museum (project grant); The Bostonian Society (Historic Markers Program); Boston Urban Youth Foundation (truancy program); City on a Hill Charter School (teacher education program); Boston Institute for Early Child Development (Reach Out and Read program); The Boston Adult Literacy Fund (program for African American men); Lesley College Center for Children (Career Paths Scholars Program); Wheelock College (Urban Teachers Program)

Grants awarded to organizations located in Massachusetts.

Typical grant range: $5,000 to $25,000

350
A.C. Ratshesky Foundation
77 Summer Street
Boston, MA 02110
(617) 426-7172

Program grants; youth; elderly; women; minorities; education; social service organizations; cultural organizations; Jewish organizations; Girl Scout Council (program for girls to explore science and mathematics); Children's Museum (program grant); Bird Street Community Center (tutoring program for middle and high school students)

Most grants awarded to organizations located in the Boston vicinity.

Typical grant range: $500 to $5,000

351
The Mabel Louise Riley Foundation
75 State Street, 6th Floor
Boston, MA 02109
(617) 951-9100

Program grants; education; youth; disabled; women; minorities; social service organizations; cultural organizations; community development; Association of Haitian Women in Boston (economic literacy training program); Generations Incorporated (literacy program); Joslin Diabetes Center (African-American Diabetes Education and Care Project); Health Care For All (Boston Health Access Project); Prevent Blindness Massachusetts (screening program); YWCA (tutorial program); Family Day Care Program, Inc. (child care and social service programs)

Most grants awarded to organizations located in the Boston vicinity.

Typical grant range: $50,000 to $225,000

352
Sawyer Charitable Foundation
200 Newbury Street, 4th Floor
Boston, MA 02116
(617) 262-3600

Program grants; disabled; youth; social service organizations; health organizations

Most grants awarded to organizations located in Massachusetts.

Typical grant range: $5,000 to $30,000

353
Gardiner Howland Shaw Foundation
56 Kearney Road
Needham, MA 02494
(781) 455-8303

Program grants; innovative projects in the criminal justice field; Boston Urban Youth Foundation (truancy prevention program); Stop It Now, Inc. (sexual abuse prevention program); Northeast Family Institute (vocational education program for youth)

Grants awarded to organizations located in Massachusetts.

Typical grant range: $2,000 to $20,000

354
State Street Foundation
225 Franklin Street, 12th Floor
Boston, MA 02215
(617) 664-3381

Program grants; social service organizations; disabled; youth; elderly; education; job training; community development

Grants awarded to organizations located in the Boston vicinity.

Typical grant range: $5,000 to $50,000

355

The Abbot and Dorothy Stevens Foundation
P.O. Box 111
N. Andover, MA 01845
(978) 688-7211

Program grants; social service organizations; youth; minorities; education; environment; cultural organizations

Grants awarded to organizations located in Massachusetts.

Typical grant range: $1,000 to $20,000

356

The Nathaniel and Elizabeth P. Stevens Foundation
P.O. Box 111
N. Andover, MA 01845
(978) 688-7211

Program grants; youth; minorities; women; social service organizations; education; health organizations; cultural organizations

Grants awarded to organizations located in Massachusetts.

Typical grant range: $1,000 to $10,000

MICHIGAN

357

Allegan County Community Foundation
P.O. Box 15
Allegan, MI 49010
(616) 673-8344

Program grants; community development; youth; education; social service organizations

Grants awarded to organizations located in Allegan County.

Typical grant range: $1,000 to $12,000

358

Battle Creek Community Foundation
One Riverwalk Center
34 W. Jackson Street
Battle Creek, MI 49017
(616) 962-2181

Program grants; social service organizations; youth; community development; health organizations; cultural organizations

Grants awarded to organizations located in the Battle Creek vicinity.

359

Bay Area Community Foundation
703 Washington Avenue
Bay City, MI 48708
(517) 893-4438

Program grants; Bay County Recreation Department (skating program); Bay Area Family Y (learn to swim program); YWCA (Empower Me, a self-esteem program for young girls); Bay County Probate Court (program for girls to learn about motherhood); Bay County Child and Senior Citizen Center (academic program for youth); The Opportunity Center (computer training program); The Conservation Fund (project grant); Holy Trinity Elementary (music program); Bush Elementary (reading program for parents)

Grants awarded to organizations located in Bay County.

Typical grant range: $500 to $10,000

360
Branch County Community Foundation
2 West Chicago Street, Suite E-1
Coldwater, MI 49036
(517) 278-4517

Program grants; Big Brothers/Big Sisters (school mentoring program); Union City Middle School (National Youth Sports Program); Coldwater Alternative High School (community project); Colon High School (planting project and reading program); Michigan State University Extension (violence prevention program)

Most grants awarded to organizations located in Branch County.

Typical grant range: $300 to $5,000

361
The Carls Foundation
333 W. Fort Street, Suite 1940
Detroit, MI 48226
(313) 965-0990

Program grants; Gilda's Club of Metro Detroit (cancer therapy program for children); Huron Valley Sinai Hospital (education program); The Detroit Institute for Children (medical care program for infants); Alternatives for Girls (program grant); Zee Computer Information Center, Inc. (education program for at-risk children); Grand Traverse Regional Land Conservation (Bowers Harbor Protection Project); L'Anse Cruese Public Schools (teen parenting program); Bay Mills Community College (nursing program)

Grants awarded to organizations located in Michigan.

Typical grant range: $4,000 to $50,000

362
Colina Foundation
One Heritage Drive, Suite 220
Southgate, MI 48195
(734) 283-8847

Program grants; Seaway Chorale & Orchestra (program for youth); Oakwood Healthcare System (program grant); Soroptimist International (sexual harassment prevention project); Taylor Teen Health Center (educational and prevention program); River Rouge High School (preschool project)

Most grants awarded to organizations located in southern Wayne County.

Typical grant range: $500 to $10,000

363
Community Foundation for Southeastern Michigan
333 W. Fort Street, Suite 2010
Detroit, MI 48226
(313) 961-6675

Program grants; National Kidney Foundation of Michigan Inc. (prevention program); Children's Hospital of Michigan (mental-health program for children with HIV); Detroit Medical Center (program for nurses); Adult Well-Being Services (substance abuse prevention program); African American Legacy Program (philanthropic giving awareness program); Sacred Heart Church (computer training program); Christ the King Catholic Parish (cultural program); Chamber Music Society (education program); Alternative for Girls (homeless prevention program); Lighthouse (child care program for homeless women); Michigan Jewish AIDS Coalition (education program); Detroit Institute of Arts Founders Society (Art Discovery Project); University of Detroit Mercy (National Youth Sports Program)

Grants awarded to organizations located in southeastern Michigan.

Typical grant range: $1,000 to $50,000

364
Community Foundation of Greater Flint
502 Church Street
Flint, MI 48502
(810) 767-8270

Program grants; Community Presbyterian Church (after school program); Catholic Social Services (summer recreation and lunch program); Girl Scout Council (summer program); Boys and Girls Club (summer project); Adams Avenue Neighborhood Association (beautification and clean up project); Cody Crime Watch (Kids at Night Project); Flint Cultural Center Corporation (Science in the Making Program); Planned Parenthood (education program); Easter Seal Society (program grant); Shelter of Flint, Inc. (program grant); Lakeville Community School District (Good Citizenship Incentive Project); Baker College of Flint (Smart Energy Program); University of Michigan (Flint Reading Center Program)

Grants awarded to organizations located in Genesee County.

Typical grant range: $500 to $35,000

365
The Community Foundation of the Holland/Zeeland Area
70 W. 8th Street, Suite 100
Holland, MI 49423-3166
(616) 396-6590

Program grants; Girl Scouts (golf program); Boys and Girls Club (after-school program); Greater Holland Youth for Christ (guidance program); Center for Women in Transition (expand program); Neighbors Plus (English tutoring program for adults); Community Health Center (infant care program); Holland Area Arts Council (youth program); Lakeshore Center for Independent Living (program to teach everyday living for people who are disabled); City of Holland (adult literacy program); Children's After School Achievement (math education program); Ottawa Area Intermediate School District (self-respect and healthy living program); American Association of University Women (Reading is Fundamental program); Pine Creek Elementary School (after-school program); Lakeshore Elementary School (Family Resource Center Outreach Program)

Grants awarded to organizations located in the Holland/Zeeland vicinity.

Typical grant range: $1,000 to $20,000

366
DaimlerChrysler Fund
CIMS 485-02-46
1000 Chrysler Drive
Auburn Hills, MI 48326
(248) 512-2502

Program grants; Eastside Emergency Center (Latchkey and Home Care Programs); Boys Club (program grant); YMCA (Black Achievers Program); Charities Aid Foundation (project grant); Traffic Improvement Association (program grant); Cornerstone Schools Association (program grant); Discovery World: The James Lovell Museum of Science Economics and Technology (A World in Motion Program)

Most grants awarded to organizations located in areas of company operations (DaimlerChrysler Corporation).

Typical grant range: $1,000 to $100,000

367
Dorothy U. Dalton Foundation, Inc.
Greenleaf Trust Building
490 W. South Street
Kalamazoo, MI 49007

Program grants; youth; women; social service organizations; hospitals; community development; cultural organizations

Grants awarded to organizations located in Kalamazoo County.

Typical grant range: $2,000 to $50,000

368
The Herbert H. and Grace A. Dow Foundation
1018 W. Main Street
Midland, MI 48640-4264
(989) 631-3699

Program grants; environment; cultural organizations; education; social service organizations; community development; Detroit Area Pre-College Engineering Program (program to increase minority enrollment in engineering)

Grants awarded to organizations located in Michigan.

Typical grant range: $50,000 to $500,000

369
DTE Energy Foundation
2000 Second Avenue, Room 1046 WCB
Detroit, MI 48226
(313) 235-9271

Program grants; Girl Scout Council (tutoring program); YMCA (Youth in Government Program); New Detroit, Inc. (employment program for youth); Chaldean-American Ladies of Charity (housing program for senior citizens); Wildlife Habitat Council (St. Clair River Project); Lyric Chamber Ensemble, Inc. (music camp program); Macomb Literacy Project, Inc. (literacy program for adults); Detroit Police Athletic League (program grant); Gleaners Community Food Bank (program grant); Turning Point, Inc. (Sexual Assault Nurse Examiner Program); Penrickton Center for Blind Children (music therapy program)

Typical grant range: $1,000 to $25,000

370
Ford Motor Company Fund
The American Road
Dearborn, MI 48121
(313) 845-8711

Program grants; minorities; disabled;
youth; cultural organizations; education;
community development; National
Society of Black Engineers (programs for
science and engineering); University of
Michigan (programs for science and
engineering)

Grants awarded to organizations located
in areas of company operations (Ford
Motor Company), with an emphasis in
Detroit.

Typical grant range: $1,000 to $50,000

371
**The Fremont Area Community
Foundation**
P.O. Box B
Fremont, MI 49412
(231) 924-5350

Program grants; community development;
cultural organizations; youth; elderly;
social service organizations

Grants awarded to organizations located
in Newaygo County.

372
Frey Foundation
40th Pearl Street, N.W., Suite 1100
Grand Rapids, MI 49503
(616) 451-0303

Program grants; East Hills Council of
Neighbors (art program); Michigan
Economic and Environmental Roundtable
(research project); Coldwater River
Watershed Council (river protection
program); Cedar Springs Public Schools
(Parents as Teachers program); Western
Michigan University (program to develop
and test curriculum)

Grants awarded to organizations located
in Kent, Emmet, and Charlevoix Counties.

Typical grant range: $5,000 to $100,000

373
General Motors Foundation, Inc.
11-134 General Motors Building
3044 W. Grand Blvd.
Detroit, MI 48202
(313) 556-4260

Program grants; youth; minorities;
disabled; cultural organizations;
environment; community development;
Warren Symphony Orchestra (Youth
Concert Program)

Grants awarded to organizations located
in areas of company operations (General
Motors Corp.).

Typical grant range: $2,000 to $75,000

374
The Gerber Foundation
4747 W. 48th Street, Suite 153
Fremont, MI 49412-8119
(231) 924-3175

Program grants; Bethany Christian
Services (project for abandoned infants);
Blue Ridge Community Health Services
(dental program); American School
Health Association (Head Start programs);
St. Andrew's Crippled Children's Clinic
(health project); Every Child by Two
(immunization program); City of Fremont
(park enhancement project); Council for
the Prevention of Child Abuse and
Neglect (prevention program); Fremont
Chamber of Commerce (volunteer
program); Fremont Area District Library
(program grant); Newaygo Public Schools
(Reading is Fundamental program);
Newaygo County (crime reduction
program in schools); Michigan State
University 4-H Council (elementary
school nutrition education program)

Grants awarded to organizations located
in areas of company operations (Gerber
Products Co.).

Typical grant range: $2,000 to $100,000

375
Irving S. Gilmore Foundation
136 E. Michigan Avenue, Suite 615
Kalamazoo, MI 49007
(616) 342-6411

Program grants; health organizations; hospitals; community development; education; higher education; youth; disabled; social service organizations; cultural organizations

Grants awarded to organizations located in the Kalamazoo vicinity.

376
Grand Haven Area Community Foundation, Inc.
One South Harbor
Grand Haven, MI 49417
(616) 842-6378

Program grants; community development; youth; disabled; education; health organizations; The People Center (emergency housing program); West Shore Committee for Jewish and Christian Dialogue (program focusing on interfaith understanding)

Grants awarded to organizations located in northwest Ottawa County, with an emphasis in Grand Haven.

Typical grant range: $500 to $20,000

377
The Grand Rapids Community Foundation
209-C Waters Building
161 Ottawa Avenue, N.W.
Grand Rapids, MI 49503
(616) 454-1751

Program grants; Grand Rapids Symphony (Artists-in-Residence program); United Cerebral Palsy Association (program grant); Creston Neighborhood Association (education program regarding home ownership); Grand Rapids Opportunities for Women (program grant); Urban Produce (summer gardening program); YMCA (program grant); Gerontology Network Services (Traveling Grannies program to provide counseling to teenage parents); SLD Learning Center, Inc. (volunteer tutoring program); Excellence in Education Day (awards program); Grand Rapids Public Schools (Effective Teams Program)

Grants awarded to organizations located in the Grand Rapids vicinity.

Typical grant range: $3,000 to $60,000

378
Hudson-Webber Foundation
333 W. Fort Street, Suite 1310
Detroit, MI 48226
(313) 963-7777

Program grants; Michigan Opera Theatre (program grant); Detroit Symphony Orchestra Hall, Inc. (program grant); Motown Historical Museum, Inc. (program grant); Detroit Hispanic Development Corp. (program grant); New Detroit, Inc. (African American Business Development Program); Michigan Partnership to Prevent Gun Violence (safety program); Volunteers in Prevention, Probation & Prisons, Inc. (Partners Against Crime Program); Planned Parenthood (education program); Cranbrook Educational Community (program grant for the Academy of Art and the Institute of Science)

Grants awarded to organizations located in the Detroit vicinity.

Typical grant range: $5,000 to $125,000

379
The Jackson County Community Foundation
One Jackson Square, Suite 110 A
Jackson, MI 49201
(517) 787-1321

Program grants; youth; disabled; education; health organizations; community development; cultural organizations

Grants awarded to organizations located in Jackson County.

Typical grant range: $1,000 to $30,000

380
Kalamazoo Community Foundation
151 S. Rose Street, Suite 332
Kalamazoo, MI 49007
(616) 381-4416

Program grants; youth; disabled; education; environment; low-income housing; community development; health organizations

Grants awarded to organizations located in Kalamazoo County.

381
Marquette Community Foundation
129 W. Baraga Avenue, Suite D
Marquette, MI 49855
(906) 226-7666

Program grants; Marquette County Sheriff's Department (Mock Drunk Driving Accident Program); Cedar Tree Institute (cedar trees for the Manitou project); NICE Family Resource Center (project for youth); United Evangelical Church (program for youth); Father Marquette Middle School (track and field program); Gwinn Area Community Schools (program grant)

Grants awarded to organizations located in Marquette County.

Typical grant range: $200 to $3,000

382
McGregor Fund
333 W. Fort Street, Suite 2090
Detroit, MI 48226
(313) 963-3495

Program grants; social service organizations; youth; minorities; women; disabled; cultural organizations; health organizations; Museum of African American History (volunteer program); Boys and Girls Republic (program grant); St. Joseph Mercy Hospital (Healthy Start Program); Wayne State University (Infant Mental Health Program)

Grants awarded to organizations located in Detroit.

Typical grant range: $20,000 to $200,000

383
Midland Area Community Foundation
P.O. Box 289
Midland, MI 48640
(989) 839-9661

Program grants; social service
organizations; youth; education;
community development

Grants awarded to organizations located
in Midland County.

Typical grant range: $250 to $12,000

384
Frances Goll Mills Fund
c/o Citizens Bank
101 N. Washington Avenue
Saginaw, MI 48607
(517) 776-7405

Program grants; social service
organizations; youth; education;
community development

Grants awarded to organizations located
in Saginaw County.

Typical grant range: $1,000 to $20,000

385
Mt. Pleasant Area Community Foundation
111 South University
P.O. Box 1283
Mt. Pleasant, MI 48858
(517) 773-7322

Program grants; youth; education;
community development; Big Brothers/
Big Sisters (mentoring program);
American Red Cross (health and safety
program)

Grants awarded to organizations located
in Isabella County.

Typical grant range: $100 to $5,000

386
Saginaw Community Foundation
100 S. Jefferson
Saginaw, MI 48607
(517) 755-0545

Program grants; social service
organizations; youth; community
development; cultural organizations

Grants awarded to organizations located
in Saginaw County.

387
The Skillman Foundation
600 Renaissance Center, Suite 1700
Detroit, MI 48243
(313) 568-6360

Program grants; youth; women;
minorities; social service organizations;
education; cultural organizations

Typical grant range: $25,000 to $250,000

388
Steelcase Foundation
P.O. Box 1967
Grand Rapids, MI 49501
(616) 246-4695

Program grants; youth; women; disabled;
social service organizations; education;
cultural organizations; community
development; health organizations

Grants awarded to organizations located
in areas of company operations (Steelcase,
Inc.).

Typical grant range: $5,000 to $150,000

389
The Harry A. and Margaret D. Towsley Foundation
140 Ashman
P.O. Box 349
Midland, MI 48640
(989) 837-1100

Program grants; youth; social service
organizations; education; health
organizations

Grants awarded to organizations located
in Michigan, with an emphasis in Ann
Arbor and Washtenaw County.

Typical grant range: $2,500 to $60,000

390
Weatherwax Foundation
P.O. Box 1111
Jackson, MI 49204
(517) 787-2117

Program grants; Hunt Elementary School
(Project Read); Hanover-Horton Middle
School (STAR program); JPS/Dibble
School (guest author program);
McCulloch School (basic skills program);
Holly Ear Institute (Village Commons
Project)

Most grants awarded to organizations
located in the Jackson vicinity.

Typical grant range: $2,500 to $35,000

391
The Whiting Foundation
901 Citizens Bank Building
328 S. Saginaw Street
Flint, MI 48502
(810) 767-3600

Program grants; medical research; cancer
research; youth; cultural organizations

Grants awarded to organizations located
in the Flint vicinity.

Typical grant range: $1,000 to $25,000

392
Lula C. Wilson Trust
c/o Bank One
1116 W. Long Lake Road
Bloomfield Hills, MI 48302
(248) 645-7308

Program grants; youth; disabled; social
service organizations; education; cultural
organizations

Grants awarded to organizations located
in the City of Pontiac and Oakland
County.

393
Matilda R. Wilson Fund
100 Renaissance Center, 34th Floor
Detroit, MI 48243
(313) 259-7777

Program grants; cultural organizations;
social service organizations; higher
education

Typical grant range: $10,000 to $75,000

MINNESOTA

394
Hugh J. Andersen Foundation
P.O. Box 204
Bayport, MN 55003
(651) 439-1557

Program grants; Evangelical Lutheran
Church of America (summer youth
program); Northwest Youth & Family
Services (teen pregnancy prevention
program); The Guthrie Theater Foundation
(educational program); The Ordway
Center for the Performing Arts (program
grant); Village of Clear Lake (park
beautification project); The Minnesota
Literacy Council (program grant); PACER
Center (Let's Prevent Abuse program);
Minnesota AIDS Project (legal program);
American Cancer Society (Friend to
Friend program); American Diabetes
Association (program grant); YMCA (teen
center project); Young Life St. Croix
Valley (tutoring program); Family
Service, Inc. (child sexual abuse program)

Typical grant range: $1,000 to $25,000

395
Bayport Foundation, Inc.
P.O. Box 204
Bayport, MN 55003
(651) 439-1557

Program grants; youth; disabled; social
service organizations; education; cultural
organizations

Most grants awarded to organizations
located in Minnesota.

Typical grant range: $500 to $25,000

396
David Winton Bell Foundation
Parkdale Plaza
1660 South Highway 100, Suite 426
St. Louis Park, MN 55416
(952) 512-1165

Program grants; environment; wildlife;
education; social service organizations

Most grants awarded to organizations
located in Minneapolis and its immediate
western suburbs.

397
The James Ford Bell Foundation
1818 Oliver Avenue South, No. 2
Minneapolis, MN 55405

Program grants; Minnesota Land Trust
(environmental education program);
American Humane Association (Caring
Connections program); Greater
Minneapolis Council of Churches (lecture
program); James Ford Bell Museum of
Natural History (science program);
Greater St. Paul Retired and Senior
Volunteer Program (program grant); Boy
Scouts of America (program grant);
Planned Parenthood (Adolescent
Pregnancy Prevention program); The
Cookie Carts, Inc. (youth employment and
mentorship program); Family Hope
Services (program for runaway
teenagers); Harriet Tubman Center
(project grant for this family violence
resource shelter); Women Venture (career
development and employment project for
women)

Last minute update: unsolicited applications
are temporarily not accepted.

Typical grant range: $1,000 to $20,000

398
F.R. Bigelow Foundation
600 Norwest Center
55 E. Fifth Street
St. Paul, MN 55101
(651) 224-5463

Program grants; cultural organizations;
community development; women; youth;
minorities; disabled; United Theological
Seminary of the Twin Cities (technology
project); Boys and Girls Club (Nature
Area Teen Project); Saint Paul Chamber
Orchestra Society (computer training
project); Ramsey Action Programs, Inc.
(Children's Literacy Project)

Grants awarded to organizations located
in the St. Paul vicinity.

Typical grant range: $5,000 to $75,000

399
The Blandin Foundation
100 Pokegama Avenue North
Grand Rapids, MN 55744
(218) 326-0523

Program grants; environment; youth;
women; disabled; social service
organizations; education; cultural
organizations; community development

Grants awarded to organizations located
in Minnesota.

400
Otto Bremer Foundation
445 Minnesota Street, Suite 2000
St. Paul, MN 55101
(651) 227-8036

Program grants; Minnesota Women's Consortium (civil rights education program); Camphor Memorial United Methodist Church (adult day program); Girl Scouts (volunteer program); Habitat for Humanity (affordable housing program); Lakeland Hospice (bereavement program); Migrant Health Service, Inc. (Hispanic Battered Women and Children's Program); Heritage Community Center, Inc. (senior nutrition program); Parents Anonymous of Minnesota, Inc. (child abuse prevention program); St. Joseph's Medical Center (Community Parish Nurse Program); The American Jewish Committee (Hands Across the Campus Program); Atwater-Cosmos-Grove City Public Schools (day care program); Northland Community and Technical College (farm management education program); St. Cloud State University (Prevention of Harassment and Hate Crimes Program)

Grants awarded to organizations located in areas of company operations (Bremer Bank).

Typical grant range: $2,000 to $30,000

401
The Bush Foundation
E-900 First National Bank Bldg.
332 Minnesota Street
St. Paul, MN 55101
(651) 227-0891

Program grants; St. Stephens Church (program for the homeless); Saint Paul Chamber Orchestra Society (program grant); Minnesota American Indian AIDS Task Force (education program); Family Service of Margaret Simpson Home (mediation program); Northwest Youth and Family Services (program for violent youth and their families); College of Saint Benedict (faculty development project); Bethel College and Seminary (program to incorporate technology into the college curriculum); Minnesota Private College Research Foundation (programs for tribal and historically black private colleges)

Typical grant range: $10,000 to $125,000

402
Patrick and Aimee Butler Family Foundation
First National Bank Building
332 Minnesota Street, E-1420
St. Paul, MN 55101
(651) 222-2565

Program grants; Upper Midwest Conservation Association (program grant); Little Sisters of the Poor (meals program); Minnesota Humanities Commission (literacy program); Neighborhood House Association (parent enrichment project); Volunteers of America (Grandparents as Parents program); Trust for Public Lands (Lower Phalen Creek project); The Friends of the Saint Paul Public Library (reading program); Division of Indian Work (Teen Indian Parent Program); Family & Children Services (Community Leadership Development Program); Communication Service for the Deaf (domestic violence program); Fairview Foundation (chemical dependency program for people who are deaf)

Grants awarded to organizations located in the Minneapolis-St. Paul vicinity.

Typical grant range: $2,000 to $50,000

403
The Cargill Foundation
P.O. Box 5690
Minneapolis, MN 55440
(612) 742-6290

Program grants; Plymouth Christian Youth Center (program grant); Our Savior's Lutheran Church (program grant); The Bridge for Runaway Youth (program grant); YMCA (program grant); Hmong American Partnership (program grant); Children's Theater Company and School (program grant); Learning Disabilities Association, Inc. (program grant); Minnesota Arboretum Foundation (program grant); St. Paul Chamber Orchestra Society (program grant); Minnesota Historical Society (program grant); Neighborhood Involvement Program, Inc. (program grant); St. David's School for Child Development and Family Services (program grant)

Most grants awarded to organizations located in the Minneapolis-St. Paul vicinity.

Typical grant range: $5,000 to $100,000

404
Carolyn Foundation
901 Marquette Avenue, Suite 2630
Minneapolis, MN 55402
(612) 596-3266

Program grants; youth; minorities; women; social service organizations; environment; education; cultural organizations; United Cambodian Association of Minnesota (program grant)

Typical grant range: $5,000 to $35,000

405
Central Minnesota Community Foundation
101 S. 7th Avenue, Suite 200
St. Cloud, MN 56301
(320) 253-4380

Program grants; youth; social service; education; cultural organizations

Grants awarded to organizations located in central Minnesota.

406
Albert W. Cherne Foundation
P.O. Box 975
Minneapolis, MN 55440
(612) 944-4378

Program grants; Girl Scout Council (program for girls who are disabled); Boy Scouts of America (program grant); Minneapolis Youth Diversion Project (off streets project); Harriet Tubman Center (employment, education and training program); Children's Theatre Company (program grant); Planned Parenthood (Reach One/Teach One Project); Lao Family Community of Minnesota, Inc. (Family English School Program)

Grants awarded to organizations located in the Minneapolis-St. Paul vicinity.

Typical grant range: $5,000 to $50,000

407
Deluxe Corporation Foundation
P.O. Box 64235
St. Paul, MN 55164
(651) 483-7842

Program grants; women; minorities; disabled; youth; elderly; social service organizations; higher education; cultural organizations

Grants awarded to organizations located in areas of company operations (Deluxe Corp.).

Typical grant range: $1,000 to $50,000

408
Ecolab Foundation
Ecolab Center
St. Paul, MN 55102
(651) 293-2658

Program grants; youth; disabled; cultural organizations; education; environment; Minnesota Zoo (educational program); Nature Conservancy (program grant); Metropolitan State University (College in the Schools program at high schools)

Grants awarded to organizations located in areas of company operations (Ecolab Inc.).

409
General Mills Foundation
P.O. Box 1113
Minneapolis, MN 55440
(763) 764-7891

Program grants; youth; minorities; women; disabled; education; social service organizations; cultural organizations; community development; Johnson City Symphony Orchestra (program grant); Big Brothers/Big Sisters (program grant)

Grants awarded to organizations located in areas of company operations (General Mills, Inc.).

Typical grant range: $2,000 to $75,000

410
Graco Foundation
P.O. Box 1441
Minneapolis, MN 55440
(612) 623-6684

Program grants; youth; disabled; women; social service organizations; community development; Employment Action Center (job training program)

Grants awarded to organizations located in areas of company operations (Graco Inc.), with an emphasis in Minneapolis.

Typical grant range: $5,000 to $50,000

411
The Greystone Foundation
730 2nd Avenue S., Suite 1450
Minneapolis, MN 55402
(612) 752-1772

Program grants; social service organizations; health organizations; cultural organizations

Most grants awarded to organizations located in Minnesota.

412
Grotto Foundation, Inc.
W. 1050 First National Bank Building
332 Minnesota Street
St. Paul, MN 55101
(651) 225-0777

Program grants; Cherokee Park United Church (program grant); Asian American Renaissance (cultural program for youth); YouthCARE, Inc. (mentoring program for women); Eco Education (environmental program for students); Person to Person (literacy program); Twin Cities Housing Development Corporation (affordable housing program for children and their families); College of Saint Thomas (Bridge for Success Emergency Student program)

Most grants awarded to organizations located in Minnesota.

Typical grant range: $2,500 to $20,000

413
The HRK Foundation
345 St. Peter Street, Suite 1200
St. Paul, MN 55102
(651) 293-9001

Project grants; Minnesota AIDS Project (project grant); New Day Shelter (project grant); Ashland-Bayfield County Healthy Families (project grant)

Previous recipients of funding from this foundation have an advantage when applying for another grant.

Typical grant range: $1,000 to $20,000

414
International Multifoods Charitable Foundation
P.O. Box 2942
Minneapolis, MN 55402
(952) 594-3568

Program grants; youth; social service organizations; education; cultural organizations

Grants awarded to organizations located in areas of company operations (International Multifoods Corp.).

Typical grant range: $500 to $10,000

415
Margaret H. and James E. Kelley Foundation, Inc.
408 St. Peter Street, Suite 425
St. Paul, MN 55102
(651) 222-7463

Program grants; cultural organizations; social service organizations; higher education

Most grants awarded to organizations located in Minnesota.

Typical grant range: $1,000 to $10,000

416
Kopp Family Foundation
7701 France Avenue South, Suite 500
Edina, MN 55435

Program grants; social service organizations; disabled; youth; education; Roman Catholic organizations; Intercommunity Ministry (volunteer program); Lutheran Social Service Respite and Caregiver (program grant)

Grants awarded to organizations located in Minnesota.

Typical grant range: $500 to $10,000

417
Marbrook Foundation
730 2nd Avenue S., Suite 1450
Minneapolis, MN 55402
(612) 752-1783

Program grants; environment; education; cultural organizations; hospitals; minorities; youth; social service organizations; Abbott-Northwestern Hospital (Associates Program); Illusion Theater (education program); Minnesota Audubon Council (Forest Demonstration Project)

Grants awarded to organizations located in the Minneapolis-St. Paul vicinity.

Typical grant range: $1,000 to $20,000

418

Mardag Foundation
600 Norwest Center
55 E. 5th Street
St. Paul, MN 55101
(651) 224-5463

Program grants; Hand in Hand
Productions (female gang education and
prevention project); Jewish Community
Action (Housing for Highland Park
Program); Duluth Playhouse (children's
program); East Metro Opportunities
Industrialization Center, Inc. (program
grant); Breaking Free, Inc. (youth
prostitution prevention project); Elim
Homes, Inc. (adult day care program);
Family Pathways (companion care
program); Genesis II for Women, Inc.
(program grant); YWCA (program grant);
Opportunities In Science, Inc. (expand
program); Independent School District
(child care program); The St. Paul
Technical College Foundation (Youth
Technical Education and Community Help
Program)

Grants awarded to organizations located
in Minnesota.

Typical grant range: $5,000 to $35,000

419

The Medtronic Foundation
7000 Central Avenue, N.E.
Minneapolis, MN 55432
(612) 514-3024

Program grants; minorities; youth;
elderly; women; cultural organizations; all
levels of education; Boy Scouts of
America (after school program); United
Hospital Foundation (violence prevention
program); Metropolitan Federation of
Alternative Schools (science project)

Grants awarded to organizations located
in areas of company operations
(Medtronic, Inc.).

Typical grant range: $1,000 to $35,000

420

The Minneapolis Foundation
A200 Foshay Tower
821 Marquette Avenue, South
Minneapolis, MN 55402
(612) 339-7343

Program grants; Big Brothers/Big Sisters
(program grant); Plymouth Christian
Youth Center (programs for at-risk youth);
Association for the Advancement of
Hmong Women (Parent-Youth Connection
program); City of Minneapolis Health and
Family Support (immunization and family
stabilization project); Friday Night Out
(child care program); Indian Child
Welfare Law Center (family stability
project); Minneapolis Youth Diversion
Program (mentorship and shelter
program); YouthCARE, Inc. (mentoring
program for young women); Hawthorne
Area Community Council (Neighborhood
Revitalization Project); Minneapolis
Public Schools (Arts for Academic
Achievement Program)

Grants awarded to organizations located
in Minnesota, with an emphasis in
Minneapolis.

Typical grant range: $10,000 to $100,000

421

Minnesota Mutual Foundation
Minnesota Mutual Life Center
400 N. Robert Street
St. Paul, MN 55101
(651) 665-3501

Program grants; social service
organizations; cultural organizations

Most grants awarded to organizations
located in the Minneapolis-St. Paul
vicinity.

422
Onan Family Foundation
310 Interchange Plaza West
435 Ford Road
Minneapolis, MN 55426
(612) 544-4702

Program grants; social service
organizations; youth; education;
cultural organizations

Most grants awarded to organizations
located in the Minneapolis-St. Paul
vicinity.

423
Ordean Foundation
501 Ordean Building
424 W. Superior Street
Duluth, MN 55802
(218) 726-4785

Program grants; disabled; women; youth;
elderly; social service organizations;
health organizations

Grants awarded to organizations located
in the Duluth vicinity.

Typical grant range: $5,000 to $90,000

424
**The Jay and Rose Phillips Family
Foundation**
Ten Second Street, N.E., Suite 200
Minneapolis, MN 55413
(612) 623-1654

Program grants; Girl Scout Council
(Activity Center Program); Boys and Girls
Club (Life Skills Program); Catholic
Charities (Success to Work program);
Minneapolis Jewish Federation
(citizenship program); Regions Hospital
Foundation Center for International
Health (health program for Russian
Jewish refugees); Simpson Housing
Services, Inc. (program for transitional
housing); Battered Women's Legal
Advocacy Project, Inc. (Native American
mentorship program); Zoological Society
(educational program); St. Vincent Senior
Citizen Nutrition Program, Inc. (Meals on
Wheels program); Minnesota Opera
Company (educational program); Ordway
Music Theatre (educational program);
American Humane Association (project
grant); Blindness: Learning in New
Dimensions (Workforce Center Project)

Grants awarded to organizations located
in Minnesota.

Typical grant range: $2,000 to $50,000

425
The Pillsbury Company Foundation
Mail Station 37X5
200 S. Sixth Street
Minneapolis, MN 55402
(612) 330-4966

Program grants; most grants are youth
related (includes child welfare, recreation
and education); Boys & Girls Clubs
(program grant)

Grants awarded to organizations located
in areas of company operations (Pillsbury,
Inc.).

Typical grant range: $1,000 to $30,000

426

Red Wing Shoe Company Foundation
314 Main Street
Red Wing, MN 55066
(651) 385-1203

Program grants; health organizations;
education; environment; Red Wing
Noontime Kiwanis (Iodine Deficiency
Project); Red Wing School District 256
Social Environmental Learning Focus
(program at a high school)

Grants awarded to organizations located
in the Red Wing vicinity.

427

Last minute update: The foundation
originally listed here has terminated.

428

The Saint Paul Foundation, Inc.
600 Norwest Center
55 East 5th Street
St. Paul, MN 55101
(651) 224-5463

Program grants; youth; elderly;
minorities; women; disabled; social
service organizations; education;
community development; cultural
organizations

Most grants awarded to organizations
located in the St. Paul vicinity.

429

Smikis Foundation
Parkdale Plaza, Suite 426
1660 South Highway 100
St. Louis Park, MN 55416
(952) 512-1165

Program grants; social service
organizations; education; environment

Grants awarded to organizations located
in Minnesota.

Typical grant range: $1,000 to $20,000

430

Star Tribune Foundation
425 Portland Avenue
Minneapolis, MN 55488
(612) 673-7051

Program grants; Learning Disabilities
Association (Learning Connections to
Reading program); Minneapolis Institute
of Arts (youth education program);
Minnesota Museum of American Art
(education programs); Minnesota
Orchestral Association (youth education
program); Big Brothers/Big Sisters
(mentoring program); Boys and Girls
Club (athletic and educational programs);
Phyllis Wheatley Community Center
(Education for Cooperative Living
program); African-American Family
Services (family preservation program);
CornerHouse Interagency Child Abuse
Evaluation (youth programs); Lyndale
Neighborhood Association (education
program); West Seventh Community
Center, Inc. (youth and senior outreach
programs); Minneapolis Public Schools:
North High Career Center (teen job
programs)

Grants awarded to organizations located
in the Minneapolis vicinity.

Typical grant range: $2,000 to $50,000

431
Supervalu Foundation
P.O. Box 990
Minneapolis, MN 55440
(952) 828-4000

Program grants; social service
organizations; food distribution;
education; cultural organizations

Most grants awarded to organizations
located in the Minneapolis-St. Paul
vicinity.

432
Target Foundation
1000 Nicollet Mall
Minneapolis, MN 55403
(612) 696-6098

Program grants; employment programs;
women; minorities; youth; social service
organizations; cultural organizations

Most grants awarded to organizations
located in Minneapolis and St. Paul.

Typical grant range: $5,000 to $50,000

433
**Archie D. and Bertha H. Walker
Foundation**
1121 Hennepin Avenue
Minneapolis, MN 55403
(612) 332-3556

Program grants; alcohol abuse; youth;
racism; women; disabled; social service
organizations; cultural organizations

Most grants awarded to organizations
located in the Minneapolis-St. Paul
vicinity.

Typical grant range: $100 to $15,000

MISSISSIPPI

434
William Robert Baird Charitable Trust
c/o Citizens National Bank
512 22nd Avenue
P.O. Box 911
Meridian, MS 39302
(601) 693-1331

Program grants; youth; social service
organizations

Typical grant range: $2,500 to $10,000

435
**Community Foundation of Greater
Jackson**
4500 I-55 N., Suite 258
Jackson, MS 39211
(601) 981-4572

Program grants; social service
organizations; youth; community
development; education; cultural
organizations

Typical grant range: $300 to $20,000

436
Foundation for the Mid South
308 E. Pearl Street, 2nd Floor
Jackson, MS 39201
(601) 355-8167

Program grants; minorities; youth;
education; community development

MISSOURI

437
The H & R Block Foundation
4435 Main Street, Suite 500
Kansas City, MO 64111
(816) 932-8324

Program grants; Mid America Heart Institute (education program); Kansas City Free Health Clinic (program grant); Heart of America Community AIDS Partnership (prevention and education program); Women's Employment Network (job training program); Kansas City Symphony (program grant); Kansas City Museum (program grant); Jewish Community Relations Bureau-American Jewish Committee (program grant); Wildwood Outdoor Education Center (program grant); Heartland Therapeutic Riding, Inc. (program grant); City Vision Ministries (program grant); Children's Center for the Visually Impaired (Infant Intervention Program); De La Salle Education Center (School-to-Career Program); Missouri Colleges Fund, Inc. (program grant)

Most grants awarded to organizations located in the Kansas City vicinity.

Typical grant range: $1,000 to $25,000

438
Community Foundation of the Ozarks
901 St. Louis Street, Suite 701
Springfield, MO 65806
(417) 864-6199

Program grants; Boys and Girls Club (music program); Girl Scouts (program grant); Congregational Health Ministries (parish nursing program); Clark Mental Health Center (program for alcoholics); Senior Employment Program (program grant); Congregational Health Ministries (program grant); Retired Senior Volunteer Program (reading program); Green County Juvenile Justice Center (program for detained youth); Harwell Art Museum (project grant); Discovery Center (science and mathematics project); Hillcrest High School Media Department (diversity program); Ozarks Technical Community College Foundation (adult education program)

Most grants awarded to organizations located in Springfield and Greene County.

Typical grant range: $500 to $7,500

439
Allen P. and Josephine B. Green Foundation
P.O. Box 523
Mexico, MO 65265
(573) 581-5568

Program grants; Epworth Children & Family Services (employment program for troubled youth); Douglas Community Center (Kids in Motion Program); Boys & Girls Clubs (Smart Moves program); Missouri River Regional Library (literacy program); Northwest Health Services (dental project); YMCA (Prime Time Program); Springfield Landmarks Preservation Trust, Inc. (project grant); St. Louis Foundation for Alcoholism & Related Dependencies (treatment program); Coalition Against Rape & Domestic Violence (program grant); ABLE Learning Center (literacy program); Stella Maris Child Center (Math & Science Improvement Project); Fairview Elementary School (Fairview Fight Free Program); Vanderschmidt School (training program for people who are underprivileged or disabled)

Grants awarded to organizations located in the Mexico, Missouri vicinity.

Typical grant range: $2,000 to $20,000

440
Hall Family Foundation
P.O. Box 419580, Mail Drop 323
Kansas City, MO 64141
(816) 274-8516

Program grants; women; youth; minorities; social service organizations; community development; cultural organizations

Grants awarded to organizations located in Kansas City.

Typical grant range: $25,000 to $500,000

441
Ewing Marion Kauffman Foundation
4801 Rockhill Road
Kansas City, MO 64110
(816) 932-1000

Program grants; Youth Opportunities Unlimited (after-school program); Diocese of Kansas City (literacy program); YWCA (program grant); Boys and Girls Club (program grant); Bethel Neighborhood Center (summer youth program); Board of Parks and Recreation (program grant); Chameleon Theatre Company (program grant); Heart of America Family Services (support program for Latino families); National Urban Technology Center, Inc. (technology education program); Kansas Unified School District (summer program); Wellesley College (child care project); Penn Valley Community College (entrepreneurship program)

Typical grant range: $50,000 to $250,000

442
The Kellwood Foundation
P.O. Box 14374
St. Louis, MO 63178
(314) 576-3431

Program grants; education; youth; social service organizations

Most grants awarded to organizations located in St. Louis.

443
R.A. Long Foundation
600 Plaza West Building
4600 Madison Avenue
Kansas City, MO 64112
(816) 561-4600

Program grants; youth; education, including elementary and secondary education; cultural organizations

Grants awarded to organizations located in the Kansas City vicinity.

Typical grant range: $1,500 to $10,000

444
Finis M. Moss Charitable Trust
108 West Walnut
P.O. Box G
Nevada, MO 64772
(417) 667-6616

Program grants; community development; education; social service organizations

Grants awarded to organizations located in Nevada, Missouri.

Typical grant range: $500 to $15,000

445
Musgrave Foundation
4035 S. Fremont
Springfield, MO 65804
(417) 883-7154

Program grants; social service organizations; youth; education; community development

Grants awarded to organizations located in the Springfield vicinity.

Typical grant range: $1,000 to $30,000

446
Sayler-Hawkins Foundation
701 Market Street, Suite 1500
St. Louis, MO 63101
(314) 982-0335

Program grants; social service organizations; cultural organizations; Christian organizations

Most grants awarded to organizations located in St. Louis.

Typical grant range: $250 to $10,000

447
The Sosland Foundation
4800 Main Street, Suite 100
Kansas City, MO 64112
(816) 756-1000

Program grants; youth; women; social service organizations; education; cultural organizations; health organizations; Jewish organizations

Most grants awarded to organizations located in the Kansas City vicinity.

Typical grant range: $1,000 to $25,000

448
St. Louis Community Foundation
319 S. N. Fourth Street, Suite 501
St. Louis, MO 63102
(314) 588-8200

Program grants; youth; elderly; women; disabled; social service organizations; education; health organizations

Grants awarded to organizations located in the St. Louis vicinity.

449
Norman J. Stupp Foundation
c/o Commerce Bank of St. Louis
8000 Forsyth Blvd.
St. Louis, MO 63105
(314) 746-8577

Program grants; women; youth; social service organizations; education; hospitals; medical research; ALIVE (domestic violence program); YMCA (literacy program); St. Louis Children's Hospital (program to prevent injuries); University of Missouri (Teacher Development Program); St. Louis University, Eye Institute (eye research program)

Most grants awarded to organizations located in the St. Louis vicinity.

Typical grant range: $2,000 to $20,000

MONTANA

450
Dufresne Foundation
P.O. Box 1929
Great Falls, MT 59403
(406) 727-2200

Program grants; youth; disabled; social service organizations; education; cultural organizations

Grants awarded to organizations located in the Great Falls area.

Typical grant range: $500 to $5,000

451
Montana Community Foundation
101 N. Last Chance Gulch, Suite 211
Helena, MT 59601
(406) 443-8313

Program grants; Native Action (voter education project); Montana Asian American Center (program grant); Great Falls Symphony Association (school program); Montana Council for Families (education prevention program for child abuse); Women's Opportunity Resource Center (teen father outreach program); Grandstreet Theatre (program grant); Council for the Arts, Inc. (program grant); Mikal Kellner Foundation for Animals (Adopt-A-Species program); Townsend Youth Council (mural project); Lodge Grass Public Schools (program for students to promote respect); Boys & Girls Club (cultural arts program); Miles Community College (summer youth program)

Grants awarded to organizations located in Montana.

Typical grant range: $500 to $5,000

452
The Sample Foundation, Inc.
14 N. 24th Street
P.O. Box 279
Billings, MT 59103
(406) 245-6342

Program grants; social service organizations; youth; elderly; education; Institute for Peace Studies (cultural program for youth); S.A.F.E. (children's program at a domestic violence center); Intermountain Children's Home (project grant); Rocky Mountain College (Academic Success Program)

Most grants awarded to organizations located in Montana.

Typical grant range: $1,000 to $15,000

NEBRASKA

453
The Theodore G. Baldwin Foundation
P.O. Box 922
Kearney, NE 68848
(308) 234-9889

Program grants; cultural organizations; education; youth; social service organizations; Saint Michael Episcopal Church (summer mission program); Kearney Area Arts Council (program grant)

Grants awarded to organizations located in Nebraska.

Typical grant range: $2,000 to $10,000

454
Oliver & Ferrol Barklage Foundation Trust
c/o Norwest Bank Nebraska, N.A.
10010 Regency Center, Suite 300
Omaha, NE 68114
(402) 536-2470

Program grants; Omaha Symphony Association (Mission Imagination Educational Program); Girl Scout Council (My Summer Place Program); Camp Fire Boys and Girls (program for children in homeless shelters); Visiting Nurse Association (program grant); Lincoln Medical Education Foundation (program to stop excessive drinking); Ollie Webb Center (program to assist children who are visually impaired)

Most grants awarded to organizations located in Omaha.

Typical grant range: $2,000 to $10,000

455

Cooper Foundation
304 Cooper Plaza
211 N. 12th Street
Lincoln, NE 68508
(402) 476-7571

Program grants; youth; cultural organizations; education; higher education

Grants awarded to organizations located in Nebraska.

Typical grant range: $1,000 to $30,000

456

May L. Flanagan Foundation
1400 First Bank Building
Lincoln, NE 68508

Program grants; Catholic Social Services (emergency services program); Lincoln Medical Education (program grant); Friendship Home of Lincoln (case management program)

Grants awarded to organizations located in Lincoln.

Typical grant range: $1,000 to $8,000

457

Fremont Area Community Foundation
605 N. Broad Street
Fremont, NE 68025
(402) 721-4252

Program grants; youth; elderly; social service organizations; education; cultural organizations; Educational Service Unit #2 (Science Fair program); Friends of Fremont Area Parks, Inc. (Keep Educating Our Seniors Program)

Grants awarded to organizations located in the Fremont vicinity.

Typical grant range: $500 to $3,000

458

Bernard K. & Norma F. Heuermann Foundation
c/o Wells Fargo Bank
Trust Department
1919 Douglas Street
Omaha, NE 68102
(402) 536-2799

Program grants; disabled; youth; higher education; agriculture, including educational programs

Grants awarded to organizations located in Nebraska.

Typical grant range: $1,000 to $20,000

459

Gilbert M. and Martha H. Hitchcock Foundation
Lamson, Dugan & Murray Building
10306 Regency Parkway Drive
Omaha, NE 68114
(402) 397-7300

Program grants; social service organizations; education; cultural organizations

Typical grant range: $1,000 to $25,000

460

Lincoln Community Foundation, Inc.
215 Centennial Mall South, Suite 200
Lincoln, NE 68508
(402) 474-2345

Program grant; cultural organizations; social service organizations; youth; environment; health organizations; The Community Blood Bank (program grant); The Hispanic Community Center (tutoring program)

Grants awarded to organizations located in the Lincoln vicinity.

Typical grant range: $100 to $15,000

461
Omaha Community Foundation
1623 Farnam Street, Suite 600
Omaha, NE 68102
(402) 342-3458

Program grants; youth; elderly; disabled; women; education; health organizations; social service organizations; community development

Grants awarded to organizations located in the Omaha vicinity.

462
Robert D. Wilson Foundation
8805 Indian Hills Drive, Suite 280
Omaha, NE 68114
(402) 390-0390

Program grants; social service organizations; youth; education; health organizations; Epilepsy Foundation (program grant); Literacy Center for the Midlands (Beyond Basic Project)

Most grants awarded to organizations located in Nebraska.

Typical grant range: $5,000 to $15,000

463
Woods Charitable Fund, Inc.
P.O. Box 81309
Lincoln, NE 68501
(402) 436-5971

Program grants; Camp Fire Boys and Girls Council (violence prevention program); Lincoln Medical Education Foundation, Inc. (Center for Family Care project); Anti-Defamation League (World of Difference program); Indian Center, Inc. (Youth Development and Cultural Education Programs); Lincoln Area Agency on Aging (Foster Grandparent Program); Lincoln Council on Alcoholism and Drugs, Inc. (Bright Futures Project); Malone Community Center (life skills program); Nebraska Humanities Council (program grant); Centerpointe, Inc. (transitional housing projects for homeless); Leadership Lincoln, Inc. (program to strengthen leadership skills of youth); University of Nebraska-Lincoln, College of Fine & Performing Arts (early childhood research project)

Most grants awarded to organizations located in Lincoln.

Typical grant range: $5,000 to $50,000

NEVADA

464
The E.L. Cord Foundation
One East 1st Street, Suite 901
Reno, NV 89501
(775) 323-0373

Program grants; youth; disabled; women; education; social service organizations; recreation; cultural organizations; YMCA (program grant)

Most grants awarded to organizations located in northern Nevada.

Typical grant range: $5,000 to $75,000

465
Greenspun Family Foundation
2290 Corporate Circle Drive, No. 250
Henderson, NV 89012

Program grants; cultural organizations; community development; Jewish organizations

Few grants awarded.

Most grants awarded to organizations located in Las Vegas.

Typical grant range: $500 to $25,000

466
Robert Z. Hawkins Foundation
One E. Liberty Street, Suite 509
Reno, NV 89501
(775) 786-1105

Program grants; social service organizations; youth; community development

Grants awarded to organizations located in Nevada.

Typical grant range: $1,000 to $30,000

467
Lied Foundation Trust
3907 W. Charleston Blvd.
Las Vegas, NV 89102
(702) 878-1559

Program grants; cultural organizations; education; higher education; youth; social service organizations

Typical grant range: $25,000 to $750,000

468
Nell J. Redfield Foundation
P.O. Box 61
1755 E. Plumb Lane, Suite 212
Reno, NV 89504
(775) 323-1373

Program grants; health organizations; children who are disabled; elderly; education; higher education

Most grants awarded to organizations located in Reno.

Typical grant range: $2,000 to $100,000

469
Donald W. Reynolds Foundation
1701 Village Center Circle
Las Vegas, NV 89134
(702) 804-6000

Program grants; SeniorNet (Seniors Media Lab Program); American Diabetes Association (program grant); United Way (program grant); Conference of Southwest Foundations, Inc. (program grant); The Philanthropy Roundtable (program grant); International Longevity Center (program grant); National Judicial College (program grant)

Typical grant range: $500,000 to $15,000,000

470
E.L. Wiegand Foundation
Wiegand Center
165 W. Liberty Street
Reno, NV 89501
(775) 333-0310

Program grants; all levels of education; hospitals; medical research; youth; women; cultural organizations; Roman Catholic organizations

Typical grant range: $5,000 to $125,000

NEW HAMPSHIRE

471
Norwin S. and Elizabeth N. Bean Foundation
c/o New Hampshire Charitable Foundation
37 Pleasant Street
Concord, NH 03301
(603) 225-6641

Program grants; social service organizations; youth; health organizations; education; cultural organizations

Most grants awarded to organizations located in Manchester and Amherst.

Typical grant range: $1,500 to $25,000

472
Alexander Eastman Foundation
c/o New Hampshire Charitable
Foundation
37 Pleasant Street
Concord, NH 03301
(603) 225-6641

Program grants; health organizations;
youth; education; social service
organizations; American Lung Association
(program grant)

Grants awarded to organizations located
in Derry, Londonderry, Windham, Chester,
Hampstead, and Sandown.

Typical grant range: $1,000 to $20,000

473
Foundation for Seacoast Health
100 Campus Drive, Suite 1
Portsmouth, NH 03801-5892
(603) 422-8200

Program grants; Seacoast HealthNet
(dental program); The AIDS Project (HIV
Health and Prevention Program); Seacoast
Mental Health Center (teen program);
Town of Eliot (Youth Bound Summer
Program); Planned Parenthood (cancer
screening program); YMCA (after school
recreation program); Educational Safety
Programs, Ltd. (martial arts program for
at-risk children); Portsmouth School
Department (leadership program for
young women)

Typical grant range: $1,000 to $100,000

474
Agnes M. Lindsay Trust
660 Chestnut Street
Manchester, NH 03104
(603) 669-1366

Program grants; health organizations;
education; youth; disabled

Typical grant range: $1,000 to $20,000

475
Mascoma Savings Bank Foundation
c/o Mascoma Savings Bank
P.O. Box 435
Lebanon, NH 03766
(603) 448-3650

Program grants; Town of Turnbridge
Recreation Association (summer camp
program); ACORN AIDS Community
Resource Network (Walk for Life
project); Easter Seals Society (program
grant); Mascoma Watershed Conservation
Council (program grant); Saint Barnabas
Church (program grant); White River
Craft Center (kayak program); Indian
River Nursery School (preschool
program); Mascoma Valley Regional
School District (Bully Prevention
Programs)

Typical grant range: $500 to $2,000

476
**The New Hampshire Charitable
Foundation**
37 Pleasant Street
Concord, NH 03301
(603) 225-6641

Program grants; health organizations;
youth; disabled; social service
organizations; environment; education;
cultural organizations

Grants awarded to organizations located
in New Hampshire.

477
Putnam Foundation
P.O. Box 323
Keene, NH 03431
(603) 352-2448

Program grants; historic preservation;
cultural organizations; environment;
education; higher education; New
England College (program grant)

Grants awarded to organizations located
in New Hampshire.

Typical grant range: $500 to $25,000

478
Last minute update: The foundation
originally listed here has terminated.

NEW JERSEY

479
Last minute update: The foundation originally listed here has terminated.

480
John Bickford Foundation
P.O. Box 1945
Morristown, NJ 07962
(973) 966-8189

Program grants; education; mental health; youth; social service; St. Paul's School (Advanced Studies Program)

Typical grant range: $1,000 to $10,000

481
Campbell Soup Foundation
Campbell Place, Box 60F
Camden, NJ 08103
(856) 342-4800

Program grants; community development; minorities; youth; health organizations

Grants awarded to organizations located in areas of company operations (Campbell Soup Co.), with an emphasis in Camden.

Typical grant range: $1,000 to $40,000

482
Geraldine R. Dodge Foundation, Inc.
163 Madison Avenue
P.O. Box 1239
Morristown, NJ 07962
(973) 540-8442

Program grants; cultural organizations; youth; minorities; environment; education

Typical grant range: $5,000 to $45,000

483
The Fund for New Jersey
94 Church Street, Suite 303
New Brunswick, NJ 08901
(732) 220-8656

Program grants; environment; minorities; community development; youth; education; Association of New Jersey Environmental Commissions (project grant); Rutgers University (summer science program)

Grants awarded to organizations located in New Jersey.

Typical grant range: $5,000 to $100,000

484
The Hyde and Watson Foundation
437 Southern Blvd.
Chatham Township, NJ 07928
(973) 966-6024

Program grants; social service organizations; youth; elderly; women; disabled; education; health organizations; cultural organizations

Typical grant range: $5,000 to $25,000

485
The James Kerney Foundation
P.O. Box 6698
Trenton, NJ 08648

Program grants; education; community development; youth; cultural organizations

Grants awarded to organizations located in the Trenton vicinity.

486
The Fanny and Svante Knistrom Foundation
229 Main Street
Chatham, NJ 07928
(973) 635-5200

Program grants; Ride on Therapeutic Horsemanship (horseback riding program for people who are disabled); Boy Scouts of America (scouting program for children who are disabled); Court Appointed Special Advocates (program advocating family court for abused children)

Typical grant range: $2,000 to $20,000

487
Blanche and Irving Laurie Foundation, Inc.
P.O. Box 53
Roseland, NJ 07068
(973) 993-1583

Program grants; Jewish organizations; cultural organizations; education; youth; disabled; social service organizations; health organizations

Most grants awarded to organizations located in New Jersey.

Typical grant range: $2,500 to $50,000

488
George A. Ohl, Jr. Trust
c/o First Union National Bank
Charitable Department
190 River Road, 2nd Floor
Summit, NJ 07901
(908) 598-3576

Program grants; health organizations; youth; elderly; homeless; social service organizations; recreation; education; secondary education

Grants awarded to organizations located in New Jersey.

Typical grant range: $1,500 to $10,000

489
Princeton Area Community Foundation, Inc.
188 Tamarack Circle
Skillman, NJ 08558
(609) 688-0300

Program grants; Passage Theatre Company (project grant); Young Audiences of New Jersey (homeless youth photography project); Big Brothers/Big Sisters (volunteer recruitment program); Womenspace (domestic violence project); Princeton Senior Resource Center (intergenerational reading program); Planned Parenthood Association (project grant); Trenton After School Program (training for teachers and parents who work with special needs children); Trenton Area Soup Kitchen (adult education program); Crawford House (transitional living program for women recovering from alcohol and drug addiction); Isles, Inc. (environmental education program); Lutheran Social Ministries (program for refugees to learn English); Trenton Area Soup Kitchen (adult education program); Trinity Counseling Service (program to prevent aggressive behavior at a high school); Notre Dame High School (community service project)

Grants awarded to organizations located in Mercer County.

490
The Prudential Foundation
751 Broad Street, 15th Floor
Newark, NJ 07102
(973) 802-7354

Program grants; AIDS Resource
Foundation for Children (after-school
program); Big Sisters (mentoring
program); Freedom Foundation of New
Jersey, Inc. (teen pregnancy prevention
program); Newark Museum Association
(educational and employment program for
youth); New Jersey Performing Arts
Center (educational program); Children's
Literacy Initiative (program grant); The
Chad School Foundation (early childhood
program)

Grants awarded to organizations located
in areas of company operations
(Prudential Insurance Co. of America).

491
Fannie E. Rippel Foundation
180 Mount Airy Road, Suite 200
Basking Ridge, NJ 07920
(908) 766-0404

Program grants; The Hastings Center
(cancer care and research project); Huron
Regional Medical Center, Inc. (cancer and
cardiac disease programs); Cancer Care,
Inc. (program grant for the elderly);
Senior Services Center (program grant);
Medical Care Development, Inc. (program
for nurses); Whitehead Institute for
Biomedical Research (research program);
The Cooper Health System (Interventional
Cardiology Program)

Typical grant range: $25,000 to $250,000

492
L.P. Schenck Fund
c/o PNC Bank
41 Oak Street
Ridgewood, NJ 07450
(201) 652-8499

Program grants; youth; girls; elderly;
social service organizations; cultural
organizations

Grants awarded to organizations located
in New Jersey.

Typical grant range: $1,000 to $25,000

493
**The Schumann Fund for New Jersey,
Inc.**
21 Van Vleck Street
Montclair, NJ 07042
(973) 509-9883

Program grants; youth; education;
environment; social service organizations;
Babyland Family Services (child care
program); Montclair Early Childhood
Corporation (prekindergarten program);
Communities in Schools of New Jersey,
Inc. (dropout prevention program)

Grants awarded to organizations located
in New Jersey.

Typical grant range: $5,000 to $50,000

494
The Westfield Foundation
301 North Avenue West
P.O. Box 2295
Westfield, NJ 07091
(908) 233-9787

Program grants; New Jersey State Opera (middle school and high school program); Arbor Chamber Music Society (mentoring program); Westfield Symphony Orchestra (education program); Lifetime Support, Inc. (guardianship program of the Association of Retarded Citizens); Summer Youth Employment Program (summer job program); Westfield High School Ice Hockey (program grant); Optimist Club (drunk driving simulator project at a high school)

Grants awarded to organizations located in the Westfield vicinity.

Typical grant range: $500 to $20,000

NEW MEXICO

495
Albuquerque Community Foundation
P.O. Box 36960
Albuquerque, NM 87176
(505) 883-6240

Program grants; Opera Southwest (free ticket program for students); Chamber Music Albuquerque (program grant); National Council on Alcoholism/Drug Dependence (intervention program); Bosque Preparatory School (environmental monitoring project); Adelante Development Center, Inc. (program for the elderly who are disabled and assist them with senior center activities)

Grants awarded to organizations located in the Albuquerque vicinity.

Typical grant range: $1,500 to $5,000

496
J.F. Maddox Foundation
P.O. Box 2588
Hobbs, NM 88241
(505) 393-6338

Program grants; youth; elderly; women; social service organizations; all levels of education; cultural organizations

Typical grant range: $3,000 to $75,000

497
McCune Charitable Foundation
345 E. Alameda Street
Santa Fe, NM 87501
(505) 983-8300

Program grants; Mesilla Valley Hospice (bereavement program); National Alliance for the Mentally Ill (education program); Santa Fe Desert Chorale (program grant); Georgia O'Keeffe Museum (Saturdays for Families program); Rio Grande Restoration (river restoration education program); Western Environmental Law Center (Concentrated Animal Feeding Operations project); Home for Women and Children (domestic violence program); Boys and Girls Club (education program); YMCA (after school programs); Behavioral Health Research Center (substance abuse and health screening programs); Adaptive Ski Program (project for children with disabilities); Santa Fe Youth 2000 (Hispanic and Native American arts program); Our Lady of Refuge Church (job program for high school students); Gathering Place (family literacy project); Agua Fria Elementary School (summer algebra program); Santa Rosa High School (Agriculture Education Career Development Program); New Mexico State University (Senior Writing Outreach project)

Grants awarded to organizations located in New Mexico.

Typical grant range: $3,000 to $50,000

498
PNM Foundation, Inc.
Alvarado Square, M.S. 1225
Albuquerque, NM 87158
(505) 241-2675

Program grants; social service
organizations; youth; elderly; minorities;
education; health organizations

Most grants awarded to organizations
located in New Mexico, with an emphasis
in areas of company operations (Public
Service Co. of New Mexico).

499
The Santa Fe Community Foundation
P.O. Box 1827
Santa Fe, NM 87504
(505) 988-9715

Program grants; youth; minorities; social
service organizations; disabled; education;
cultural organizations; animal welfare;
environment; health organizations; Santa
Fe Teen Arts Center (art program);
Presbyterian Medical Services Teen
Health Center (pregnancy prevention
program)

Most grants awarded to organizations
located in the Santa Fe vicinity.

Typical grant range: $2,000 to $14,000

NEW YORK

500
The Achelis Foundation
767 Third Avenue, 4th Floor
New York, NY 10017
(212) 644-0322

Program grants; Catholic Big Brothers
(Sports Buddies mentoring program);
New York Theological Seminary
(program grant for youth); American
Women's Economic Development
Corporation (entrepreneurship program);
Girls Incorporated (program grant); New
York City Opera (program grant);
Brooklyn Academy of Music (Increased
Access Programs); League for the Hard of
Hearing (career mentoring program);
Madison Square Boys & Girls Club
(employment program); National Center
for Neighborhood Enterprise (Distant
Learning Program); Pierpont Morgan
Library (program grant); Institute for
Responsible Fatherhood and Family
Revitalization (fatherhood program);
Metropolitan Museum of Art (High
School Apprenticeships Program)

Grants awarded to organizations located
in New York City.

Typical grant range: $10,000 to $50,000

501
Altman Foundation
521 5th Street, 35th Floor
New York, NY 10175
(212) 682-0970

Program grants; United Hospital Fund of New York (Families and Health Care Project); Little Sisters of the Assumption Family Health Service, Inc. (Family Life Program); Visiting Nurse Service (Mental Health Program); Catholic Big Brothers (Sports Buddies of New York program); Big Brothers/Big Sisters (program grant); Council of Senior Centers and Services (program grant); Federation of Protestant Welfare Agencies, Inc. (program grant); The Hope Program, Inc. (Job Readiness Project for homeless); The Nature Conservancy of New York (Internship Program for City Youth); The Brooklyn Children's Museum (after-school program); The Wildlife Conservation Society (Marine Teen Program); Wave Hill Incorporated (environmental education program); Literacy Partners, Inc. (Family Literacy Program); Saint Joseph School (extended day program)

Grants awarded to organizations located in New York City.

Typical grant range: $10,000 to $75,000

502
J. Aron Charitable Foundation, Inc.
126 E. 56th Street, Suite 2300
New York, NY 10022
(212) 832-3405

Program grants; cultural organizations; youth; education; hospitals; health organizations; social service organizations; Boy Scouts (program grant)

Typical grant range: $1,000 to $50,000

503
AXA Foundation
1290 Avenue of the Americas
New York, NY 10104
(212) 314-2566

Program grants; youth; cultural organizations; YMCA (program grant); Brooklyn Children's Museum (educational program)

Typical grant range: $2,000 to $25,000

504
The Baird Foundation
P.O. Box 1210, Ellicott Station
Buffalo, NY 14205
(716) 883-2429

Project grants; education; youth; environment; community development; cultural organizations

Most grants awarded to organizations located in the Buffalo vicinity.

505
The Barker Welfare Foundation
P.O. Box 2
Glen Head, NY 11545
(516) 759-5592

Program grants; Council on Aging (transportation program); Girl Scouts (program grant); YWCA (young parents program); Boys and Girls Club, Inc. (program grant); National Dance Institute (program grant); Brooklyn Public Library (Kids Connection Program); City Parks Foundation (tennis program for youth); Grosvenor Neighborhood House, Inc. (summer camp program); Partnership for the Homeless, Inc. (program grant); Visiting Nurse Association (Security Escort Program); Saint Vincent's Hospital and Medical Center (parent education program); International Center for the Disabled (Direct Care Training program)

Typical grant range: $5,000 to $30,000

506
Bethesda Foundation, Inc.
P.O. Box 296
North Hornell, NY 14843
(607) 324-1616

Program grants; Net Domestic Abuse Program (project grant); Institute for Human Services (program grant); Steuben County Office for the Aging (Grandparents Raising Grandchildren program); Planned Parenthood (program grant); Kinship Family & Youth Services, Inc. (Healthy Families Program); YMCA (Cardiac Rehabilitation Program); Home and Health Care Services (home health aide training program)

Grants awarded to organizations located in the Hornell vicinity.

Typical grant range: $1,000 to $8,000

507
The Bodman Foundation
767 Third Avenue, 4th Floor
New York, NY 10017
(212) 644-0322

Program grants; New York Hall of Science (Science Career Ladder program); Long Island Children's Museum (program grant); American Lyme Disease Foundation (education program); Animal Medical Center (Guide Dog Program); Broadway Community (employment program for the homeless); Girls Incorporated (program grant); YWCA (Youth Entrepreneur Program); Jewish Board of Family and Children's Services (cult rehabilitation program); Teen Challenge (drug rehabilitation program); St. Matthew's and St. Timothy's Neighborhood Center (Star Learning Program); Theatre Development Fund (Talking Hands-Theatre Access Project for students who are hearing impaired); Goodwill Industries (mathematics and science program for children and parents)

Grants awarded to organizations located in the New York City vicinity.

Typical grant range: $15,000 to $100,000

508
Booth Ferris Foundation
60 Wall Street, 46th Floor
New York, NY 10260
(212) 809-1630

Program grants; cultural organizations; youth; women; minorities; social service organizations; community development; Boys & Girls Club (Teen Time program); Center for Children and Families (program grant); Merchants Block Association (employment program); Lincoln Center for the Performing Arts (program grant); Long Island Philharmonic (program grant); New Visions for Public Schools (library program); City University of New York (Teacher Opportunity Project)

Grants awarded to organizations located in the New York City vicinity.

Typical grant range: $25,000 to $150,000

509
The Robert Bowne Foundation, Inc.
345 Hudson Street
New York, NY 10014
(212) 229-7223

Program grants; literacy programs; youth; Literacy Assistance Center (project grant); Foundation for Children and the Classics (project grant); Brooklyn Children's Museum (project grant); The Partnership for Afterschool Education (project grant)

Grants awarded to organizations located within one of the five boroughs of New York City.

Typical grant range: $10,000 to $40,000

510

The Bristol-Myers Squibb Foundation, Inc.
345 Park Avenue, 43rd Floor
New York, NY 10154
(212) 546-4566

Program grants; health organizations; women; youth; education; cultural organizations; women; minorities; Boys and Girls Clubs (program grant)

Grants awarded to organizations located in areas of company operations (Bristol-Myers Squibb Co.).

Typical grant range: $3,000 to $100,000

511

The Louis Calder Foundation
230 Park Avenue, Room 1525
New York, NY 10169
(212) 687-1680

Program grants; Boys and Girls Club (after school program); Big Brothers/Big Sisters (mentoring program); Little Orchestra Society (educational program for youth); Brooklyn Youth Chorus (educational program); Libraries for the Future (after school program); Literacy Assistance Center, Inc. (program grant); Catholic Charities (after school program); Saint Francis Xavier Church (after school program); Staten Island Children's Museum (educational program); Friends of Green Chimneys, Inc. (environmental education program); Wildlife Conservation Society (educational program); Xaverian High School (program to introduce laptop technology into the classroom); All Hallows High School (leadership development program)

Most grants awarded to organizations located in New York City.

Typical grant range: $5,000 to $50,000

512

Mary Flagler Cary Charitable Trust
122 East 42nd Street, Room 3505
New York, NY 10168
(212) 953-7700

Program grants; The Diller-Quaile School of Music, Inc. (music and dance summer program for children from Harlem); The Brooklyn Academy of Music, Inc. (program grant); Miller Theatre, Columbia University (contemporary music and jazz program); Brooklyn Botanic Garden (GreenBridge program); Citizens Committee for New York City (Neighborhood Environmental Action Program); The Nature Conservancy (Conservation Internship Program for City Youth)

Typical grant range: $5,000 to $50,000

513

Central New York Community Foundation, Inc.
500 S. Salina Street, Suite 428
Syracuse, NY 13202
(315) 422-9538

Program grants; Alzheimer's Association (program grant); Westcott East Neighborhood Association (ceramic mosaic mural project); Partnership for Community Development, Ltd. (small business mentoring program); Dunbar Association, Inc. (adoptive homes for minority children program); Native American Service Agency (program for people who are developmentally disabled); Exceptional Family Resources (massage therapy program for children who are disabled); Madison Family Outreach (visitation program for parents involved in child abuse cases); Canastota Central School District (summer program); Bishop Ludden Junior/Senior High School (music program); Syracuse City School District (Syracuse Early Reading Project)

Grants awarded to organizations located in Onondaga and Madison Counties.

Typical grant range: $4,000 to $20,000

514

Charitable Venture Foundation
c/o Lavelle & Finn
450 New Karner Road
Albany, NY 12205
(518) 271-1134

Program grants; Catholic Charities (Caring Companion Volunteer Program); United Ministries (Computers for Kids Program); Hispanic Outreach Program (program grant); Affordable Housing Partnership (program grant); EBA Dance Theater (educational program); Alzheimer's Association (program grant); Family and Children's Service (program for at-risk students); The Ark (Computers and Communications Technology Summer Employment and Training Program)

Most grants awarded to organizations located in Albany.

Typical grant range: $10,000 to $100,000

515

Chase Manhattan Foundation
The Chase Manhattan Bank, N.A.
One Chase Manhattan Plaza
New York, NY 10081
(212) 552-1112

Program grants; youth; minorities; social service organizations; disabled; cultural organizations; education; community development; New Visions for Public Schools (Chase Active Learning Program)

Grants awarded to organizations located in areas of company operations (Chase Manhattan Bank), with an emphasis in New York City.

Typical grant range: $1,000 to $50,000

516

Chautauqua Region Community Foundation, Inc.
418 Spring Street
Jamestown, NY 14701-5332
(716) 661-3390

Program grants; social service organizations; youth; education; cultural organizations; Chautauqua Regional Youth Symphony, Inc. (program grant); Patterson Library (program grant); Frewsburg Community Pride Group (recreation program)

Grants awarded to organizations located in southern Chautauqua County.

Typical grant range: $1,000 to $9,000

517

The Edna McConnell Clark Foundation
250 Park Avenue, Suite 900
New York, NY 10017
(212) 551-9100

Program grants; Big Brothers/Big Sisters (mentoring program); New York Botanical Gardens (program grant); Fund for the City of New York (summer employment project); Women's Housing and Economic Development Corporation (employment program); Friends of Island Academy, (expand employment program)

Typical grant range: $20,000 to $250,000

518

The Clark Foundation
One Rockefeller Plaza
New York, NY 10020
(212) 977-6900

Program grants; youth; minorities; disabled; social service organizations; education; community development; cultural organizations

Most grants awarded to organizations located in New York City and in Cooperstown, New York.

Typical grant range: $15,000 to $125,000

519

Robert Sterling Clark Foundation, Inc.
135 East 64th Street
New York, NY 10021
(212) 288-8900

Program grants; cultural organizations; women; youth; community development; environment; Brooklyn Botanic Garden (project grant)

Typical grant range: $10,000 to $80,000

520

The Community Foundation for the Capital Region, N.Y.
Executive Park Drive
Albany, NY 12203
(518) 446-9638

Program grants; disabled; youth; elderly; social service organizations; health organizations; Joseph's House & Shelter, Inc. (program for homeless adults who have a mental illness); Bottomless Closet of Schenectady, Inc. (program for women that supplies clothing and job readiness training)

Grants awarded to organizations located in Albany, Rensselaer, Saratoga and Schenectady Counties.

Typical grant range: $5,000 to $50,000

521

The Community Foundation of Herkimer and Oneida Counties, Inc.
270 Genesee Street
Utica, NY 13502
(315) 735-8212

Program grants; education; higher education; animal welfare; youth; disabled; social service organizations; environment; cultural organizations; health organizations; Little Falls Hospital (Health and Safety Awareness Program); Glimmerglass Opera (program grant); Girl Scout Council (program grant); United Cerebral Palsy & Handicapped Persons (golf program); Thomas R. Proctor Senior High School (mentoring program); Hamilton College (liberal arts education project for women leaving the welfare rolls)

Grants awarded to organizations located in Oneida and Herkimer Counties.

Typical grant range: $500 to $30,000

522

The Community Foundation of the Elmira-Corning Area
307 B East Water Street, Box 714
Elmira, NY 14901
(607) 734-6412

Program grants; Corning Area Humane Society (spay and neuter program); Tanglewood Nature Center & Museum (program grant); Tri-Cities Opera (program grant); Community Dispute Resolution Center (CHOICES program); Southern Tier Interfaith Coalition (religious diversity program); Association for the Visually Impaired (Adaptive Skills Training Program); Junior Achievement (program grant); YWCA (single moms program to build self-esteem and to prevent child abuse); Chemung County Chamber of Commerce (leadership program); Rolling Readers USA (Read Aloud program); The Salvation Army (homework assistance program)

Grants awarded to organizations located in Chemung County and southeastern Stueben County.

Typical grant range: $500 to $10,000

523

Corning Incorporated Foundation
MP-LB-02-1
Corning, NY 14831
(607) 974-8746

Program grants; Alliance of New York State Arts Councils (rural arts program); Frederic Remington Art Museum (project grant); Chemung County Performing Arts (program grant); Boy Scouts of America (outreach program); Women's Center (program grant); Aurelia Osborn Fox Memorial Hospital Foundation (project grant); AIDS Rochester (program grant); New York Public Library (program grant); Partnership for a Drug-Free America (program grant); Southern Tier Association for the Visually Impaired Corporation (adaptive skills training project); Junior Achievement (economic education program); Regional Science and Discovery Center (educational project); Corning City School District (Kids Sake program)

Grants awarded to organizations located in areas of company operations (Corning Inc.).

Typical grant range: $1,000 to $20,000

524
The Frances L. & Edwin L. Cummings Memorial Fund
501 Fifth Avenue, Suite 708
New York, NY 10017
(212) 286-1778

Program grants; Boys & Girls Club (pregnancy prevention program); Big Brothers/Big Sisters (program grant); Goodwill Industries (program grant); The Hope Program, Inc. (Job Retention Project for the homeless); The Partnership for the Homeless, Inc. (project grant); Cypress Hills Local Development Corporation, Inc. (employment program); Urban Justice Center (Family Violence Prevention Project); The Women's Prison Association and Home, Inc. (Youth Services Program); Community Healthcare Network, Inc. (pregnancy prevention program); Village Center for Care (treatment program for new AIDS therapies); The Teachers Network, Inc. (on-line projects); New York School for the Deaf (Career Education and Transition Program); St. John's University (Paraeducator Pathway to Teaching Program)

Grants awarded to organizations located in the New York City vicinity.

Typical grant range: $1,500 to $40,000

525
The Nathan Cummings Foundation, Inc.
475 10th Avenue, 14th Floor
New York, NY 10018
(212) 787-7300

Program grants; disabled; minorities; youth; social service organizations; environment; cultural organizations; Jewish organizations

Typical grant range: $5,000 to $75,000

526
The Charles A. Dana Foundation, Inc.
745 Fifth Avenue, Suite 700
New York, NY 10151
(212) 223-4040

Program grants; The Carter Center (mental health program); New York Presbyterian Hospital (medical research project); Lady Bird Johnson National Wildflower Center (education program); The Barbara Bush Foundation for Family Literacy (literacy program)

Typical grant range: $50,000 to $250,000

527
Dr. G. Clifford & Florence B. Decker Foundation
8 Riverside Drive
Binghamton, NY 13905
(607) 722-0211

Program grants; cultural organizations; youth; disabled; education; health organizations; social service organizations; The Children's Home (Wilderness Adventure Project); YWCA (program grant); Tioga Association for Retarded Citizens (educational program)

Grants awarded to organizations located in Broome County.

528
Deutsche Bank Americas Foundation
130 Liberty Street, MS 2107
New York, NY 10006
(212) 250-7065

Program grants; Sponsors for Educational Opportunity (college program); WGBH Educational Foundation (Africans in America Project); American Museum of Natural History (Great Gull Island project); New York Housing Partnership (program grant); New York University (Professional Development Laboratory Program)

Most grants awarded to organizations located in New York City.

Typical grant range: $2,500 to $50,000

529
Cleveland H. Dodge Foundation, Inc.
670 W. 247th Street
Bronx, NY 10471
(718) 543-1220

Program grants; environment; education; youth; disabled; social service organizations; Boys and Girls Club (performing arts program); YWCA (Young Parents Program); Bank Street College of Education (Teens and Tots program)

Most grants awarded to organizations located in New York City.

Typical grant range: $2,000 to $100,000

530
Last minute update: The foundation originally listed here has terminated.

531
Fred L. Emerson Foundation, Inc.
5654 S. Street Road
P.O. Box 276
Auburn, NY 13021
(315) 253-9621

Program grants; hospitals; youth; higher education; social service organizations; cultural organizations; community development; Cayuga County Sheriff's Department (DARE program)

Most grants awarded to organizations located in Auburn, Cayuga County, and upstate New York.

Typical grant range: $1,000 to $100,000

532
Helene Fuld Health Trust
50 E. 42nd Street, 19th Floor
New York, NY 10017
(212) 681-1237

Program grants; Owensboro Community College (nursing program); Samuel Merritt College (nursing program); Center for the Health Professions (Nursing Education Program)

Typical grant range: $10,000 to $100,000

533
Gebbie Foundation, Inc.
110 W. 3rd Street, Suite 308
Jamestown, NY 14701
(716) 487-1062

Program grants; social service organizations; youth; hospitals; education; cultural organizations; environment; Woman's Christian Association Hospital (education program)

Grants awarded to organizations located in Chautauqua County and surrounding areas.

Typical grant range: $1,000 to $100,000

534

The Rosamond Gifford Charitable Corporation
518 James Street, Suite 280
Syracuse, NY 13203
(315) 474-2489

Program grants; youth; elderly; social service organizations; health organizations; cultural organizations

Grants awarded to organizations located in Onondaga County and Syracuse.

535

The Glens Falls Foundation
237 Glen Street
Glens Falls, NY 12801
(518) 792-1151

Program grants; Big Brothers/Big Sisters (program grant); Alzheimer's Association (educational program for children); Prosect Child and Family Center (adoption program for children who are disabled); Glens Falls City School District (program for at risk youth)

Grants awarded to organizations located in Warren, Washington, and Saratoga Counties.

Typical grant range: $1,500 to $10,000

536

Herman Goldman Foundation
61 Broadway, 18th Floor
New York, NY 10006
(212) 797-9090

Program grants; youth; disabled; social service organizations; education; higher education; health organizations; hospitals; cultural organizations

Grants awarded to organizations located in the New York City vicinity.

Typical grant range: $5,000 to $40,000

537

Hasbro Children's Foundation
32 W. 23rd Street
New York, NY 10010
(212) 645-2400

Program grants; Bicycle Action Project (Earn-A-Bike Program); Children's Hope Foundation (health program); NYU Children's Oncology Center (program grant); Police Athletic League (education program); Hour Children (education programs); Canine Companions for Independence (program grant)

Typical grant range: $5,000 to $65,000

538

The F.B. Heron Foundation
100 Broadway, Suite 17
New York, NY 10005
(212) 404-1835

Program grants; East Harlem Employment Services, Inc. (job training program); New Economics for Women (business related program); Citizen Policy & Education Fund (program for increased home ownership and financial literacy); New School University (technical assistance program on alternative financing strategies for nonprofits)

Typical grant range: $25,000 to $100,000

539

Stewart W. & Willma C. Hoyt Foundation, Inc.
300 Security Mutual Building
80 Exchange Street
Binghamton, NY 13901
(607) 722-6706

Program grants; cultural organizations; social service organizations; youth; disabled; health organizations; higher education

Grants awarded to organizations located in Broome County.

Typical grant range: $2,500 to $25,000

540
The JM Foundation
60 E. 42nd Street, Room 1651
New York, NY 10165
(212) 687-7735

Program grants; Phoenix House
Foundation (educational program for the
Children of Alcoholics Foundation);
National Council on Alcoholism and Drug
Dependence (project grant); Life Issues
Youth Forums (mentoring program for
disadvantaged youth); Independent
Women's Forum (project grant); New
York Botanical Garden (internship
program); Personality Disorders
Foundation (public information program);
International Center for the Disabled
(project grant); Wildlife Conservation
Society (Summer Training and
Employment Program)

Typical grant range: $5,000 to $25,000

541
Daisy Marquis Jones Foundation
1600 South Avenue, Suite 250
Rochester, NY 14620
(716) 461-4950

Program grants; Westside Health Services,
Inc. (program for parents of newborn
children); Public Broadcasting Council
(Broadcast Trainee Program); Rochester
General Hospital Foundation (Health Care
Youth Apprenticeship Program); Rushville
Health Center, Inc. (program grant);
Bishop Sheen Ecumenical Housing
Foundation, Inc. (home repair program);
Corpus Christi Church (program to help
women go from jail to work); Catholic
Family Center (program providing
services for the elderly); Rochester
Association of Performing Arts (after
school program for performing arts);
Urban League (Black Scholars
Recognition Program); Friends of School
of the Arts, Inc. (program to reduce
teenage pregnancy)

Grants awarded to organizations located
in Monroe and Yates Counties.

Typical grant range: $1,000 to $40,000

542
The J.M. Kaplan Fund, Inc.
261 Madison Avenue, 19th Floor
New York, NY 10116
(212) 767-0630

Program grants; youth; minorities; women;
social service organizations; education;
environment; cultural organizations;
community development; City Harvest,
Inc. (food program); Bronx Museum of
Art (program grant); The Chancellor's
Literacy Campaign (Fill-a-Bookshelf
Program); New York AIDS Coalition, Inc.
(program grant)

Most grants awarded to organizations
located in New York City.

Typical grant range: $2,000 to $75,000

543
Josiah Macy, Jr. Foundation
44 E. 64th Street
New York, NY 10021
(212) 486-2424

Program grants; New York Public Library
(Community Health Onsite Information
Centers program); Roswell Park Cancer
Institute (project to increase the
availability of nurses); Amfar AIDS
Research Foundation (research program);
Partners in Prevention of Substance Abuse
(program to prevent substance abuse)

544
**James J. McCann Charitable Trust and
McCann Foundation, Inc.**
35 Market Street
Poughkeepsie, NY 12601
(845) 452-3085

Program grants; social service
organizations; higher education; cultural
organizations; Christian organizations

Grants awarded to organizations located
in the Poughkeepsie vicinity.

Typical grant range: $1,000 to $50,000

545

J.P. Morgan Charitable Trust
60 Wall Street, 46th Floor
New York, NY 10260
(212) 648-9673

Program grants; minorities; youth;
women; social service organizations;
education; health organizations;
community development; cultural
organizations

Grants awarded to organizations located
in the New York City vicinity.

Typical grant range: $5,000 to $100,000

546

NEC Foundation of America
Eight Corporate Center Drive
Melville, NY 11747
(516) 753-7021

Program grants; Institute for Deaf and
Blind (project grant); Association for
Women in Science (program grant);
Center for Applied Special Technology
(Family and Community Literacy Project)

Typical grant range: $10,000 to $50,000

547

New York Foundation
350 5th Avenue, No. 2901
New York, NY 10118
(212) 594-8009

Program grants; minorities; women;
elderly; youth; disabled; community
development

Most grants awarded to organizations
located in the New York City vicinity.

Typical grant range: $5,000 to $45,000

548

**The New York Times Company
Foundation, Inc.**
229 W. 43rd Street
New York, NY 10036
(212) 556-1091

Program grants; New York Hall of
Science (education program); The
Museum of Jewish Heritage (program
grant); American Museum of the Moving
Image (film studies program); New York
City Opera (program grant); New York
Shakespeare Festival (Directors in
Residence Program); Pierpont Morgan
Library (education program for children);
Mote Marine Laboratory (science program
for children and adults); Recording for the
Blind and Dyslexic (digital audio project);
East Harlem Tutorial Program (after
school program); Villa Montessori School
(minority education project); Barnard
College (minority science and writing
program); College of Physicians &
Surgeons Columbia University (summer
laboratory program)

Most grants awarded to organizations
located in New York City.

Typical grant range: $1,000 to $30,000

549

**Northern New York Community
Foundation, Inc.**
120 Washington Street
Watertown, NY 13601
(315) 782-7110

Program grants; youth; disabled; social
service organizations; environment; health
organizations; cultural organizations;
community development; Alcohol &
Substance Abuse Council (First Night
Program); Literacy Volunteers (program
grant); YMCA (project grant); Jefferson
Community College (paramedic program)

Grants awarded to organizations located
in Jefferson and Lewis Counties.

Typical grant range: $1,000 to $25,000

550
The John R. Oishei Foundation
One HSBC Center, Suite 3650
Buffalo, NY 14203
(716) 856-9490

Program grants; health organizations; disabled; youth; elderly; secondary and higher education; cultural organizations; social service organizations; The Center for Hospice and Palliative Care (demonstration project); Canisius College (program to encourage innovative and effective learning and teaching)

Grants awarded to organizations located in the Buffalo vicinity.

Typical grant range: $5,000 to $150,000

551
The Pinkerton Foundation
630 Fifth Avenue, Suite 1755
New York, NY 10111
(212) 332-3385

Program grants; Brooklyn Youth Chorus (education program); The ArtsConnection, Inc. (after school art program for youth); Azusa Christian Community (employment project and educational program for at-risk girls); The Catholic Big Sisters (mentoring, counseling and educational programs); Highbridge Community Life Center (violence prevention program); Boy Scouts of America (program grant); Homes for the Homeless, Inc. (after school program); The New York Foundling Hospital (mother-child program for teenage mothers); Wildlife Conservation Society (after school science enhancement program); Wave Hill (summer environmental education program); Brooklyn College Foundation (summer mathematics and science program for girls)

Grants awarded to organizations located in New York City.

Typical grant range: $5,000 to $50,000

552
The Prospect Hill Foundation, Inc.
99 Park Avenue, Suite 2200
New York, NY 10016
(212) 370-1165

Program grants; environment; cultural organizations; education; National Audubon Society (Important Bird Areas Program); Inwood House (pregnancy prevention program for teenagers)

Typical grant range: $5,000 to $50,000

553
Rochester Area Community Foundation
500 East Avenue
Rochester, NY 14607
(716) 271-4100

Program grants; social service organizations; youth; elderly; women; environment; education; cultural organizations; Oak Orchard Community Health Center (Women, Infants and Children Supplemental Food Program); Nazareth College (mentoring program)

Grants awarded in the following counties: Monroe, Genesee, Livingston, Ontario, Orleans and Wayne.

554
The Dorothea Haus Ross Foundation
1036 Monroe Avenue
Rochester, NY 14620
(716) 473-6006

Program grants; social service organizations; youth; disabled; education; cancer research; health organizations; hospitals; research projects to treat children with burns; Big Brothers/Big Sisters (program grant)

Typical grant range: $1,000 to $20,000

555
Helena Rubinstein Foundation, Inc.
477 Madison Avenue, 7th Floor
New York, NY 10022
(212) 750-7310

Program grants; Figure Skating in Harlem
(after school sports and tutoring program
for girls); Dance Theatre of Harlem
(education program); Police Athletic
League (after school cultural programs);
HIV/AIDS Technical Assistance Project
(education program); American-Italian
Cancer Foundation (mobile mammography
program); Phoenix House Foundation
(drug abuse prevention and treatment
program); The Children's Storefront
(preschool program); Planned Parenthood
(education program); The Jewish Museum
(education program); Coalition for the
Homeless (job readiness program);
Brooklyn College of the City University
of New York, School of Education
(Eureka! Teen Achievement Program)

Grants awarded to organizations located
in New York City.

Typical grant range: $5,000 to $25,000

556
The Scherman Foundation, Inc.
16 E. 52nd Street, Suite 601
New York, NY 10022
(212) 832-3086

Program grants; women; minorities;
disabled; elderly; youth; social service
organizations; education; environment;
community development; Women's
Housing and Economic Development
Corporation (Urban Horizons Program);
Fund for the City of New York (HIV/
AIDS Technical Assistance Project for the
New York City Public Schools)

Most grants awarded to organizations
located in New York City.

Typical grant range: $10,000 to $60,000

557
Emma A. Sheafer Charitable Trust
c/o J.P. Morgan Chase & Co.
Philanthropic Services
60 Wall Street
New York, NY 10260

Program grants; performing arts; Pan
Asian Repertory Theatre (training
program)

Grants awarded to organizations located
in New York City.

Typical grant range: $15,000 to $25,000

558
Ralph C. Sheldon Foundation, Inc.
P.O. Box 417
Jamestown, NY 14702
(716) 664-9890

Program grants; social service
organizations; youth; community
development; cultural organizations

Most grants awarded to organizations
located in southern Chautauqua County.

Typical grant range: $5,000 to $50,000

559
The Valentine Perry Snyder Fund
c/o J.P. Morgan Chase & Co.
Philanthropic Services
60 Wall Street
New York, NY 10260
(212) 648-9673

Program grants; women; youth; social
service organizations; job training;
community development; Women In Need
(project grant); Neighborhood Coalition
for Shelter (JobWorks project)

Grants awarded to organizations located
in New York City.

Typical grant range: $15,000 to $30,000

560
Surdna Foundation, Inc.
330 Madison Avenue, 30th Floor
New York, NY 10017
(212) 557-0010

Program grants; New York Youth
Symphony (training program); 92nd
Street YM-YWHA (art program);
Rheedlen Centers for Children and
Families (Effective Citizenry Program);
Defenders of Wildlife (project grant);
St. Nicholas Neighborhood Preservation
Corporation (training program for a
nursing facility); Cooper-Hewitt, National
Design Museum (program to have
professional designers work with high
school students)

Typical grant range: $30,000 to $150,000

561
Taconic Foundation
c/o J.P. Morgan Chase & Co.
Philanthropic Services
60 Wall Street
New York, NY 10260

Program grants; Concord Community
Development Corporation (Home
Retention Program); Low Income
Housing Fund (program grant); Careers
Through Culinary Arts Program (program
grant); Per Scholas (computer technician
training program); Nature Conservancy
(youth internship program); Lower
Eastside Girls Club (We Mean Business-
training program)

Most grants awarded to organizations
located in New York City.

Typical grant range: $10,000 to $25,000

562
The Teagle Foundation Incorporated
Ten Rockefeller Plaza, Suite 920
New York, NY 10020
(212) 373-1970

Program grants; The HealthCare
Chaplaincy (education program); Alfred
University (planned gifts program);
St. Thomas Aquinas College (enrollment
management program); Hilbert College
(strengthen the institutional advancement
program)

Typical grant range: $20,000 to $250,000

563
Texaco Foundation
2000 Westchester Avenue
White Plains, NY 10650
(914) 253-4000

Program grants; Lawrence Hall of Science
(program grant); American Museum of
Natural History (science and nature
programs for children); Bank Street
College of Education (science program);
Merit Music Program (tuition free music
program); Children's Museum (Parent
Stars Program); Junior Achievement
(education program); Levine School of
Music (Early Childhood Music Program);
Metropolitan Opera Association
(education program); University of
Rochester (music program)

Most grants awarded to organizations
located in areas of company operations
(Texaco, Inc.).

Typical grant range: $10,000 to $100,000

564
Tiger Foundation
101 Park Avenue
New York, NY 10178
(212) 984-2565

Program grants; New York Society for the Prevention of Cruelty to Children (program grant); Project Reach Youth (education program for children); Church Avenue Merchants Block Association (youth employment program); Women's Housing and Economic Development Corporation (employment program); Little Sisters of the Assumption Family Health Service (early childhood program); YMCA (program grant); Franciscan Community Center (tutorial program)

Most grants awarded to organizations located in New York City.

Typical grant range: $20,000 to $100,000

565
Tompkins County Foundation, Inc.
P.O. Box 97
Ithaca, NY 14851

Program grants; social service organizations; youth; education; cultural organizations; health organizations; Family and Children's Services (Crisis Outreach Project); The Learning Web (Homeless Youth Outreach Program)

Grants awarded to organizations located in Tompkins County.

Typical grant range: $2,500 to $11,000

566
Mildred Faulkner Truman Foundation
212 Front Street
P.O. Box 236
Owego, NY 13827
(607) 687-0225

Program grants; cultural organizations; youth; community development; environment; Christian organizations; Alzheimer's Association (program grant); Newark Valley Historical Society (Herrick Barn project)

Grants awarded to organizations located in Tioga County, with an emphasis in the Owego vicinity.

Typical grant range: $1,500 to $25,000

567
van Ameringen Foundation, Inc.
509 Madison Avenue
New York, NY 10022
(212) 758-6221

Program grants; Saint Vincent's Hospital and Medical Center (psychiatric outreach project); Morningside Retirement and Health Services, Inc. (Mental Health Services Project); Bronx-Lebanon Hospital (after school program); Catholic Charities (after school program for children who are emotionally disturbed); Jewish Board of Family and Children's Services, Inc. (bereavement program for children); University Settlement Society (Attention Deficit/Hyperactivity Disorder Project); Dorot, Inc. (program to prevent homelessness); The Family Center, Inc. (program for children whose parents have AIDS); Project Reach Youth (program to reduce the number of children dropping out of school); Trustees of Columbia University/Department of Pediatrics (parent-child counseling program)

Typical grant range: $10,000 to $150,000

568

The Western New York Foundation
Main Seneca Building, Suite 1402
237 Main Street
Buffalo, NY 14203
(716) 847-6440

Program grants; women; youth; cultural
organizations; community development;
health organizations; social service
organizations

Grants awarded to organizations located
in western New York State (Allegany,
Cattaraugus, Chautauqua, Erie, Genesee,
Niagara and Wyoming Counties).

569

**Marie C. and Joseph C. Wilson
Foundation**
160 Allens Creek Road
Rochester, NY 14618
(716) 461-4699

Program grants; youth; elderly; social
service organizations; education; health
organizations; cultural organizations

Grants awarded to organizations located
in Rochester.

Typical grant range: $2,000 to $30,000

NORTH CAROLINA

570

**Mary Reynolds Babcock Foundation,
Inc.**
2522 Reynolda Road
Winston-Salem, NC 27106
(336) 748-9222

Program grants; Penn Center (program for
African American children); Educational
Development Corporation (employment
program); Surging Into the Future Today
(after school tutoring and summer
enrichment program); Project Proud
(youth diversion program); Princeville
Tourism and Historic Society (program
grant); Sewee to Santee Economic Forum
(project planning for economic
development and conservation)

Typical grant range: $3,000 to $60,000

571

Bank of America Foundation
401 N. Tryon Street, NC1-007-18-01
Charlotte, NC 28255

Program grants; youth; women; minorities
disabled; social service organizations;
health organizations; cultural organizations;
Berkeley Repertory Theater (educational
program); Battered Women's Association
(program grant); AIDS Project
(educational program)

Grants awarded to organizations located
in areas of company operations (Bank of
America Corp.).

572

The Blumenthal Foundation
P.O. Box 34689
Charlotte, NC 28234
(704) 377-9237

Program grants; cultural organizations;
youth; elderly; social service
organizations; environment; animal
welfare; Jewish organizations; Jewish
Federation of Charlotte (project grant);
Carolina Agency of Jewish Education
(program grant)

Most grants awarded to organizations
located in North Carolina, with an
emphasis in the Charlotte vicinity.

Typical grant range: $1,000 to $50,000

573

The Cannon Foundation, Inc.
P.O. Box 548
Concord, NC 28026
(704) 786-8216

Program grants; hospitals; youth; social
service organizations; secondary and
higher education; cultural organizations;
Cabarrus County Schools (literacy
program)

Grants awarded to organizations located
in North Carolina, with an emphasis in
Cabarrus County.

Typical grant range: $10,000 to $100,000

574
Cape Fear Community Foundation
P.O. Box 119
Wilmington, NC 28402
(910) 251-3911

Program grants; youth; women; social
service organizations; education; health
organizations

Most grants awarded to organizations
located in the Cape Fear vicinity.

Typical grant range: $500 to $3,000

575
The Cemala Foundation, Inc.
122 N. Elm Street, Suite 816
Greensboro, NC 27401
(336) 274-3541

Program grants; Hospice at Greensboro
(pediatric care program); Green Hill
Center for North Carolina Art (program
grant); Greensboro Symphony (Instrument
Loan and Scholar Program); Greensboro
Children's Museum (education program);
Haw River Assembly (conservation
project); Black Child Development
Institute (tutoring program); Mental
Health Association (treatment program); A
Healthy Start (teen pregnancy prevention
program); Guilford County Public Health
Department (Childhood Lead Poisoning
Prevention program)

Most grants awarded to organizations
located in Guilford County.

Typical grant range: $10,000 to $60,000

576
**Community Foundation of Greater
Greensboro, Inc.**
100 S. Elm Street, Suite 307
Greensboro, NC 27401
(336) 379-9100

Program grants; social service
organizations; youth; education; cultural
organizations; community development

Grants awarded to organizations located
in the Greensboro vicinity.

Typical grant range: $3,000 to $10,000

577
**The Community Foundation of
Henderson County, Inc.**
Fourth Avenue and Main Street
P.O. Box 1108
Hendersonville, NC 28793
(704) 697-6224

Program grants; youth; women; disabled;
social service organizations; education;
community development; cultural
organizations

Grants awarded to organizations located
in Henderson County.

Typical grant range: $100 to $10,000

578
**Cumberland Community Foundation,
Inc.**
P.O. Box 2171
Fayetteville, NC 28302
(910) 483-4449

Program grants; youth; social service
organizations; education; environment;
community development; cultural
organizations; Tiffany Pines Community
Watch Association (project grant);
Cumberland County Public Library
(summer program for teenagers);
Communities United for Youth
Development (after-school tutorial
program)

Grants awarded to organizations located
in Cumberland County.

Typical grant range: $500 to $10,000

579
The Duke Endowment
100 N. Tryon Street, Suite 3500
Charlotte, NC 28202
(704) 376-0291

Program grants; Scotland Health Care System (program for prenatal care); Charlotte-Mecklenburg Hospital Authority (health program for immigrants); Ronald McDonald House (program grant); FirstHealth of the Carolinas (dental health program); Presbyterian Healthcare (Healthy Steps for Young Children program); Christ Church (child care program); Baptist Children's Homes (Family Preservation Services program); Regional AIDS Interfaith Network (program grant)

Typical grant range: $10,000 to $150,000

580
Durham Merchants Association Charitable Foundation
P. O. Box 52016
Durham, NC 27717
(919) 489-7921

Program grants; education; youth; social service organizations; cultural organizations

Grants awarded to organizations located in the Durham vicinity.

Typical grant range: $1,000 to $7,000

581
Janirve Foundation
One North Pack Square, Suite 416
Asheville, NC 28801
(828) 258-1877

Program grants; Brevard Chamber Orchestra Association, Inc. (musical education program for elementary school students); The Eblen Foundation (dental program for uninsured children); One Youth at a Time (mentoring and tutoring program for at-risk students); Creative Communications Youth and Family Services (program for teenage mothers who are homeless); Western Carolina Rescue Mission (substance abuse program); Ashe Services for Aging, Inc. (health program); Catholic Social Services (program to prepare immigrants to become U.S. citizens); Second Chance Wildlife Rehabilitation Center, Inc. (wildlife preservation educational program); Southern Appalachian Highlands Conservancy (project to protect high elevation ecosystems); Appalachian Wilderness Experience, Inc. (after school program for at-risk students)

Typical grant range: $10,000 to $100,000

582
North Carolina GlaxoSmithKline Foundation
Five Moore Drive
Research Triangle Park, NC 27709
(919) 483-2140

Program grants; Duke University (Health Sector Management Program); North Carolina Central University (research training program); Shaw University (Science and Mathematics Program); Meredith College (Undergraduate Research Opportunities Program)

Grants awarded to organizations located in North Carolina.

Typical grant range: $50,000 to $1,000,000

583

Outer Banks Community Foundation, Inc.
P.O. Box 1100
Kill Devil Hills, NC 27948
(252) 261-8839

Program grants; youth; social service organizations; education; cultural organizations; Children & Youth Partnership (School Readiness Program)

Grants awarded to organizations located in the Outer Banks vicinity.

Typical grant range: $1,500 to $15,000

584

Kate B. Reynolds Charitable Trust
128 Reynolda Village
Winston-Salem, NC 27106
(336) 723-1456

Program grants; Hospice of Davidson County, Inc. (program grant); Guilford County Health Department (dental care program for children); Rutherford Hospital, Inc. (cancer screening and educational program); AIDS Service Agency (program grant); Campbell University (diabetes care program); YWCA (pregnancy prevention program); Girl Scouts (pregnancy prevention program); Seniors Call to Action Team, Inc. (program grant); Rockingham County School (school nurse program); University of North Carolina (program for people who are disabled)

Grants awarded to organizations located in North Carolina.

Typical grant range: $20,000 to $200,000

585

Z. Smith Reynolds Foundation, Inc.
101 Reynolda Village
Winston-Salem, NC 27106
(336) 725-7541

Program grants; Linda Lavin Arts Foundation (after school program for girls); Salvation Army (after school and summer day program); Boys and Girls Club (Native American program); Cape Lookout Environmental Education Center (educational program); Neuse River Foundation (river protection program); Citizens Against Domestic Violence (educational program); Family Abuse Services (housing program for women and children); Sandy Grove A.M.E. Zion Church (career camp project); Sickle Cell Disease Association (Adolescent Pregnancy Prevention Project); Young Life of Forsyth County (tutoring program); YWCA (racial justice project); Community of Excellence (tutoring program for youth); North Carolina Central University (middle school achievement project); East End Elementary School (Young Scholars Project); Appalachian State University (mentoring program for at-risk girls)

Grants awarded to organizations located in North Carolina.

Typical grant range: $10,000 to $200,000

586
Triangle Community Foundation
100 Park Offices, Suite 209
P.O. Box 12834
Research Triangle Park, NC 27709
(919) 549-9840

Program grants; New Bethel Baptist
Church (mentoring program); Church of
the Holy Family (tutoring program);
YWCA (program grant); YMCA (summer
program); North Carolina Museum of Art
Foundation (student project); Chatham
Education Foundation (Shakespeare
program); Mental Health Association
(program grant); North Carolina
Occupational Safety and Health Project
(education program)

Grants awarded to organizations located
in Durham, Orange, and Wake Counties.

Typical grant range: $2,000 to $20,000

NORTH DAKOTA

587
Fargo-Moorhead Area Foundation
609-1/2 First Avenue North, Suite 205
Fargo, ND 58102
(701) 234-0756

Program grants; social service
organizations; youth; women; education;
cultural organizations; community
development

Grants awarded to organizations located
in Cass County, North Dakota and Clay
County, Minnesota.

588
**Tom and Frances Leach Foundation,
Inc.**
P.O. Box 1136
Bismarck, ND 58502
(701) 255-0479

Program grants; Salvation Army (after-
school program); Burleigh County Senior
Adults Center (computer training
program); YMCA (program grant); Big
Brothers/Big Sisters Program (mentor
program); Bismarck Gymnastics Academy
Inc. (program grant); Bismarck Public
Schools Foundation (Art Gallery
program); Sleepy Hollow Summer
Theatre (summer program); Dacotah
Foundation (foster grandparent program);
Fort Abraham Lincoln Foundation (Native
American Interpretive Program); Gateway
to Science Center, Inc. (work mentorship
program); Prairie Learning Centers, Inc.
(drug and alcohol recovery program)

Most grants awarded to organizations
located in North Dakota.

Typical grant range: $2,000 to $25,000

589
Alex Stern Family Foundation
609-1/2 First Avenue North, Suite 205
Fargo, ND 58102
(701) 237-0170

Program grants; youth; elderly; women;
social service organizations; education;
cultural organizations

Grants awarded to organizations located
in Fargo, North Dakota and Moorhead,
Minnesota.

Typical grant range: $1,000 to $40,000

OHIO

590
The Abington Foundation
c/o Foundation Management Services, Inc.
1422 Euclid Avenue, Suite 627
Cleveland, OH 44115
(216) 621-2901

Program grants; The Cleveland Christian Home for Children (program grant); Cleveland Hearing and Speech Center (educational program for children); Northeast Ohio Coalition for the Homeless (program grant); YMCA (after school program for girls); Rainbow Children's Museum (Museum-on-Wheels program); Cleveland Public Theatre (program grant); East End Neighborhood House (cultural and educational program); Villa Montessori Center (kindergarten program); Central School of Practical Nursing, Inc. (program for at-risk students)

Most grants awarded to organizations located in Cuyahoga County.

Typical grant range: $5,000 to $40,000

591
Akron Community Foundation
345 W. Cedar Street
Akron, OH 44307
(330) 376-8522

Program grants; Children's Hospital Foundation (children's immunization project); Alzheimer's Disease & Related Disorders (program grant); Battered Women's Shelter (program to prevent domestic violence); Girl Scout Council (program grant); Boys and Girls Club (program grant); Greater Akron Musical Association, Inc. (educational program); Ohio Chamber Ballet (educational program); Northcoast Food Rescue (food distribution program); Northeastern Ohio University College of Medicine (program to reduce youth smoking)

Most grants awarded to organizations located in the Akron vicinity.

Typical grant range: $2,000 to $20,000

592
Bicknell Fund
c/o Advisory Services, Inc.
1422 Euclid Avenue, Suite 1010
Cleveland, OH 44115
(216) 363-6482

Program grants; social service organizations; disabled; education; health organizations

Most grants awarded to organizations located in the Cleveland vicinity.

Typical grant range: $1,000 to $15,000

593
The William Bingham Foundation
20325 Center Ridge Road, Suite 629
Cleveland, OH 44116-3554
(440) 331-6350

Program grants; cultural organizations; youth; education; social service organizations; Western Reserve Historical Society (program grant); Cuyahoga Valley Preservation and Scenic Railway Association (education program for students at elementary and secondary schools)

Typical grant range: $5,000 to $60,000

594
Britton Fund
1422 Euclid Avenue, Room 1010
Cleveland, OH 44115
(216) 363-6489

Program grants; Salvation Army (summer camp program); Northcoast Food Rescue (meal program); YMCA (child care program); Alzheimer's Association (respite program); Cleveland Museum of Art (program grant); Cleveland Playhouse (educational program)

Grants awarded to organizations located in Ohio.

Typical grant range: $2,000 to $50,000

595

Eva L. and Joseph M. Bruening Foundation
1422 Euclid Avenue, Suite 627
Cleveland, OH 44115
(216) 621-2632

Program grants; Lutheran Metropolitan Ministry Association (program for ex-offender women); The Open House (program for women with HIV/AIDS); Transitional Housing, Inc. (dental care program); West Side Catholic Center (shelter program); Cleveland Opera (program for the elderly); Cleveland Public Theatre (educational program); Rainbow Children's Museum and TRW Early Learning Center (hands-on learning program); Goodrich Gannet Neighborhood Center (preschool program); Office of Catholic Education (Urban Math Initiative program); Notre Dame College (Junior Experience program); Ursuline College (program offering therapy for children with emotional difficulties)

Grants awarded to organizations located in Cuyahoga County.

Typical grant range: $5,000 to $75,000

596

Cinergy Foundation, Inc.
139 E. 4th Street
2604 Atrium II
Cincinnati, OH 45202
(513) 287-2410

Program grants; youth; disabled; community development; education; cultural organizations; Good Samaritan Hospital Foundation (educational program); The Inclusion Network (Employment Inclusion Project); Neighborhood Housing Services, Inc. (educational program for home ownership); University of Cincinnati (precollegiate program)

Grants awarded to organizations located in areas of company operations (Cinergy Corporation).

Typical grant range: $10,000 to $50,000

597

The Cleveland Foundation
1422 Euclid Avenue, Suite 1300
Cleveland, OH 44115
(216) 861-3810

Program grants; youth; elderly; disabled; minorities; social service organizations; community development; education; health organizations; cultural organizations

Grants awarded to organizations located in the Cleveland vicinity.

598

The George W. Codrington Charitable Foundation
3900 Key Center
127 Public Square
Cleveland, OH 44114
(216) 566-5837

Program grants; youth; disabled; education; cultural organizations

Grants awarded to organizations located in Cuyahoga County.

Typical grant range: $500 to $25,000

599

The Columbus Foundation and Affiliated Organizations
1234 E. Broad Street
Columbus, OH 43205
(614) 251-4000

Program grants; youth; disabled; women; social service organizations; education; cultural organizations; community development

Grants awarded to organizations located in the Columbus vicinity.

600
Columbus Medical Association Foundation
431 E. Broad Street
Columbus, OH 43215-3820
(614) 240-7420

Program grants; Columbus AIDS Task Force (education program); Central Ohio Area Agency on Aging (program grant); Children's Hospital (project to control asthma); Ohio Hispanic Coalition (prenatal education program); Ohio Hunger Task Force (nutrition education project); St. Joseph Montessori School (nicotine addiction program); Mount Carmel Health System Foundation (immunization project); Commission on Minority Health (program for African-Americans to stop smoking); Amethyst, Inc. (health education project for women and children)

Grants awarded to organizations located in Franklin County.

Typical grant range: $15,000 to $150,000

601
The Community Foundation of Greater Lorain County
1865 N. Ridge Road East, Suite A
Lorain, OH 44055
(440) 277-0142

Program grants; youth; disabled; women; social service organizations; health organizations; minorities; community development; cultural organizations

Grants awarded to organizations located in the Lorain County vicinity.

Typical grant range: $2,000 to $25,000

602
The Corbett Foundation
127 W. Ninth Street, Suite 3
Cincinnati, OH 45202
(513) 241-3320

Program grants; cultural organizations; youth; education

Most grants awarded to organizations located in the Cincinnati vicinity.

Typical grant range: $2,500 to $50,000

603
The Mary S. & David C. Corbin Foundation
910 Society Building
159 S. Main Street
Akron, OH 44308
(330) 762-6427

Program grants; Pastoral Counseling Service of Summit County (Alternative School Program); Akron Zoological Park (Tiger Valley Project); The Salvation Army (Family Service Department's Emergency Assistance Program)

Most grants awarded to organizations located in Akron.

Typical grant range: $3,000 to $30,000

604
Coshocton Foundation
P.O. Box 55
Coshocton, OH 43812
(740) 622-0010

Program grants; education; youth; health organizations; recreation; community development; cultural organizations; National Child Safety Council (program grant); South Lawn Elementary School (accelerated reader program)

Grants awarded to organizations located in Coshocton County.

Typical grant range: $2,000 to $30,000

605

Charles H. Dater Foundation, Inc.
602 Main Street, Suite 302
Cincinnati, OH 45202
(513) 241-1234

Program grants; North Presbyterian Church (program for children); Children's Museum (project grant); Ensemble Theatre of Cincinnati (educational program); Hamilton County Special Olympics (program grant); YMCA (program grant); Parkinson's Disease Support Network (educational program for children); Literacy Network (dyslexia program for children); Stepping Stones Center (early childhood education program); Holy Cross High School (special education program)

Grants awarded to organizations located in the Cincinnati vicinity.

606

The Dayton Foundation
2100 Kettering Tower
Dayton, OH 45423
(937) 222-0410

Program grants; AIDS Foundation (Protecting Our Youth project); Hospice of Dayton (program grant); Green County Combined Health District (immunization program); Dayton Philharmonic Orchestra Association (program to enhance the music curriculum at elementary schools); Aullwood Audubon Center and Farm (program grant); Montgomery County Health Outreach Consortium (program grant); Girl Scouts of America (Camp Dayton Program); Camp Fire Council (after school program); Catholic Social Services (educational and counseling program); The Other Place (program to help the homeless); Dayton Metropolitan Housing Authority (program grant)

Most grants awarded to organizations located in the Dayton vicinity.

607

The GAR Foundation
50 S. Main Street
P.O. Box 1500
Akron, OH 44309-1500
(330) 643-0201

Program grants; youth; disabled; women; social service organizations; cultural organizations; education; higher education; Law Enforcement Foundation (program to reduce drug abuse); University of Akron (literacy program)

Typical grant range: $5,000 to $100,000

608

Benjamin S. Gerson Family Foundation
c/o Foundation Management Services
1422 Euclid Avenue, Suite 627
Cleveland, OH 44115
(216) 696-7273

Program grants; Cleveland Mediation Center (Homeless Prevention Project); Cleveland Film Society (program grant); Cleveland Public Theatre (program grant); Planned Parenthood (educational program); Cleveland Rape Crisis Center (educational program)

Grants awarded to organizations located in Cuyahoga County.

Typical grant range: $1,000 to $15,000

609

The Greater Cincinnati Foundation
200 W. 4th Street
Cincinnati, OH 45202
(513) 241-2880

Program grants; youth; elderly; disabled; social service organizations; environment; health organizations; cultural organizations; Women's Research and Development Center (program grant); Cincinnati Health Network (Pediatric Care Project)

Grants awarded to organizations located in the Cincinnati vicinity.

Typical grant range: $1,000 to $30,000

610
The George Gund Foundation
1845 Guildhall Building
45 Prospect Avenue West
Cleveland, OH 44115
(216) 241-3114

Program grants; all levels of education;
youth; minorities; women; social service
organizations; cultural organizations;
environment; community development;
Rainbow Hospital (Child Advocacy and
Protection Program); Cleveland Heights-
University Heights City School District
(training project for teachers); The Ohio
State University Foundation (Urban
Gardening Program)

Most grants awarded to organizations
located in the Cleveland vicinity.

Typical grant range: $5,000 to $100,000

611
**The Hamilton Community Foundation,
Inc.**
319 North Third Street
Hamilton, OH 45011
(513) 863-1389

Program grants; Senior Citizens, Inc. (art
program); Fitton Center for Creative Arts
(program grant); Summertime for Kids
(summer program); Booker T. Washington
Community Center (tutoring program for
Hispanics); Hamilton Chamber of
Commerce (School to Work Program)

Grants awarded to organizations located
in Butler County.

Typical grant range: $4,000 to $25,000

612
**George M. and Pamela S. Humphrey
Fund**
c/o Advisory Services, Inc.
1422 Euclid Avenue, Suite 1010
Cleveland, OH 44115
(216) 363-6483

Program grants; health organizations;
education; cultural organizations; youth;
disabled; social service organizations

Most grants awarded to organizations
located in the Cleveland vicinity.

Typical grant range: $1,000 to $30,000

613
The Invacare Foundation
One Invacare Way
Elyria, OH 44035
(440) 329-6000

Program grants; disabled; education;
youth; cultural organizations; community
development

Grants awarded to organizations located
in areas of company operations (Invacare
Corporation).

614

The Martha Holden Jennings Foundation
710 Halle Building
1228 Euclid Avenue
Cleveland, OH 44115
(216) 589-5700

Program grants; Beck Center for the Cultural Arts (education program); Boys & Girls Club (music program); Amherst Historical Society (education program); Cuyahoga Valley Preservation and Scenic Railway Association (school field trip program); Cleveland Center for Contemporary Art (program grant); Columbus Symphony Orchestra (education program); Cleveland Zoological Society (program grant); Epilepsy Foundation (education project); Cleveland Society for the Blind (youth education program); Parents Volunteer Association for Retarded Children and Adults, Inc. (project grant); Ashtabula County Educational Service Center (Distance Learning Project); Cleveland Municipal Schools (literacy program); University of Rio Grande (Girls Emerging in Mathematics and Science Program)

Grants awarded to organizations located in Ohio.

Typical grant range: $5,000 to $100,000

615

Kulas Foundation
50 Public Square, Suite 924
Cleveland, OH 44113
(216) 623-4770

Program grants; cultural organizations; education; youth; social service organizations

Most grants awarded to organizations located in the Cleveland vicinity.

Typical grant range: $1,000 to $50,000

616

The Lubrizol Foundation
29400 Lakeland Blvd., Suite 53A
Wickliffe, OH 44092
(440) 943-4200

Program grants; Cleveland Zoological Society (composting program); Access to the Arts (special arts program); NAACP (back-to-school/stay-in-school program); Center of Science and Industry (interactive chemistry program); Family Life Education (Parents as Teachers program); Leadership Lake County, Inc. (youth program); Ohio University (Minority Women in Engineering and Technology Outreach Program)

Grants awarded to organizations located in areas of company operations (The Lubrizol Corp.).

Typical grant range: $1,000 to $15,000

617

Mathile Family Foundation
6450 Sand Lake Road, Suite 200
Dayton, OH 45414-2645
(937) 264-4600

Program grants; The Camp Fire Council of the Greater Dayton Area (Safety of Kids Program); The Dayton Urban League (Girls Self-Expression Program); YMCA (Black Achievers Program); Epilepsy Foundation (prescription assistance program); Hospice of Dayton (program grant); Wesley Community Center (Nutrition Services Program); The Cincinnati Zoo and Botanical Garden (program grant); Law Enforcement Foundation (D.A.R.E. Program); Ohio Hunger Task Force (food program); Project READ Coalition (reading program); Chaminade-Julienne Catholic High School (retreat program for high school seniors); Boys Hope/Girls Hope (Success for College Program)

Most grants awarded to organizations located in Dayton.

Typical grant range: $2,000 to $125,000

618

Montgomery Foundation

365 N. Whitewoman Street
Coshocton, OH 43812
(740) 622-2696

Program grants; National Marrow Donor Program (registration program); First Step Family Intervention Service (family intervention program); Pomerene Center for Fine Arts (program grant); Ridgewood Local School District (reading program); River View Local School District (child care program)

Grants awarded to organizations located in Coshocton.

619

The Murphy Family Foundation

25800 Science Park Drive, Suite 200
P.O. Box 22747
Beachwood, OH 44122
(216) 831-7320

Program grants; Northeast Ohio Coalition for the Homeless (program grant); Cleveland Foodbank (delivery program); West Side Ecumenical Ministry (program grant); Salvation Army (hunger and shelter programs); Youth Opportunities Unlimited (Business Education Team Program); Seeds of Literacy (adult literacy program); Ohio Boys Town (independent living program for teenage boys); Cleveland Housing Network (eviction prevention project); Lexington Bell Community Center (arts education program)

Most grants awarded to organizations located in the Cleveland vicinity.

Typical grant range: $5,000 to $20,000

620

The Nord Family Foundation

347 Midway Blvd., Suite 312
Elyria, OH 44035
(440) 324-2822

Program grants; youth; women; disabled; social service organizations; education; health organizations; cultural organizations; community development; Girls Incorporated (educational program for girls); Kidney Foundation of Ohio, Inc. (program grant); Senior Citizens Association (foster grandparent program)

Grants awarded to organizations located in Cuyahoga and Lorain Counties.

Typical grant range: $5,000 to $60,000

621

The Nordson Corporation Foundation

28601 Clemens Road
Westlake, OH 44145
(440) 892-1580

Program grants; Salvation Army (emergency assistance program); Cleveland Public Theatre (program grant); Northern Ohio Youth Orchestras (program grant); Harrison Cultural Community Centre (after school youth program); National Multiple Sclerosis Society (counseling program); YMCA (Youth Sport Basketball Program); Girl Scout Council (Girls are Great Program); Sandstone Office on Aging (socialization program); Wilberforce University (summer program)

Typical grant range: $1,000 to $30,000

622

The William J. and Dorothy K. O'Neill Foundation, Inc.

30195 Chagrin Blvd., Suite 310
Cleveland, OH 44124
(216) 831-9667

Program grants; Cleveland Botanical Garden (Green Corps Program); Kingsbridge Heights Community Center (project grant); Youth Challenge (volunteer service program); Young Audiences (program grant); YMCA (LIFE program); Adoption Network Cleveland (project grant); Center for Chemical Addictions Treatment (project grant); Services United for Mothers and Adolescents (program for young fathers); West Side Ecumenical Ministry (program grant); Cleveland Christian Home (Safe and Sound Project); Crittenton Family Services (project grant); Teen Health Clinic (project grant); National Multiple Sclerosis Society (respite care program); Cleveland Clinic Children's Hospital for Rehabilitation (Champs Adaptive Sports Program)

Typical grant range: $1,000 to $15,000

623

The Elisabeth Severance Prentiss Foundation

c/o National City Bank
1900 E. 9th Street, LOC-2066
Cleveland, OH 44114
(216) 575-2760

Program grants; Cleveland Rape Crisis Center (Sexual Assault Nurse Examiner Program); Women's Center of Greater Cleveland (Intensive Outpatient Chemical Dependency Treatment Program); Achievement Centers for Children (preschool program); American Red Cross (emergency medical technician training program); West Side Ecumenical Ministry (health care program for the elderly); Gathering Place (program assisting cancer survivors); Hanna Perkins Center for Child Development (Psychotherapeutic Treatment Program); Hospice of the Western Reserve (project grant); United Cerebral Palsy (vocational project); Frances Payne Bolton School of Nursing (Nurse Practitioner Program)

Grants awarded to organizations located in the Cleveland vicinity.

Typical grant range: $25,000 to $300,000

624

The Helen Steiner Rice Foundation

221 E. Fourth Street, Suite 2100, Atrium 2
P.O. Box 0236
Cincinnati, OH 45201
(513) 451-9241

Program grants; youth; disabled; education; social service organizations; Christian organizations

Grants awarded to organizations located in Lorain, Ohio and the Cincinnati vicinity.

Typical grant range: $1,000 to $20,000

625
Richland County Foundation
24 W. Third Street, Suite 100
Mansfield, OH 44902
(419) 525-3020

Program grants; Med Central Health
Systems (Community Health Access
Program); Area Agency on Aging
(Alzheimer's Caregiver Respite Program);
Plymouth Area Historical Society (project
grant); YWCA (program grant); Big
Brothers/Big Sisters (summer program);
Mansfield Richland County Public
Library (program grant); Culliver Reading
Center (tutoring program); Madison Local
Schools (Nutrition and Information
Program); Eastview Elementary (First
Grade Accelerated Reader Program)

Grants awarded to organizations located
in Richland County.

Typical grant range: $500 to $25,000

626
Last minute update: The foundation
originally listed here has terminated.

627
Jacob G. Schmidlapp Trust No. 1 and No. 2
38 Fountain Square Plaza
Mail Drop 1090 D7
Cincinnati, OH 45263
(513) 579-6034

Program grants; youth; elderly; education;
disabled; social service organizations;
health organizations

Grants awarded to organizations located
in the Cincinnati vicinity.

Typical grant range: $5,000 to $80,000

628
The Scioto County Area Foundation
National City Bank Building, Room 801
800 Gallia Street
Portsmouth, OH 45662
(740) 354-4612

Program grants; SOMC Adult Daily
Living Services (memory stimulation
program using music); Southern Ohio
Light Opera (program grant); Portsmouth
Public Library (Shakespeare Birthday
Celebration project); Portsmouth City
School District (book program); South
Central Ohio Educational Service Center
(summer program)

Grants awarded to organizations located
in Scioto County.

Typical grant range: $500 to $10,000

629
The Sears-Swetland Foundation
2700 Eaton Road
Shaker Heights, OH 44118

Program grants; social service
organizations; health organizations;
environment; cultural organizations

Grants awarded to organizations located
in the Cleveland vicinity.

Typical grant range: $500 to $3,500

630

The Sisler McFawn Foundation
P.O. Box 149
Akron, OH 44309
(330) 849-8887

Program grants; Children's Ballet Theatre (education program); Akron Symphony Orchestra (education program); Twinsburg Public Library (project grant); Big Brothers/Big Sisters (program grant); Battered Women's Shelter (program grant); Crown Point Ecology Center (project grant); Mental Health Association (suicide prevention program); Very Special Arts (school workshop program); Catholic Youth Organization and Community Services (program grant); Jerome Lippman Jewish Community Day School (program grant); Northeastern Educational Television of Ohio (Ready to Learn Program); Portage Path School of Technology (project grant); Hiram College (technology project); University of Akron, Center for Economic Education (entrepreneurship program for educators)

Grants awarded to organizations located in Summit County.

Typical grant range: $3,000 to $25,000

631

The Stocker Foundation
559 Broadway Avenue, 2nd Floor
Lorain, OH 44052
(440) 246-5719

Program grants; Big Brothers/Big Sisters (high school mentoring program); Boy Scouts of America (program grant); Lyric Opera Cleveland (educational program); Cleveland Museum of Natural History (Adopt-a-Student Internship Program); Cleveland Public Theater (program grant); Building a Solid Foundation (after school program); Catholic Charities Services Corporation (transportation program for the Senior Achievement Center); Lutheran Metropolitan Ministry (program for at-risk youth); Salvation Army (after school program); Lorain County Community Action Agency (foster grandparent program); Lorain County Urban League (mentoring program for girls); Heartland Circle (substance abuse program for women)

Typical grant range: $2,000 to $20,000

632
The Stranahan Foundation
4159 Holland-Sylvania Road, Suite 206
Toledo, OH 43623
(419) 882-6575

Program grants; Toledo Botanical Gardens (educational program for children); Toledo Opera Association (educational program); Arts Commission of Greater Toledo (summer work program for high school students); Boys and Girls Club (program grant); Advocates for Victims and Justice (crime prevention program for youth); Hospice of Northwest Ohio (project grant); Sunshine Foundation (vocational program for people who are developmentally disabled); David's House of Compassion, Inc. (program for people who have HIV/AIDS); Central City Ministries of Toledo (program grant); University of Toledo Foundation (summer work project); Ohio Foundation of Independent Colleges (distance learning project)

Most grants awarded to organizations located in the Toledo vicinity.

Typical grant range: $5,000 to $125,000

633
The Frank M. Tait Foundation
Courthouse Plaza, S.W., 5th Floor
Dayton, OH 45402
(937) 222-2401

Program grants; The Salvation Army (program grant); Artemis Center for Alternatives to Domestic Violence (children's program); Community Blood Center (education program); Girl Scouts of Buckeye Trails Council (program grant); Dayton Boys Club, Inc. (program grant); Miami Valley Child Development Centers (The Wonder of Plants project); TeenWorks (teen entrepreneurial program); Dayton Visual Arts Center (Art for Youth program); K12 Gallery for Young People (Artist in Training program); Huber Heights Southwest Neighborhood Association (program grant)

Grants awarded to organizations located in Montgomery County.

Typical grant range: $1,000 to $25,000

634
Toledo Community Foundation, Inc.
608 Madison Avenue, Suite 1540
Toledo, OH 43604
(419) 241-5049

Program grants; Greater Toledo Urban League (after school program); Anthony Wayne Area Youth Center (program grant); Planned Parenthood (program grant); Toledo Zoological Society (program grant); YMCA (pregnancy prevention program); Arts Commission of Greater Toledo (Latino Community Art Program); Family Service of Northwest Ohio (For Girls Only Program)

Most grants awarded to organizations located in the Toledo vicinity.

635
The Troy Foundation
910 W. Main Street
Troy, OH 45373
(937) 335-8513

Program grants; Troy Recreation
(program for before and after school);
Dorothy Love Retirement Community
(program grant); Troy Christian School
(project to help an orphanage); Hook
Elementary School (project to provide
food and clothing to families)

Grants awarded to organizations located
in the Troy vicinity.

Typical grant range: $250 to $25,000

636
The Thomas H. White Foundation
1422 Euclid Avenue, Suite 627
Cleveland, OH 44115
(216) 696-7273

Program grants; St. Paul's Community
Church (preschool program); Metro
Catholic Parish School (day care
program); Old Brooklyn Montessori
School (Early Childhood Pilot Program);
Musical Arts Association (Learning
Through Music program); Beck Center for
the Cultural Arts (educational program);
AIDS Task Force (program grant);
Cleveland Rape Crisis Center (educational
program); El Barrio (tutoring program for
Hispanic children)

Grants awarded to organizations located
in Cuyahoga County.

Typical grant range: $2,000 to $25,000

OKLAHOMA

637
**Mary K. Ashbrook Foundation for
El Reno, Oklahoma**
P.O. Box 627
El Reno, OK 73036
(405) 262-4684

Program grants; community development;
education; social service organizations

Grants awarded to organizations located
in El Reno.

638
The Mervin Bovaird Foundation
100 W. Fifth Street, Suite 800
Tulsa, OK 74103
(918) 583-1777

Program grants; social service
organizations; youth; elderly; women;
disabled; cultural organizations

Most grants awarded to organizations
located in the Tulsa vicinity.

Typical grant range: $2,000 to $50,000

639
**H.A. and Mary K. Chapman
Charitable Trust**
6100 South Yale, Suite 1816
Tulsa, OK 74136
(918) 496-7882

Program grants; medical research;
education; higher education; youth;
elderly; women; social service
organizations

Most grants awarded to organizations
located in Tulsa.

Typical grant range: $5,000 to $100,000

640
The Helmerich Foundation
1579 E. 21st Street
Tulsa, OK 74114
(918) 742-5531

Program grants; social service organizations; youth; education; environment; cultural organizations; AIDS

Grants awarded to organizations located in the Tulsa vicinity.

Typical grant range: $5,000 to $75,000

641
Inasmuch Foundation
P.O. Box 2325
Oklahoma City, OK 73101-2325
(405) 235-1356

Program grants; youth; disabled; social service organizations; education; cultural organizations

642
The Merrick Foundation
2932 N.W. 122nd Street
Bradley Square, Suite 19
Oklahoma City, OK 73120
(405) 755-5571

Program grants; youth; hospitals; higher education

Grants awarded to organizations located in Oklahoma, with an emphasis in south central Oklahoma.

Typical grant range: $1,000 to $20,000

643
The Samuel Roberts Noble Foundation, Inc.
2510 Sam Noble Parkway
P.O. Box 2180
Ardmore, OK 73402
(580) 223-5810

Program grants; Diabetes Foundation of Oklahoma (camping program for children); Education and Employment Ministry, Inc. (education project); Boy Scouts of America (program grant); C.B. Goddard Center for Visual and Performing Arts, Inc. (program grant); Greater Oklahoma City Tree Bank Foundation (Tornado Re-Leaf project); Communities in Schools (summer program); Oklahoma State University Foundation (Agriculture Leadership Program)

Typical grant range: $5,000 to $200,000

644
Puterbaugh Foundation
215 E. Choctaw, Suite 114
P.O. Box 729
McAlester, OK 74502
(918) 426-1591

Program grants; McAlester Police Department DARE Program (educational program on drug awareness); American Red Cross (program grant); American Cancer Society (program grant); Boys and Girls Club (program grant); McAlester Public Library (summer program for children); Make a Wish Foundation (program grant); Oklahoma Foundation for Excellence (educational program); Eastern Oklahoma State College (nursing program)

Grants awarded to organizations located in Oklahoma.

Typical grant range: $500 to $25,000

645

Robert Glenn Rapp Foundation

2301 N.W. 39th Expressway, Suite 300
Oklahoma City, OK 73112
(405) 525-8331

Program grants; Center for Psychotherapy
(residency program); Regional Food Bank
(project grant); Community Literacy
(program grant); Christian Heritage
Academy (project grant)

Grants awarded to organizations located
in Oklahoma, with an emphasis in
Oklahoma City.

Typical grant range: $5,000 to $50,000

646

Sarkeys Foundation

530 E. Main Street
Norman, OK 73071
(405) 364-3703

Program grants; higher education;
education; disabled; social service
organizations; cultural organizations;
health organizations

Grants awarded to organizations located
in Oklahoma.

Typical grant range: $5,000 to $100,000

647

**The Anne and Henry Zarrow
Foundation**

401 S. Boston Avenue, Suite 900
Tulsa, OK 74103
(918) 295-8004

Program grants; social service
organizations; elderly; youth; disabled;
women; hospitals; health organizations

Most grants awarded to organizations
located in the Tulsa vicinity.

Typical grant range: $500 to $25,000

OREGON

648

The Carpenter Foundation

711 E. Main Street, Suite 10
Medford, OR 97504-7139
(541) 772-5851

Program grants; Oregon Ballet & Theatre
(program grant); Boys & Girls Club
(theater program); Girl Scout Council
(program grant); CASA (Hispanic
advocate program); Mediation Works
(family mediation program); Britt
Festivals (project to increase classical
concert attendance); CERVS (program for
the homeless); Start Making a Reader
Today (reading program); Dome School
(delinquency prevention program)

Grants awarded to organizations located
in Jackson and Josephine Counties.

Typical grant range: $2,000 to $20,000

649

The Collins Foundation

1618 S.W. First Avenue, Suite 505
Portland, OR 97201
(503) 227-7171

Program grants; The Nature Conservancy
(program grant); Community Connection
of Northeast Oregon (Meals on Wheels
program); Hollywood Senior Center
(program grant); Boys & Girls Clubs
(program grant); Northwest Pilot Project
(independent living program for the
elderly and people who are disabled);
Shelter/Domestic Violence Resource
Center (program grant); Columbia River
Maritime Museum (program grant);
Ecumenical Ministries (program for
mothers who have completed drug and
alcohol treatment); Oregon Association
for Children with Learning Disabilities
(program grant); Oregon Children's
Foundation (reading and book program);
Central School District (family reading
program); Pacific University
(environmental science program)

Grants awarded to organizations located
in Oregon.

Typical grant range: $3,000 to $70,000

650

The Ford Family Foundation
1600 N.W. Stewart Parkway
Roseburg, OR 97470
(541) 957-5574

Program grants; youth; disabled; social service organizations; all levels of education; cultural organizations; Boy Scouts of America (program grant); Oregon Symphony Association (program grant)

Typical grant range: $5,000 to $150,000

651

The Samuel S. Johnson Foundation
P.O. Box 356
Redmond, OR 97756
(541) 548-8104

Program grants; youth; elderly; education; social service organizations; animal welfare; cultural organizations; Columbia County Council of Senior Citizens (Dial-a-Ride program); Columbia Humane Society (Companion Adoption Program); Oregon Symphony (program grant); Crook County Library (Hooked on Books Project); William Temple House (program for dental care and prescription medication)

Grants awarded to organizations located in Oregon.

Typical grant range: $500 to $7,500

652

McKay Family Foundation
P.O. Box 70313
Eugene, OR 97401
(541) 686-5963

Program grants; youth; social service organizations

Most grants awarded to organizations located in Lane County.

653

Meyer Memorial Trust
1515 S.W. Fifth Avenue, Suite 500
Portland, OR 97201
(503) 228-5512

Program grants; Oregon Humane Society (educational programs); Feed the Hungry (hot meal program); Oregon Symphony Association (rural touring program); Lane Arts Council (summer program); Oregon Children's Foundation (book and reading program); Southern Oregon Child and Family Council (literacy project); Cascade AIDS Project (program grant); Neighborhood Health Clinics (education program); Boys and Girls Aid Society (teen pregnancy prevention program); Homestead Youth Lodge (program for troubled youth); Pioneer House (transitional housing program); Safe Haven Maternity Home (vocational program for pregnant teens); Salvation Army (after school program); Open Meadow Learning Center (natural resource education program); John Tuck Elementary School (reading program); Churchill Alternative High School (student project to produce a play)

Most grants awarded to organizations located in Oregon.

Typical grant range: $5,000 to $200,000

654

The Oregon Community Foundation
1221 S.W. Yamhill Street, Suite 100
Portland, OR 97205
(503) 227-6846

Program grants; social service organizations; youth; women; disabled; health organizations; cultural organizations

Grants awarded to organizations located in Oregon.

Typical grant range: $5,000 to $50,000

655
Rose E. Tucker Charitable Trust
900 S.W. Fifth Avenue, 24th Floor
Portland, OR 97204
(503) 224-3380

Program grants; Oregon Children's
Theater Company (program grant);
Regional Arts & Cultural Council (Arts in
Education Program); Boys & Girls Club
(program grant); Camp Fire Boys and
Girls (Hispanic program); Natural
Resources Defense Council (energy
project); Community Energy Project
(senior weatherization project); Northwest
Nurse Parish Ministries (medication
education program); Lutheran Family
Services (program grant); National
Alliance for the Mentally Ill (education
program); Oregon Zoo Foundation
(project grant); Oregon Chapter of the
Alexander Graham Bell Association for
the Deaf (summer camp program);
Portland After-School Tennis (program
grant); Wetlands Conservancy (technical
assistance program); Community
Traditional School (transportation
program); Forest Grove School District
(T.E.A.M. program)

Most grants awarded to organizations
located in Oregon, with an emphasis in
the Portland vicinity.

Typical grant range: $1,000 to $20,000

PENNSYLVANIA

656
Alcoa Foundation
Alcoa Corporate Center
201 Isabella Street
Pittsburgh, PA 15212
(412) 553-2348

Program grants; youth; elderly;
minorities; social service organizations;
education; health organizations; cultural
organizations

Grants awarded to organizations located
in areas of company operations.

Typical grant range: $1,000 to $25,000

657
Allegheny Foundation
One Oxford Centre
301 Grant Street, Suite 3900
Pittsburgh, PA 15219
(412) 392-2900

Program grants; cultural organizations;
youth; disabled; education; community
development

Most grants awarded to organizations
located in western Pennsylvania, with an
emphasis in Pittsburgh.

Typical grant range: $5,000 to $100,000

658
The Annenberg Foundation
St. Davids Center
150 Radnor-Chester Road, Suite A-200
St. Davids, PA 19087
(610) 341-9066

Program grants; all levels of education;
youth; cultural organizations

659
The Arcadia Foundation
105 E. Logan Street
Norristown, PA 19401
(610) 275-8460

Program grants; cultural organizations;
youth; elderly; disabled; education;
animal welfare

Grants awarded to organizations located
in eastern Pennsylvania.

Typical grant range: $2,500 to $25,000

660
Barra Foundation, Inc.
8200 Flourtown Avenue, Suite 12
Wyndmoor, PA 19038
(215) 233-5115

Program grants; cultural organizations;
health organizations; youth; education;
social service organizations

Most grants awarded to organizations
located in the Philadelphia vicinity.

Typical grant range: $2,500 to $50,000

661
Bayer Foundation
100 Bayer Road
Pittsburgh, PA 15205
(412) 777-5791

Program grants; cultural organizations; youth; education; higher education

Grants awarded to organizations located in areas of company operations (Bayer Corporation).

662
Will R. Beitel Childrens Community Foundation
P.O. Box 292
Nazareth, PA 18064
(610) 861-8929

Program grants; emphasis on youth; South Bethlehem Neighborhood Center (after-school program)

Grants awarded to organizations located in Northampton County.

Typical grant range: $1,000 to $10,000

663
Claude Worthington Benedum Foundation
1400 Benedum-Trees Building
Pittsburgh, PA 15222
(412) 288-0360

Program grants; Junior Achievement (Staying in School Project); YWCA (prevention program for violence and drug abuse); Literacy Volunteers (program grant); Pennsylvania Trolley Museum, Inc. (education program); Conservation Fund (program grant); Pittsburgh Council on Public Education (youth employment program)

Typical grant range: $5,000 to $100,000

664
The Buhl Foundation
Center City Tower
650 Smithfield Street, Suite 2300
Pittsburgh, PA 15222
(412) 566-2711

Program grants; Bach Choir of Pittsburgh (educational project); The Pittsburgh Symphony Society (educational program); Goodwill Industries (computer recycling program); National Organization on Disability (school-to-work program); National Assoc. of Minority Contractors and Black Contractors Association (training workshop for the Incubator Project); Quaker Valley School District (kindergarten program for children who are developmentally delayed); Carnegie Library of Homestead (Heritage Project for Children); University of Pittsburgh (disaster management project); Carnegie Mellon University (tutoring program)

Most grants awarded to organizations located in southwestern Pennsylvania, with an emphasis in the Pittsburgh vicinity.

Typical grant range: $2,000 to $70,000

665
Centre County Community Foundation
P.O. Box 824
State College, PA 16804
(814) 237-6229

Program grants; The Music Academy (program grant); Bellefonte Museum (after school arts and crafts program); Habitat for Humanity (project grant); Keystone Legal Services (education project); YMCA (basketball program); Clear Water Conservancy (Thompson Woods Preservation Project)

Most grants awarded to organizations located in Centre County.

Typical grant range: $500 to $10,000

666
The Anne L. and George H. Clapp Charitable and Educational Trust
c/o Mellon Bank
Three Mellon Bank Center, Room 4000
Pittsburgh, PA 15259
(412) 234-1634

Program grants; Pittsburgh Action Against Rape (program grant); Rainbow Kitchen (anti-hunger program); YMCA (program grant); Boys Scouts of America (program for scouts who are mentally disabled); Pittsburgh Civic Light Opera (program grant); River City Brass Band (student ticket program); Beaver County CSC (preschool and daycare programs); Up for Reading (after school literacy program); Derry Area School District (reading program); Greater Pittsburgh Literacy Council (English as Second Language Program); Reading is Fundamental (after school program); St. Phillips School (technology program); Chatham College (student and faculty research program)

Grants awarded to organizations located in the Pittsburgh vicinity.

Typical grant range: $2,000 to $15,000

667
Connelly Foundation
One Tower Bridge, Suite 1450
West Conshohocken, PA 19428
(610) 834-3222

Program grants; youth; elderly; women; minorities; disabled; social service organizations; cultural organizations; education; Christian organizations

Grants awarded to organizations located in Philadelphia and the greater Delaware Valley.

668
The Douty Foundation
P.O. Box 540
Plymouth Meeting, PA 19462
(610) 828-8145

Program grants; education; youth; women; social service organizations

Most grants awarded to organizations located in the Philadelphia vicinity, with an emphasis in Montgomery and Philadelphia Counties.

669
The Eberly Foundation
Two W. Main Street, Suite 600
Uniontown, PA 15401
(724) 438-3789

Program grants; Historical Society of Western Pennsylvania (program grant); Family Abuse Council (program grant); Ohiopyle-Stewart Community Center (program grant); Wharton Township (baseball and soccer programs for youth); Spina Bifida Association (Woodlands Summer Development Program); Communities in Schools in Fayette County (program grant)

Typical grant range: $1,000 to $100,000

670
Eden Hall Foundation
600 Grant Street, Suite 3232
Pittsburgh, PA 15219
(412) 642-6697

Program grants; cultural organizations; higher education; youth; women; social service organizations; health organizations

Grants awarded to organizations located in western Pennsylvania, with an emphasis in Pittsburgh.

Typical grant range: $10,000 to $150,000

671

The Erie Community Foundation

127 W. Sixth Street
Erie, PA 16501
(814) 454-0843

Program grants; social service organizations; youth; education; cultural organizations

Grants awarded to organizations located in Erie County.

672

Samuel S. Fels Fund

1616 Walnut Street, Suite 800
Philadelphia, PA 19103
(215) 731-9455

Program grants; cultural organizations; youth; women; minorities; social service organizations; education; community development

Grants awarded to organizations located in Philadelphia.

Typical grant range: $1,000 to $20,000

673

The Greater Harrisburg Foundation

200 N. 3rd Street, 8th Floor
P.O. Box 678
Harrisburg, PA 17108
(717) 236-5040

Program grants; youth; disabled; social service organizations; education; environment; health organizations; Girl Scout Council (program grant); Hamilton Health Center, Inc. (Homeless Children's Health Care Project)

Grants awarded to organizations located in the following Counties: Dauphin, Perry, Franklin, Cumberland and Lebanon.

Typical grant range: $100 to $5,000

674

Howard Heinz Endowment

30 CNG Tower
625 Liberty Avenue
Pittsburgh, PA 15222
(412) 281-5777

Program grants; Clean Water Fund (Good Neighbor Project); Western Pennsylvania Conservancy (watershed program); Air and Water Management Association (Sister Cities Program); Pittsburgh Dance Council (project grant); Community Human Services Corporation (program grant); Ecumenical Institute on Racism (Building Bridges to the 21st Century project); Carnegie Mellon University (teacher-training program); Westmoreland County Community College (electronics technician development program); Community College of Allegheny County Educational Foundation (alternative education program)

Grants awarded to organizations located in Pennsylvania, with an emphasis in Pittsburgh and southwestern Pennsylvania.

Typical grant range: $5,000 to $300,000

675

Vira I. Heinz Endowment
30 CNG Tower
625 Liberty Avenue
Pittsburgh, PA 15222
(412) 281-5777

Program grants; Museum of Fine Arts
(exhibition and catalog project); Gateway
to the Arts (Ready for Life program);
Western Pennsylvania Conservancy
(Urban Gardening Program); East End
Cooperative Ministry (literacy program);
Pittsburgh Board of Public Education
(literacy program); Youth Enhancement
and Support, Inc. (basketball program for
girls); Pittsburgh Dynamo Youth Soccer
Association (program grant); National
Foundation for Teaching Entrepreneurship
to Disadvantaged and Handicapped
Youths, Inc. (education program);
Carnegie Mellon University (teacher
training program)

Most grants awarded to organizations
located in the Pittsburgh vicinity.

Typical grant range: $5,000 to $200,000

676

The Hillman Foundation, Inc.
2000 Grant Building
Pittsburgh, PA 15219
(412) 338-3466

Program grants; youth; disabled; women;
education; environment; cultural
organizations; community development;
East End Cooperative Ministry (substance
abuse recovery program for homeless
men); Robert Morris College
(Communications Skills Program)

Most grants awarded to organizations
located in the Pittsburgh vicinity.

Typical grant range: $25,000 to $150,000

677

The Stewart Huston Charitable Trust
50 S. First Avenue, 2nd Floor
Coatesville, PA 19320
(610) 384-2666

Program grants; Olivet United Methodist
Church (summer camp project); Lan-
Chester Christian School (kindergarten
program); Christ Church (project for the
children's school); People's Light and
Theatre Company (Project Discovery);
YMCA (program grant); Family Planning
Council (program grant); Chester County
Chamber of Business and Industry
(welfare to work mentoring program)

Typical grant range: $3,000 to $50,000

678

Independence Foundation
200 S. Broad Street, Suite 1101
Philadelphia, PA 19102
(215) 985-4009

Program grants; Episcopal Community
Services (meal program); Frankford
Group Ministry (Emergency Assistance
Program); Catholic Social Services
(project grant); Women's Resource Center
(project grant); Visiting Nurses
Association (project grant); Abington Art
Center (project grant); Arden Theater
(project grant); Library Company of
Philadelphia (project grant); Zoological
Society of Philadelphia (project grant);
Domestic Violence Center (project grant);
Little Brothers-Friends of the Elderly
(program grant); Montgomery County
Association for the Blind (project grant);
Special Olympics (adult athlete program)

Typical grant range: $500 to $100,000

679

The Mary Hillman Jennings Foundation

2203 Allegheny Tower
625 Stanwix Street
Pittsburgh, PA 15222
(412) 434-5606

Program grants; hospitals; health organizations; youth; women; disabled; education; environment; cultural organizations

Most grants awarded to organizations located in the Pittsburgh vicinity.

Typical grant range: $5,000 to $50,000

680

The Jewish Healthcare Foundation of Pittsburgh

Centre City Tower, Suite 2330
650 Smithfield Street
Pittsburgh, PA 15222
(412) 261-1400

Program grants; National Council of Jewish Women (project grant); Jewish Residential Services (club house program); Pittsburgh AIDS Task Force (Medications Buddy Project); Pittsburgh Mercy Health Foundation (project to care for the elderly); Greater Pittsburgh Community Food Bank (project grant); Allegheny County Human Services (project grant); Youth Enhancement Support, Inc. (exercise program); The American Cancer Society (smoking prevention program for teens); University of Pittsburgh (Youth Empowerment Project)

Grants awarded to organizations located in western Pennsylvania, with an emphasis in Pittsburgh.

Typical grant range: $500 to $100,000

681

T. James Kavanagh Foundation

234 E. State Street
Sharon, PA 16146

Program grants; Great Valley Nature Center (environmental education program for children); Salvation Army (program grant); Allegheny Highlands Regional Theatre (program for children); Boy Scouts of America (program grant); Keystone Blind Association (educational program); Liberty Museum (educational program); Valley Arts Guild, Inc. (after school art program); Lower Merion Senior Center (meal program); St. Mary's Church (food and clothing program); Tolentine Community Center & Development Corp. (after school program for latchkey children); Pennsylvania Moose Association (drug abuse education program for youth); Cumberland College (Mountain Outreach Program)

Typical grant range: $1,000 to $7,500

682

Josiah W. and Bessie H. Kline Foundation, Inc.

515 S. 29th Street
Harrisburg, PA 17104
(717) 561-4373

Program grants; Humane Society (program grant); Association for Retarded Citizens (vocational training program); Music At Gretna, Inc. (program grant); Salvation Army (program grant); Pinnacle Health Hospice (bereavement program for children); Easter Seal Society (recreational therapy program); Project Forward Leap (program that assists middle school students from disadvantaged backgrounds)

Grants awarded to organizations located in south central Pennsylvania.

Typical grant range: $2,000 to $50,000

683
Laurel Foundation
Two Gateway Center, Suite 1800
Pittsburgh, PA 15222
(412) 765-2400

Program grants; Light of Life Ministries
(program for the homeless); Community
Outreach Ministries (educational
program); Women's Christian Renewal,
Inc. (program for female former
offenders); Boy Scouts of America
(Learning for Life/Exploring program);
Family Health Council Center for
Adolescent Pregnancy Prevention
(program for teenagers); Gateway to
Music and the Performing Arts (program
grant); Carnegie Library (Beginning with
Books Early Literacy Training Program);
One Small Step, Inc. (after-school
program for at-risk children); Community
Environmental Legal Defense Fund
(program grant); Pennsylvania Resources
Council (resource conservation program);
PA Clean Ways (educational programs
regarding illegal dump sites)

Typical grant range: $5,000 to $50,000

684
Lehigh Valley Community Foundation
961 Marcon Blvd., Suite 110
Allentown, PA 18103
(610) 266-4284

Program grants; social service
organizations; youth; women; cultural
organizations; community development

Grants awarded to organizations located
in Lehigh and Northampton Counties.

Typical grant range: $1,000 to $5,000

685
Samuel P. Mandell Foundation
1735 Market Street, Suite 3410
Philadelphia, PA 19103
(215) 979-3404

Program grants; cultural organizations;
social service organizations; education;
hospitals; health organizations

Most grants awarded to organizations
located in Pennsylvania.

686
McCune Foundation
6 PPG Place, Suite 750
Pittsburgh, PA 15222
(412) 644-8779

Program grants; disabled; minorities;
youth; social service organizations; health
organizations; education; community
development; cultural organizations

Most grants awarded to organizations
located in southwestern Pennsylvania,
with an emphasis in the Pittsburgh
vicinity.

Typical grant range: $25,000 to $400,000

687
McFeely-Rogers Foundation
1110 Ligonier Street, Suite 300
P.O. Box 110
Latrobe, PA 15650
(724) 537-5588

Program grants; East Liberty Family
Health Care Center (dental program for
children); Leukemia Society of America
(program grant); Girl Scout Council
(program grant); Presbyterian Media
Mission (project grant); Westmoreland
Symphony Orchestra (student ticket
program); Community Foundation of
Westmoreland County (project for a
one-room schoolhouse)

Typical grant range: $500 to $10,000

688
**Katherine Mabis McKenna
Foundation, Inc.**
P.O. Box 186
Latrobe, PA 15650
(724) 537-6900

Program grants; environment; cultural
organizations; youth; disabled;
community development

Grants awarded to organizations located
in Westmoreland County.

Typical grant range: $2,500 to $50,000

689

Philip M. McKenna Foundation, Inc.
P.O. Box 186
Latrobe, PA 15650
(724) 537-6900

Program grants; Center for Immigration Studies (research and writing program); Faith and Reason Institute for the Study of Religion and Culture (education project); National Center for Policy Analysis (education project); Social Philosophy and Policy Foundation (visiting scholars program); Carnegie Science Center (elementary school program); National Association of Scholars (Academic Leadership Project)

Typical grant range: $5,000 to $50,000

690

Richard King Mellon Foundation
One Mellon Bank Center
500 Grant Street, Suite 4106
Pittsburgh, PA 15219
(412) 392-2800

Program grants; St. Mary's Lawrenceville Arts Program (summer program); Friendship Ministries (education and youth program); Garfield Youth Sports (program grant); Alice Paul House (rape crisis program); Crime Victims Services (program grant); Youth Enrichment Services (mentoring program); Bethel Church of God in Christ (after-school program); Carnegie Library of Pittsburgh (Beginning with Books project); Keystone Oaks High School (Project Succeed); Hosanna House (after-school program for elementary school students); Carnegie Mellon University (InfoLink Program)

Most grants awarded to organizations located in the Pittsburgh vicinity.

Typical grant range: $10,000 to $250,000

691

Howard E. & Nell E. Miller Charitable Foundation
Two PNC Plaza
620 Liberty Avenue, 25th Floor
Pittsburgh, PA 15222
(412) 762-3502

Program grants; youth; cultural organizations; education; social service organizations

Most grants awarded to organizations located in Pittsburgh.

Typical grant range: $2,000 to $20,000

692

The William Penn Foundation
2 Logan Square, 11th Floor
100 N. 18th Street
Philadelphia, PA 19103
(215) 988-1830

Program grants; Women's Christian Alliance (parent education project); Big Brothers/Big Sisters Association (mentoring program); Crime Prevention Association (child abuse prevention and parenting education program); Wildlife Information Center, Inc. (environmental education summer camp program); Pennsylvania Environmental Council, Inc. (GreenSpace Alliance Project); Rosenbach Museum and Library (educational program); Pennsylvania Ballet Association (educational program); Children's Hospital (Parents Against Drugs project); AIDS Information Network (educational project); School District of Philadelphia (program for school reform); Rosemont College (Summer Success Program)

Typical grant range: $10,000 to $250,000

693
The Pew Charitable Trusts
One Commerce Square
2005 Market Street, Suite 1700
Philadelphia, PA 19103
(215) 575-9050

Program grants; Delaware County Women Against Rape (prevention and educational program); Big Sisters (mentoring program); Women's Christian Alliance (Adolescent Life Skills Training Program); Retired Senior Volunteer Program (program grant); American Cancer Society (mobile mammography program); Epilepsy Foundation (employment program); American National Red Cross (AIDS Home Care Program); Episcopal Hospital (Life Skills and Education Program); Day Care Association of Montgomery County, Inc. (child care project); Homeless Advocacy Project (Children's Education and Outreach Project); Please Touch Museum (educational project); The Free Library of Philadelphia (Learning, Enjoyment and Play Program); Allegheny University of the Health Sciences (Eating Good Eating Right project)

Typical grant range: $100,000 to $1,000,000

694
The Philadelphia Foundation
1234 Market Street, Suite 1800
Philadelphia, PA 19107
(215) 563-6417

Program grants; youth; minorities; women; disabled; social service organizations; health organizations; cultural organizations

Most grants awarded to organizations located in the Philadelphia vicinity.

Typical grant range: $2,000 to $50,000

695
The Pittsburgh Foundation
One PPG Place, 30th Floor
Pittsburgh, PA 15222
(412) 391-5122

Program grants; cultural organizations; education; disabled; youth; minorities; social service organizations; health organizations; community development

Grants awarded to organizations located in the Pittsburgh vicinity.

696
PNC Charitable Trust
c/o PNC Bank, N.A.
1 PNC Plaza
249 5th Avenue, 29th Floor
Pittsburgh, PA 15222
(412) 762-7076

Program grants; disabled; women; youth; social service organizations; community development; cultural organizations

Grants awarded to organizations located in areas of company operations (PNC Bank, N.A.).

697
PPG Industries Foundation
One PPG Place
Pittsburgh, PA 15272
(412) 434-2453

Program grants; social service organizations; disabled; minorities; women; youth; higher and secondary education; cultural organizations; Langley High School (Project Aspire)

Grants awarded to organizations located in areas of company operations (PPG Industries, Inc.), with an emphasis in Pittsburgh.

Typical grant range: $500 to $50,000

698

Herbert M. Rehmeyer Trust
c/o The York Bank & Trust Co.
21 E. Market Street
York, PA 17401
(717) 846-9800

Program grants; youth; social service organizations; cultural organizations; community development; Salvation Army (program grant); YWCA (program grant)

Grants awarded to organizations located in York County.

Typical grant range: $1,000 to $10,000

699

S & T Bancorp Charitable Foundation
c/o S & T Bank, Trust Department
P.O. Box 220
Indiana, PA 15701
(724) 465-1443

Program grants; social service organizations; youth; recreation; community development; cultural organizations

Grants awarded to organizations located in areas of company operations (S & T Bank).

Typical grant range: $700 to $10,000

700

Adam and Maria Sarah Seybert Institution for Poor Boys and Girls
P.O. Box 8228
Philadelphia, PA 19101
(610) 828-8145

Program grants; emphasis on children (including education, minorities, and child welfare organizations)

Grants awarded to organizations located in Philadelphia.

Typical grant range: $2,000 to $6,000

701

W.W. Smith Charitable Trust
3515 W. Chester Pike, Suite E
Newton Square, PA 19073-3705
(610) 359-1811

Program grants; Episcopal Community Services (meal delivery program for the elderly); First United Methodist Church (food for adolescents program); Silver Springs Martin Luther School (meal program); The Domestic Violence Center (program grant); Delco Blind/Sight Center (program for the elderly); Energy Coordinating Agency of Philadelphia, Inc. (Cool Aid Program); Bethanna Christian Home for Boys and Girls (Residential Treatment Program)

Typical grant range: $5,000 to $150,000

702

Staunton Farm Foundation
Centre City Tower, Suite 210
650 Smithfield Street
Pittsburgh, PA 15222
(412) 281-8020

Program grants; Pittsburgh Black Action Drug Abuse Center, Inc. (education program); Catholic Charities (counseling program); Center Against Domestic and Sexual Violence (program grant); North Side Common Ministries (counseling program for homeless men); Best Friends, Inc. (recreation program); Family Hospice (bereavement program); Butler Memorial Hospital Foundation (treatment program for children with special needs); KidsPeace (Internet program); Planned Parenthood (education program); Schenley Heights Community Development Program (after school tutoring program); Clelian Heights School for Exceptional Children (work transition project); University of Pittsburgh (respite care program)

Grants awarded to organizations located in southwestern Pennsylvania.

Typical grant range: $10,000 to $85,000

703
The Helen F. Whitaker Fund
4718 Old Gettysburg Road, Suite 209
Mechanicsburg, PA 17055
(717) 763-1600

Program grants; Curtis Institute of Music
(conducting program); Central City Opera
(training program); Chamber Music
America (program grant); Academy of
Vocal Arts (training program); American
Composers Orchestra, Inc. (program
grant); Association of Performing Arts
(Classical Connections Project); American
Symphony Orchestra League (orchestra
management fellowship program)

Typical grant range: $5,000 to $100,000

704
Williamsport-Lycoming Foundation
220 West 4th Street, Suite C, 3rd Floor
Williamsport, PA 17701
(570) 321-1500

Program grants; Partners in Golf
(mentoring and tutoring program for
youth); Lycoming County Historical
Society (program grant); City of
Williamsport (Downtown Facade
Improvement Project); Lycoming County
Housing Authority (program grant);
Community Theater League (program
grant); YWCA (program grant); Lycoming
County Health Improvement Coalition
and Children's Advocacy Initiative
(program grant)

Grants awarded to organizations located
in Lycoming County.

Typical grant range: $1,000 to $40,000

705
York Foundation
20 W. Market Street
York, PA 17401
(717) 848-3733

Program grants; youth; education; cultural
organizations; community development

Grants awarded to organizations located
in York County.

PUERTO RICO

706
Puerto Rico Community Foundation
P.O. Box 70362
San Juan, PR 00936
(787) 721-1037

Program grants; cultural organizations;
social service organizations; youth;
community development; education;
health organizations; AIDS

Grants awarded to organizations located
in Puerto Rico.

RHODE ISLAND

707
The Champlin Foundations
300 Centerville Road, Suite 300S
Warwick, RI 02886
(401) 736-0370

Program grants; Roger Williams Hospital
(bone marrow transplant program); Rhode
Island Prevention Coalition (fitness and
walking program); YMCA (summer
program); University of Rhode Island
(program grant)

Grants awarded to organizations located
in Rhode Island.

Typical grant range: $5,000 to $150,000

708
Hasbro Charitable Trust, Inc.
c/o Hasbro, Inc.
1027 Newport Avenue
Pawtucket, RI 02862
(401) 727-5429

Program grants; health organizations;
education; youth; social service
organizations

Grants awarded to organizations located
in areas of company operations.

Typical grant range: $1,000 to $25,000

709

Mary E. Hodges Fund
c/o Masonic Grand Lodge Charities
222 Taunton Avenue
East Providence, RI 02914
(401) 435-4650

Program grants; social service
organizations; women; hospitals; health
organizations; AIDS

Grants awarded to organizations located
in Rhode Island.

Typical grant range: $1,000 to $5,000

710

The Rhode Island Foundation
One Union Station
Providence, RI 02903
(401) 274-4564

Program grants; Hope Center for Cancer
Support (leadership program); Mother of
the Servant Academy (farm program for
inner-city families); Sail Newport
(summer sailing program); South
Providence Neighborhood Ministries
(youth program); Women's Health &
Education Fund (program for low-income
women); Pawtucket School Department
(Start with Arts Program); Public
Education Fund (Parents Making A
Difference Program); Next Step (visitation
program for children and families
separated as a result of divorce, substance
abuse or domestic abuse)

Grants awarded to organizations located
in Rhode Island.

Typical grant range: $2,500 to $100,000

SOUTH CAROLINA

711

**Central Carolina Community
Foundation**
P.O. Box 11222
Columbia, SC 29211
(803) 254-5601

Program grants; health organizations;
hospitals; youth; elderly; social service
organizations; education; community
development; Salvation Army (program
grant); Boy Scouts of America (Learning
for Life Program)

712

**Community Foundation of Greater
Greenville, Inc.**
27 Cleveland Street, Suite 101
Greenville, SC 29601
(864) 233-5925

Program grants; education; youth; social
service organizations

Grants awarded to organizations located
in Greenville County.

713

**The Community Foundation Serving
Coastal South Carolina**
90 Mary Street
Charleston, SC 29403
(843) 723-3635

Program grants; social service
organizations; youth; elderly; community
development; education; cultural
organizations

Grants awarded in the following counties:
Berkeley, Charleston, Dorchester,
Georgetown, Beaufort, Colleton, Hampton
and Jasper.

714
The Fullerton Foundation, Inc.
515 W. Buford Street
Gaffney, SC 29340

Program grants; Memorial Mission Medical Center (program for molecular genetics); Medical University of South Carolina (program for cancer detection and prevention)

Typical grant range: $10,000 to $125,000

715
Hilton Head Island Foundation, Inc.
4 Northridge Drive, Suite A
P.O. Box 23019
Hilton Head Island, SC 29925
(803) 681-9100

Program grants; youth; disabled; social service organizations; community development; cultural organizations; Special Olympics (program grant); Meals on Wheels (expand food program)

Grants awarded to organizations located in Hilton Head Island.

Typical grant range: $3,000 to $35,000

716
The Joanna Foundation
P.O. Box 308
Sullivan's Island, SC 29482
(843) 883-9199

Program grants; environment; community development; higher education; youth; social service organizations; The Nature Conservancy (landscape project)

Grants awarded in the following counties: Berkeley, Charleston, Dorchester, Laurens and Newberry.

Typical grant range: $1,000 to $10,000

717
The Self Family Foundation
P.O. Drawer 1017
Greenwood, SC 29648
(864) 941-4036

Program grants; Liberty Police Department (child safety program); Greenwood Community Children's Center (Healthy Beginnings Program); PALS (Entrepreneurship Youth Enterprise program); St. Nicholas Speech and Hearing Center (program grant); Greenwood Community Improvement Foundation (program grant); Special Olympics (sports program); Arts Council (summer program); Teens Under Fire (drug, alcohol and seat belt awareness program); Greenwood Literacy Council (program grant); Education Enrichment Foundation (Authors Reaching Kids program)

Grants awarded to organizations located in South Carolina, with an emphasis in the Greenwood vicinity.

Typical grant range: $5,000 to $75,000

718

The Spartanburg County Foundation
320 E. Main Street, Suite 3
Spartanburg, SC 29302
(864) 582-0138

Program grants; The Salvation Army (program grant); Carolina Counseling, Inc. (abuse prevention program); Spartanburg Little Theatre (program grant); Music Foundation of Spartanburg (program grant); Spartanburg Regional Hospital System (nursing program); TASC/Rotary (Youth at Risk Tennis Program); Girl Scouts (program grant); YMCA (program grant for Family Recreation and Play Center); Urban League (program grant); Greenville Literacy Association (literacy project); Adult Learning Center (program grant); Spartanburg Science Center (program grant); Spartanburg Animal Shelter and Humane Society (program grant)

Grants awarded to organizations located in Spartanburg County.

Typical grant range: $500 to $50,000

SOUTH DAKOTA

719

Sioux Falls Area Community Foundation
300 N. Phillips Avenue, Suite 102
Sioux Falls, SD 57104-6035
(605) 336-7055

Program grants; environment; education; social service organizations; cultural organizations; health organizations; Girl Scout Council (program grant); McKennan Hospital (grief training program); Roosevelt High School (summer school program)

Grants awarded to organizations located in the Sioux Falls vicinity.

Typical grant range: $1,000 to $3,000

720

South Dakota Community Foundation
207 East Capitol
P.O. Box 296
Pierre, SD 57501
(605) 224-1025

Program grants; cultural organizations; health organizations; youth; women; social service organizations; community development; Native Americans; Rapid City Fine Arts Council, Inc. (program grant)

Grants awarded to organizations located in South Dakota.

Typical grant range: $2,000 to $20,000

721

Watertown Community Foundation
1200 33rd Street SE, Suite 309A
Watertown, SD 57201
(605) 882-3731

Program grants; recreation; youth; social service organzations; education; cultural organzations

Grants awarded to organizations located in Watertown.

TENNESSEE

722

The Community Foundation of Greater Chattanooga, Inc.
1270 Market Street
Chattanooga, TN 37402
(423) 265-0586

Program grants; Camp Fire Boys and Girls (after-school program); Inner-City Ministries (Family Advocacy Project); Chattanooga Parks & Recreation (dance program); YMCA (Youth Leadership Exchange Program); Dalewood Middle School (summer program); Hamilton County Department of Education (parenting program)

Grants awarded to organizations located in the Chattanooga vicinity.

723
Community Foundation of Greater Memphis
1900 Union Avenue
Memphis, TN 38104-4029
(901) 728-4600

Program grants; community development; youth; disabled

724
Joe C. Davis Foundation
908 Audubon Road
Nashville, TN 37204
(615) 297-1030

Program grants; youth; elderly; social service organizations; education; health organizations; Girl Scouts (program grant); Immanuel Baptist Church (program grant)

Grants awarded to organizations located in the Nashville vicinity.

Typical grant range: $1,000 to $50,000

725
East Tennessee Foundation
550 W. Main Street, Suite 550
Knoxville, TN 37902
(865) 524-1223

Program grants; social service organizations; youth; community development; cultural organizations

Typical grant range: $500 to $5,000

726
The Frist Foundation
3319 W. End Avenue, Suite 900
Nashville, TN 37203
(615) 292-3868

Program grants; youth; women; disabled; education; social service organizations; Tennessee Police Athletic League (inner-city youth program); Junior Achievement (economic education program)

Most grants awarded to organizations located in Nashville.

Typical grant range: $2,000 to $30,000

727
Lyndhurst Foundation
517 E. 5th Street
Chattanooga, TN 37403
(423) 756-0767

Program grants; The Nature Conservancy of Tennessee (project grant); The Wilderness Society (forest management project); South Wings (public lands protection project); Volunteer Center of Memphis (reading program)

Most grants awarded to organizations located in Chattanooga.

Typical grant range: $10,000 to $150,000

728
Plough Foundation
6410 Poplar, Suite 710
Memphis, TN 38119-4863
(901) 761-9180

Program grants; social service organizations; youth; health organizations; education; cultural organizations

Grants awarded to organizations located in Memphis and in Shelby County.

Typical grant range: $10,000 to $200,000

729
The Thompson Charitable Foundation
P.O. Box 10516
Knoxville, TN 37939
(865) 588-0491

Program grants; social service organizations; youth; education; health organizations; Knoxville College (work study program)

Typical grant range: $10,000 to $75,000

TEXAS

730
Abell-Hanger Foundation
P.O. Box 430
Midland, TX 79702
(915) 684-6655

Program grants; Mercy Regional Medical Center (program grant for the domestic violence shelter); American Lung Association (asthma education program); Boys and Girls Club (program grant); Southwest Guide Dog Foundation (dog training program); Midland Community Theatre, Inc. (educational program); Ellen Noel Art Museum (project grant); Northside Community Action League (summer basketball program); Friends of the Howard County Library (program grant); Odessa College (program on philanthropy and volunteerism); Greenwood Independent School District (High School Project Graduation); Schreiner College (Community Internship Work Study Program); University of Texas (Thermal Bioengineering research program); Midland College (Students-In-Philanthropy Program)

Grants awarded to organizations located in Texas.

Typical grant range: $2,000 to $60,000

731
Albert and Margaret Alkek Foundation
1221 McKinney, Suite 4525
Houston, TX 77010
(713) 951-0019

Program grants; medical research; all levels of education; cultural organizations; Houston Symphony Orchestra (program grant); Baylor College of Medicine (program grant)

Grants awarded to organizations located in Texas.

Typical grant range: $20,000 to $150,000

732
M.D. Anderson Foundation
P.O. Box 2558
Houston, TX 77252
(713) 216-1451

Program grants; health organizations; youth; education; social service organizations; cultural organizations; YMCA (program grant); Baylor University (program grant at the law library)

Grants awarded to organizations located in Texas, with an emphasis in the Houston vicinity.

Typical grant range: $5,000 to $75,000

733
Lee and Ramona Bass Foundation
309 Main Street
Fort Worth, TX 76102
(817) 336-0494

Program grants; Valley Zoological Society (Students Teaching Students program); The Forever Foundation for Texas Wildlife, Inc. (Texas Big Game Awards Program)

Grants awarded to organizations located in Texas.

734
The Brown Foundation, Inc.
P.O. Box 130646
Houston, TX 77219
(713) 523-6867

Program grants; youth; disabled; minorities; women; social service organizations; education; cultural organizations; Society for Performing Arts (educational program); Houston Museum of Natural Science (project grant); San Antonio Public Library Foundation (program grant); San Antonio Amateur Sports Foundation, Inc. (program grant)

Grants awarded to organizations located in Texas, with an emphasis in Houston.

735

William and Catherine Bryce Memorial Fund
c/o Bank One, Texas, N.A.
P.O. Box 2050
Fort Worth, TX 76113
(817) 884-4151

Program grants; social service organizations; youth; education; cultural organizations

Grants awarded to organizations located in Texas, with an emphasis in Fort Worth.

736

The Burnett Foundation
801 Cherry Street, Suite 1400
Ft. Worth, TX 76102
(817) 877-3344

Program grants; AIDS Outreach Center (program for minorities); Women's Center of Tarrant County, Inc. (employment program); Crime Prevention Resource Center (violence prevention program); Southside Area Ministries, Inc. (food program); Santa Fe Counseling Centre, Inc. (substance abuse education and counseling program); National Association for the Advancement of Colored People (leadership program for youth); Santa Fe Opera (project support); Santa Fe Community Foundation (Technical Assistance Connection project)

Most grants awarded to organizations located in the Ft. Worth vicinity.

737

Amon G. Carter Foundation
P.O. Box 1036
Ft. Worth, TX 76101
(817) 332-2783

Program grants; youth; elderly; women; disabled; social service; education; community development; cultural organizations; health organizations; American Lung Association (program grant)

Most grants awarded to organizations located in Ft. Worth and Tarrant County.

Typical grant range: $1,000 to $100,000

738

The CH Foundation
P.O. Box 16458
Lubbock, TX 79490
(806) 799-3250

Program grants; all levels of education; youth; women; social service organizations; community development; health organizations; cultural organizations

Grants awarded to organizations located in Lubbock County and surrounding counties.

Typical grant range: $5,000 to $60,000

739

The Cockrell Foundation
1600 Smith, Suite 3900
Houston, TX 77002
(713) 209-7500

Program grants; youth; women; disabled; social service organizations; hospitals; cultural organizations; Texas Children's Hospital Library (program for children); The Women's Home (program grant); YMCA (program grant); Nehemiah Community Center (program grant); Homes of St. Mark (programs for foster care and maternity care); Houston Museum of Natural Science (Technology Improvement Program)

Grants awarded to organizations located in the Houston vicinity.

Typical grant range: $1,500 to $50,000

740
Communities Foundation of Texas, Inc.
4605 Live Oak Street
Dallas, TX 75204
(214) 826-5231

Program grants; youth; social service organizations; education; cultural organizations; health organizations; North Texas Food Bank (meal program)

Most grants awarded to organizations located in the Dallas vicinity.

741
Dave Coy Foundation
c/o Bank of America, NA
P.O. Box 121
San Antonio, TX 78291
(210) 270-5371

Program grants; social service organizations; youth; elderly; disabled

Most grants awarded to organizations located in the San Antonio vicinity.

Typical grant range: $5,000 to $30,000

742
The Cullen Foundation
601 Jefferson, 40th Floor
Houston, TX 77002
(713) 651-8837

Program grants; youth; women; social service organizations; education; higher education; cultural organizations

Grants awarded to organizations located in Texas, with an emphasis in Houston.

Typical grant range: $50,000 to $400,000

743
Dodge Jones Foundation
P.O. Box 176
Abilene, TX 79604
(915) 673-6429

Program grants; youth; women; disabled; social service organizations; education; cultural organizations

Grants awarded to organizations located in Abilene.

Typical grant range: $1,000 to $100,000

744
El Paso Community Foundation
310 N. Mesa, 10th Floor
El Paso, TX 79901
(915) 533-4020

Program grants; disabled; youth; women; social service organizations; environment; education; cultural organizations

Grants awarded to organizations located in the El Paso vicinity.

745
ExxonMobil Foundation
5959 Las Colinas Blvd.
Irving, TX 75039
(972) 444-1104

Program grants; Memorial Sloan Kettering Cancer Center (cancer vaccine development program); Children of Alcoholics Foundation (program grant); American Heart Association (awareness program); Dallas Opera (program grants); Children's Museum of Houston (after school program); Southwest Museum of Science and Technology (project grant); Student Conservation Association (career development program); National Council of Teachers of Mathematics (educational program); Harris County Education Foundation (Energy Industry Program); Barbers Hill Independent School District (recycling program); Houston Independent School District (High School Teachers Reform Effort Program)

Typical grant range: $3,000 to $50,000

746
The Favrot Fund
1770 St. James Place, Suite 510
Houston, TX 77056
(713) 622-1442

Program grants; environment; animal welfare; youth; social service organizations; education; health organizations; cultural organizations; Garrison Art Center, Inc. (program grant); Galveston Historical Foundation (internship program); Tree People, Inc. (urban environmental project)

Typical grant range: $5,000 to $60,000

747
Leland Fikes Foundation, Inc.
3050 Lincoln Plaza
500 N. Akard, Suite 3050
Dallas, TX 75201
(214) 754-0144

Program grants; youth; women; disabled; social service organizations; health organizations; all levels of education; cultural organizations; Camp Fire Boys and Girls (program grant)

Grants awarded to organizations located in Dallas.

Typical grant range: $5,000 to $75,000

748
The Fondren Foundation
P.O. Box 2558
Houston, TX 77252-2558
(713) 216-4513

Program grants; youth; disabled; social service organizations; secondary and higher education; health organizations; cultural organizations

Most grants awarded to organizations located in Texas, with an emphasis in Houston.

Typical grant range: $10,000 to $200,000

749
The George Foundation
304 Morton Street, Suite C
Richmond, TX 77469
(281) 342-6109

Program grants; youth; women; disabled; social service organizations; education; health organizations

Most grants awarded to organizations located in Ft. Bend County.

Typical grant range: $5,000 to $50,000

750
Paul and Mary Haas Foundation
P.O. Box 2928
Corpus Christi, TX 78403
(361) 887-6955

Program grants; youth; social service organizations; education; cultural organizations; health organizations; AIDS

Grants awarded to organizations located in the Corpus Christi vicinity.

751
The Donald D. Hammill Foundation
8700 Shoal Creek Blvd.
Austin, TX 78757
(512) 451-0784

Program grants; elderly; disabled; education; social service organizations; health organizations

Most grants awarded to organizations located in the Austin vicinity.

Typical grant range: $250 to $10,000

752
Hoblitzelle Foundation
5956 Sherry Lane, Suite 901
Dallas, TX 75225
(214) 373-0462

Program grants; secondary and higher education; youth; cultural organizations; disabled; social service organizations; health organizations; AIDS; North Dallas Shared Ministries (program grant); Southwestern Medical Foundation (program grant); Contact Counseling and Crisis Line (program for teenagers)

Grants awarded to organizations located in Texas, with an emphasis in Dallas.

Typical grant range: $25,000 to $200,000

753
Houston Endowment, Inc.
600 Travis, Suite 6400
Houston, TX 77002
(713) 238-8100

Program grants; youth; women; disabled; minorities; social service organizations; cultural organizations; environment; animal welfare; education; higher education

Grants awarded to organizations located in Houston.

Typical grant range: $5,000 to $250,000

754
Harris and Eliza Kempner Fund
P.O. Box 119
Galveston, TX 77553
(409) 762-1603

Program grants; Associated Catholic Charities (food program); Girl Scout Area Council (project grant); Boy Scouts of America (program grant); Houston Children's Chorus, Inc. (apprentice project); Clean Galveston (project to develop a community garden); American Red Cross (hurricane disaster relief project); Environmental Defense Fund (project grant); Senior Citizen's Center (storytelling project); Methodist Retirement Services (Meals On Wheels program); St. Vincent's House (preschool program); Project Graduation, Inc. (drug free graduation project); Galveston Independent School District (Fine Arts Project); Texas A & M University (Ecology Field Trips Project)

Most grants awarded to organizations located in the Galveston vicinity.

Typical grant range: $500 to $15,000

755
The Eugene McDermott Foundation
3808 Euclid Avenue
Dallas, TX 75205
(214) 521-2924

Program grants; youth; education; minorities; cultural organizations

Grants awarded to organizations located in Dallas.

Typical grant range: $1,000 to $50,000

756
Meadows Foundation, Inc.
Wilson Historic Block
3003 Swiss Avenue
Dallas, TX 75204
(214) 826-9431

Program grants; Boy Scouts of America (program grant); Austin Groups for the Elderly (day care program for the elderly); Advocacy Center for Crime Victims and Children (program for victims of child abuse); Austin Symphony Orchestra Society (educational program); National Audubon Society (educational program); American Lung Association (educational program); AIDS Foundation (program grant); First Presbyterian Church of Dallas (Community Ministries Program); Alamo Community College (distance-learning program); University of Texas at Austin for Texas Center for Reading and Language Arts (faculty training program)

Grants awarded to organizations located in Texas.

Typical grant range: $10,000 to $200,000

757

The Moody Foundation
2302 Postoffice Street, Suite 704
Galveston, TX 77550
(409) 763-5333

Program grants; Dallas Supporters of the
Fort Worth/Dallas Ballet, Inc. (educational
program); Dallas Museum of Art
(educational program); Gulf Coast
Alliance for the Mentally Ill (program
grant); Transitional Learning Center
(programs serving people who are
neurologically impaired); The University
of Texas Southwestern Medical Center
(Texas Medication Algorithm Project)

Grants awarded to organizations located
in Texas.

Typical grant range: $5,000 to $150,000

758

B.B. Owen Trust
P.O. Box 830068
Richardson, TX 75083
(972) 238-8537

Program grants; social service
organizations; youth; disabled

Most grants awarded to organizations
located in the Dallas vicinity.

Typical grant range: $1,000 to $50,000

759

Howard Earl Rachofsky Foundation
8201 Preston Road, Suite 400
Dallas, TX 75225
(214) 890-8800

Program grants; social service
organizations; youth; education; cultural
organizations; Jewish organizations

Grants awarded to organizations located
in Dallas.

Typical grant range: $1,000 to $20,000

760

Sid W. Richardson Foundation
309 Main Street
Ft. Worth, TX 76102
(817) 336-0494

Program grants; Fort Worth Museum of
Science and History (education program);
Arts Council of Fort Worth (Neighborhood
Arts Program); Cassata Learning Center
(Reading Improvement Program);
First Texas Council of Camp Fire, Inc.
(Kindergarten Readiness Program);
Southside Area Ministries (mentoring
program); Baylor Health Care System
(TEAM Diabetes Self-Management
Training Program); Dental Health for
Arlington, Inc. (program grant); Texas
Scottish Rite Hospital for Crippled
Children (program grant); Boy Scouts of
America (program grant); Circle T Girl
Scout Council (program grant); YWCA
(after school program); National Audubon
Society, Inc. (program grant); Women's
Center (employment program); National
Society to Prevent Blindness (Glaucoma
Alert program); Texas Engineering
Foundation (educational program); Texas
Woman's University (Project TEACH);
Texas Wesleyan University (Courage to
Teach program)

Grants awarded to organizations located
in Texas.

Typical grant range: $5,000 to $250,000

761

Rockwell Fund, Inc.
1330 Post Oak Blvd., Suite 1825
Houston, TX 77056
(713) 629-9022

Program grants; youth; elderly; women;
disabled; social service organizations;
cultural organizations; all levels of
education; Greater Houston Community
Foundation (Rusk School Health
Promotion Project)

Grants awarded to organizations located
in Texas, with an emphasis in Houston.

Typical grant range: $5,000 to $100,000

762
Harold Simmons Foundation
Three Lincoln Center
5430 LBJ Freeway, Suite 1700
Dallas, TX 75240
(972) 233-2134

Program grants; youth; social service organizations; education; community development; health organizations; cultural organizations

Grants awarded to organizations located in the Dallas vicinity.

Typical grant range: $1,000 to $30,000

763
Bob and Vivian Smith Foundation
1900 W. Loop South, Suite 1050
Houston, TX 77027
(713) 986-8030

Program grants; Communities in Schools, Inc. (Acres Homes program); University of Texas M.D. Anderson Cancer Center (Prostate Cancer Research Program)

Most grants awarded to organizations located in Houston.

Typical grant range: $10,000 to $50,000

764
Vivian L. Smith Foundation
1900 W. Loop South, Suite 1050
Houston, TX 77027
(713) 964-6661

Program grants; social service organizations; education; Christian organizations

Grants awarded to organizations located in Texas, with an emphasis in Houston.

Typical grant range: $5,000 to $100,000

765
Strake Foundation
712 Main Street, Suite 3300
Houston, TX 77002
(713) 216-2400

Program grants; youth; minorities; women; disabled; social service organizations; health organizations; education; cultural organizations; Roman Catholic organizations

Grants awarded to organizations located in Texas, with an emphasis in Houston.

Typical grant range: $2,500 to $20,000

766
Swalm Foundation
11511 Katy Freeway, Suite 430
Houston, TX 77079
(281) 497-5280

Program grants; First Baptist Church of Lubbock (employment program for women); Houston Area Women's Center (program for battered women and their children); Catholic Charities (parenting program); Christ Church Cathedral (program grant); Jewish Community Center (Senior Companion Program); Houston Symphony Society (Community Connections Program); Art Museum of Southeast Texas (educational program); Boys and Girls Club (program grant); Girl Scouts (program grant); Association for Citizens with Handicaps (Early Childhood Intervention Program); Houston Hospice (program grant); Friends of Hermann Park (Environmental and Natural Science Education Programs); Houston Independent School District (Even Start Program)

Grants awarded to organizations located in Texas.

Typical grant range: $3,000 to $100,000

767

The Trull Foundation
404 Fourth Street
Palacios, TX 77465
(361) 972-5241

Program grants; social service
organizations; youth; elderly; women;
environment; all levels of education;
community development; cultural
organizations; Protestant organizations

Typical grant range: $500 to $10,000

768

Rachael & Ben Vaughan Foundation
P.O. Box 2233
Austin, TX 78768
(512) 477-4726

Program grants; Friends of the Texas
Historical Commission, Inc. (LaSalle
Shipwreck Project); Austin Museum of
Art, Inc. (summer program for children);
Center for Battered Women (Children's
Therapeutic Program); YWCA (Women's
Enterprise Program); Marywood (African
American Adoption Program); Goodwill
Industries of South Texas, Inc. (Job
Readiness Training and Placement
Services Program); National Wildlife
Federation (wetlands permitting program);
Sabal Palm Audubon Center & Sanctuary
(volunteer program); Seton Fund of the
Daughters of Charity of St. Vincent de
Paul (Diabetes Management Program);
Therapy Pet Pals of Texas, Inc. (program
for animals to visit nursing homes and
other health care organizations); Saint
Edward's University (College Assistance
Migrant Program)

Typical grant range: $500 to $8,000

UTAH

769

**The Katherine W. Dumke and Ezekiel
R. Dumke, Jr. Foundation**
P.O. Box 776
Kaysville, UT 84037
(801) 544-4626

Program grants; youth; education; higher
education; environment; Boys and Girls
Club (after school program); University of
Utah, College of Nursing (EDNET
program)

Typical grant range: $1,000 to $25,000

770

**The George S. and Dolores Dore Eccles
Foundation**
Deseret Building, 12th Floor
79 S. Main Street
Salt Lake City, UT 84111
(801) 246-5336

Program grants; youth; disabled; social
service organizations; cultural
organizations; environment; higher
education

Most grants awarded to organizations
located in Utah.

Typical grant range: $3,000 to $80,000

771

**Herbert I. and Elsa B. Michael
Foundation**
c/o U.S. Bank
15 West South Temple, Suite 200
Salt Lake City, UT 84101
(801) 534-6085

Program grants; youth; social service
organizations; education; Legal Aid
Society (program grant)

Grants awarded to organizations located
in Utah.

Typical grant range: $1,000 to $10,000

772
Dr. W. C. Swanson Family Foundation
2955 Harrison Blvd., Suite 201
Ogden, UT 84403
(801) 392-0360

Program grants; social service
organizations; child welfare; education;
cultural organizations

Most grants awarded to organizations
located in Utah, with an emphasis in
Weber County.

VERMONT

773
Lamson-Howell Foundation
R.D. 2, Box 48
Randolph, VT 05060

Program grants; cultural organizations;
education; higher education; youth;
Vermont Symphony Orchestra (program
grant)

Grants awarded to organizations located
in the Randolph vicinity.

Typical grant range: $500 to $5,000

774
Lintilhac Foundation
886 North Gate Road
Shelburne, VT 05482
(802) 985-4106

Program grants; Flynn Theatre
(performing arts program for school
children); Vermont Historical Society
(Vermont History Day Program); The
Nature Conservancy (Natural Area
Interpretive Project); Sara Holbrook
Community Center (preschool program);
Central Vermont Adult Basic Education
(program grant); Lyman C. Hunt Middle
School (music literacy and composition
program); Shelburne Community School
(Music Keyboarding Program); South
Burlington High School (Humanities and
Technology Work Station Project)

Typical grant range: $500 to $10,000

775
Merchants Bank Foundation, Inc.
c/o Merchants Bank
P.O. Box 1009
Burlington, VT 05402-1009

Program grants; youth; education; social
service organizations; health organizations

Grants awarded to organizations located
in Vermont.

Typical grant range: $250 to $5,000

776
The Vermont Community Foundation
P.O. Box 30
Middlebury, VT 05753
(802) 388-3355

Program grants; Bonnyvale
Environmental Education Center, Inc.
(equipment loan program); American
Farmland Trust (farmland conservation
program); VINS North Branch Nature
Center (environmental education program
for teenagers); Gilman Housing Trust
(pilot program); Vermont Campaign to
End Childhood Hunger (project grant);
Vermont CARES (HIV prevention
program); Vermont Museum of Natural
History (program grant); Women's Small
Business Program (business training
program); Retired & Senior Volunteer
Program (exercise program); Milton
Family Community Center (infant and
toddler program); Middlebury Teen
Empowerment (project to train youth
organizers)

Grants awarded to organizations located
in Vermont.

Typical grant range: $2,000 to $7,500

VIRGINIA

777
Beazley Foundation, Inc.
3720 Brighton Street
Portsmouth, VA 23707
(757) 393-1605

Program grants; youth; disabled; social
service organizations; community
development; education; cultural
organizations; health organizations;
American Lung Association (educational
program)

Most grants awarded to organizations
located in the South Hampton Roads
vicinity.

Typical grant range: $5,000 to $75,000

778
The Community Foundation Serving Richmond & Central Virginia
7325 Beaufont Springs Drive, Suite 210
Richmond, VA 23225-5546
(804) 330-7400

Program grants; youth; homeless;
disabled; social service organizations;
community development; education;
cultural organizations

Grants awarded to organizations located
in the Richmond vicinity and central
Virginia.

779
Mars Foundation
6885 Elm Street
McLean, VA 22101
(703) 821-4900

Program grants; John F. Kennedy Center
for the Performing Arts (educational
program); Arlington Symphony (program
to provide tickets to students); Girl Scout
Council (camping program); Boy Scouts
of America (camping program); World
Wildlife Fund (education project);
Humane Society (program grant); Mid-
Atlantic Multicultural Alliance (teacher
training program); IONA Senior Services
(program grant); Student Conservation
Association, Inc. (volunteer service
program); Arlington Community
Temporary Shelter, Inc. (program for
abused or homeless women); Church of
the Epiphany (Sunday breakfast program);
Columbia Road Health Services (health
care program); Samaritan Inns, Inc.
(program for homeless addicts and
alcoholics); Reading Connection
(children's reading program at shelters);
Virginia Foundation for Independent
Colleges (Fund for the Future program)

Typical grant range: $1,000 to $20,000

780
Mitsubishi Electric America Foundation
1560 Wilson Blvd., Suite 1150
Arlington, VA 22209-2409
(703) 276-8240

Program grants; Youth Service America
(volunteer program); Paul Hearne
Leadership Awards (program for young
leaders who are disabled); Gallaudet
University (national training program)

Most grants awarded to organizations
located in areas of company operations
(Mitsubishi Electric Corp.).

781
The Norfolk Foundation
One Commercial Place, Suite 1410
Norfolk, VA 23510
(757) 622-7951

Program grants; Virginia Air & Space Center (educational program); The Children's Center (Early Head Start program); CIVIC Leadership Institute (community leadership program); Chesapeake Bay Foundation (Oyster Aquaculture Program); Norfolk State University (honors program); Old Dominion University, Diehn Center for Fine Arts and Performing Arts (residency program)

Grants awarded to organizations located in the Norfolk vicinity.

Typical grant range: $5,000 to $75,000

782
The Portsmouth Community Foundation
P.O. Box 1394
Portsmouth, VA 23705
(757) 397-5424

Program grants; Girl Scout Council (program grant); Portsmouth Public Library (program for youth); Portsmouth Educare Project (program to diagnose depression in the elderly)

Grants awarded to organizations located in the Portsmouth vicinity.

Typical grant range: $500 to $5,000

783
C.E. Richardson Benevolent Foundation
P.O. Box 1120
Pulaski, VA 24301
(540) 980-6628

Program grants; women; youth; disabled; cultural organizations; higher education; Women's Resource Center (domestic violence and sexual assault program); Virginia Mountain Housing, Inc. (program for homeless women and children); YMCA (program grant); Camp Virginia Jaycee, Inc. (respite program for people who are mentally disabled); Pulaski County 4-H (educational program); Science Museum of Western Virginia (educational program); American Red Cross (Youth Services and Emergency Disaster Relief Program)

Most grants awarded to organizations located in Virginia.

Typical grant range: $1,000 to $10,000

784
Robins Foundation
P.O. Box 1124
Richmond, VA 23218
(804) 697-6917

Program grants; First Baptist Church (Rites of Passage program for teenage boys); Commonwealth Girl Scout Council (program grant); Action Alliance for Virginia's Children and Youth (Kids Count project); Friends Association for Children (Community Leadership Development Program); Preservation Alliance (program for endangered historic places); Metropolitan Junior Baseball League (educational program); University of Richmond (Living and Learning Leadership program)

Most grants awarded to organizations located in Virginia.

Typical grant range: $10,000 to $100,000

785

The Virginia Beach Foundation
P.O. Box 4629
Virginia Beach, VA 23454
(757) 422-5249

Program grants; Edmarc Hospice for
Children (bereavement program); YMCA
(leadership program); Boy Scouts of
America (program grant); Easter Seals
(recreation program); Making a
Difference Foundation (Hispanic outreach
program); Virginia Beach Ballet (dance
program); Young Audiences (music
appreciation project); Virginia Zoological
Society (Zoo to You Program); Help and
Emergency Response (program
concerning domestic violence at the
workplace)

Grants awarded to organizations located
in the Virginia Beach vicinity.

Typical grant range: $500 to $2,000

786

Virginia Environmental Endowment
Three James Center
1051 East Cary Street, Suite 1400
Richmond, VA 23219
(804) 644-5000

Program grants; Hoffler Creek Wildlife
Foundation (Public Environmental
Education Program); The Wintergreen
Nature Foundation (Stream Monitoring
Project); Virginia Department of
Environmental Quality (Virginia Oyster
Heritage Program); Virginia Institute of
Marine Science (Oyster Gardener
Monitoring Project); The Potomac
Conservancy (Potomac Watershed
Protection Program); Western Virginia
Land Trust (project grant); Friends of the
North Fork of the Shenandoah River
(Headwaters Education Program);
Smithsonian Institution Conservation &
Research Center (Forest Biodiversity
Project); Grundy High School (Slate
Creek Project); The George Washington
University (Loudoun County
Environmental Indicators Project)

Typical grant range: $1,000 to $50,000

787

Washington Forrest Foundation
2300 S. Ninth Street
Arlington, VA 22204
(703) 920-3688

Program grants; Voyager Reading
Program; Arlington Young Fathers
Program; Wakefield Band Instrumental
Music Education Program; 4-H Character
Club (camp program for youth); Arlington
Public Schools (photography project);
Child Development Center of Northern
Virginia (playgroup project); Bethany
House (family assistance program);
United Methodist Homes (Samaritan
Program)

Grants awarded to organizations located
in northern Virginia, with an emphasis in
south Arlington.

Typical grant range: $500 to $15,000

WASHINGTON

788

The Bullitt Foundation, Inc.
1212 Minor Avenue
Seattle, WA 98101
(206) 343-0807

Program grants; Kettle Range
Conservation Group (project to protect the
wilderness); Cold Spring Conservancy
(project to protect ancient forest);
Groundworks Institute (Citizens for
Environmental Education project); Land
Conservancy (project to protect habitats
along streams and rivers); Audubon
Society (project to secure permanent
protection of land); Northwest Natural
Resource Group (forest management
project); Olympic Environmental Council
(cleanup monitoring project); Puget
Sound Farm Trust (project to protect
farmland for future generations)

Typical grant range: $10,000 to $60,000

789

Ben B. Cheney Foundation, Inc.
1201 Pacific Avenue, Suite 1600
Tacoma, WA 98402
(253) 572-2442

Program grants; youth; elderly; disabled;
social service organizations; education;
cultural organizations; health
organizations

Typical grant range: $2,000 to $50,000

790

**Greater Wenatchee Community
Foundation**
Seven N. Wenatchee Avenue, Suite 201
P.O. Box 3332
Wenatchee, WA 98807
(509) 663-7716

Program grants; youth; elderly; women;
health organizations; education; cultural
organizations; community development;
Children's Discovery Museum (summer
program)

Typical grant range: $500 to $5,000

791

Horizons Foundation
4020 E. Madison Street, Suite 322
Seattle, WA 98112
(206) 323-8061

Program grants; environment; women;
domestic violence; sexual assault; social
service organizations; cultural
organizations

Most grants awarded to organizations
located in Washington, with an emphasis
on the Puget Sound vicinity.

792

**Florence B. Kilworth Charitable
Foundation**
c/o KeyTrust Company
P.O. Box 11500, MS: WA31-01-0310
Tacoma, WA 98411-5052
(253) 305-7215

Program grants; social service
organizations; youth; education;
recreation; cultural organizations

Most grants awarded to organizations
located in Tacoma and in Pierce County.

Typical grant range: $1,000 to $10,000

793

Medina Foundation
1300 Norton Building
801 Second Avenue, 13th Floor
Seattle, WA 98104
(206) 464-5231

Program grants; women; disabled; youth;
elderly; meal programs; social service
organizations; education; community
development

Grants awarded to organizations located
in the Puget Sound vicinity.

Typical grant range: $500 to $25,000

794

Northwest Fund for the Environment
1904 3rd Avenue, Suite 615
Seattle, WA 98101
(206) 386-7220

Program grants; Friends of the Earth
(Puget Sound Salmon Recovery Project);
Northwest Environmental Advocates
(restoration project); Environmental
Media Services (project grant); Lake
Forest Park Stewardship Foundation
(Brookside Creek Headwaters Protection
Project); Western Environmental Law
Center (Confined Animal Feeding
Operation and Pollution Control Project)

Grants awarded to organizations located
in Washington.

Typical grant range: $5,000 to $20,000

795
Wasmer Foundation
422 West Riverside, Suite 1100
Spokane, WA 99201
(509) 624-5265

Program grants; higher education; cultural organizations; youth; social service organizations; Cancer Patient Care (home outreach program); Spokane Art School (program grant); Central Washington University (music program)

Typical grant range: $1,000 to $20,000

WEST VIRGINIA

796
Beckley Area Foundation, Inc.
129 Main Street, Suite 203
Beckley, WV 25801
(304) 253-3806

Program grants; youth; women; social service organizations; education; cultural organizations; community development; American Cancer Society (emergency fund program); Raleigh Co. School Service Personnel Association (school bus safety education project)

Grants awarded to organizations located in the Beckley vicinity.

Typical grant range: $1,000 to $5,000

797
James B. Chambers Memorial
P.O. Box 3047
Wheeling, WV 26003
(304) 243-9373

Program grants; youth; social service organizations; education; recreation; health organizations; YMCA (program grant)

Most grants awarded to organizations located in the Wheeling vicinity.

Typical grant range: $500 to $20,000

798
Clay Foundation, Inc.
1426 Kanawha Blvd., East
Charleston, WV 25301
(304) 344-8656

Program grants; cultural organizations; youth; all levels of education

Grants awarded to organizations located in West Virginia, with an emphasis in the greater Kanawha Valley vicinity.

Typical grant range: $5,000 to $60,000

799
Daywood Foundation, Inc.
1600 Bank One Center
Charleston, WV 25301
(304) 345-8900

Program grants; Covenant House, Inc. (emergency assistance program); Girl Scout Council (camping program); Boy Scouts of America (program grant); YWCA (program grant); American National Red Cross (program grant); Children's Home Society (program grant); Family Refuge Center (program grant); Fund for the Arts (program grant); Greenbrier County Library (program grant); National Youth Science Camp (program grant); Education Alliance, Inc. (educational improvement program)

Grants awarded to organizations located in Kanawha, Greenbrier and Barbour Counties.

Typical grant range: $2,000 to $50,000

800

The Greater Kanawha Valley Foundation

P.O. Box 3041
Charleston, WV 25331-3041
(304) 346-3620

Program grants; Big Brothers/Big Sisters (mentoring program); YWCA (program for abused women); Girl Scout Council (program grant); Sunrise Museum (educational program); Valley Christian Assembly (food program); West Virginia Welfare Reform Coalition (welfare to work program); Gauley Bridge Community Center (nutrition program for the elderly); The Salvation Army (program grant); Putnam County Humane Society, Inc. (program grant); Putnam County Community Action Council, Inc. (in-school reading program); Belvil Elementary School (Accelerated Reader Program); Pinch Elementary School (after school reading program); West Virginia University School of Nursing (graduate nursing program)

Grants awarded to organizations located in the Greater Kanawha Valley.

Typical grant range: $1,500 to $10,000

801

Parkersburg Area Community Foundation

P.O. Box 1762
Parkersburg, WV 26102
(304) 428-4438

Program grants; youth; disabled; social service organizations; education; community development; health organizations; MOV Symphony Society (school project); Volunteer Action Center (Family Matters Program); Alzheimer's Association (Getting Started Program)

Grants awarded to organizations located in the Parkersburg vicinity.

Typical grant range: $1,000 to $5,000

WISCONSIN

802

Judd S. Alexander Foundation, Inc.

500 Third Street, Suite 320
P.O. Box 2137
Wausau, WI 54402
(715) 845-4556

Program grants; all levels of education; disabled; youth; social service organizations; health organizations; community development; cultural organizations

Grants awarded to organizations located in Marathon County.

Typical grant range: $1,000 to $30,000

803

Helen Bader Foundation, Inc.

233 N. Water Street
Milwaukee, WI 53202
(414) 224-6464

Program grants; dementia; youth; minorities; disabled; education; community development; cultural organizations; social service organizations; Capital Christian Center, Inc. (child care program); Mount Olive Evangelical Lutheran Church (adult day care program); Athletes for Youth, Inc. (basketball program); Matt Talbot Recovery Center, Inc. (employment program for people in a substance abuse program); Legal Aid Society (program for free legal service); United Performing Arts Fund, Inc. (program grant); All Saints Catholic Church (after school tutoring program); Milwaukee Public Schools (Waterford Early Reading program); University of Wisconsin Foundation (dementia care program)

Most grants awarded to organizations located in the Milwaukee vicinity.

Typical grant range: $5,000 to $100,000

804

The Lynde and Harry Bradley Foundation, Inc.
P.O. Box 510860
Milwaukee, WI 53203
(414) 291-9915

Program grants; Center for Blind and Visually Impaired Children (educational program); Alliance for Children and Families (project grant); Council for Spanish Speaking (program for youth); American Diabetes Association (program grant); Encounter for Culture and Education (book program); Engineers and Scientists of Milwaukee (Career Guidance Program); F.A.C.E. Foundation (Gang Related Tattoo Removal Program)

Typical grant range: $5,000 to $150,000

805

L.C. Christensen Charitable and Religious Foundation, Inc.
c/o Hostak, Henzl & Bichler, S.C.
P.O. Box 516
Racine, WI 53401
(262) 632-7541

Program grants; community development; education; youth; social service organizations; Protestant organizations; YMCA (program grant)

Grants awarded to organizations located in Racine and Abbotsford, Wisconsin.

Typical grant range: $500 to $3,000

806

Community Foundation for the Fox Valley Region, Inc.
P.O. Box 563
Appleton, WI 54912
(920) 830-1290

Program grants; Boys & Girls Club (after school program); Big Brothers/Big Sisters (mentoring program); Goodwill Industries (program grant); Habitat for Humanity (program grant); Attic Theater (program for children); American Red Cross (project grant); Family Service Association (project to assist trauma and torture survivors); Financial Information Service Center (program assisting homeless families); Wisconsin Center for Academically Talented Youth (Accelerated Learning Program); Fremont Elementary School (School, Family, Community Partnership Program)

Grants awarded to organizations located in the Fox Valley vicinity.

Typical grant range: $2,500 to $10,000

807

Madison Community Foundation
615 E. Washington Avenue
P.O. Box 71
Madison, WI 53701
(608) 255-0503

Program grants; cultural organizations; youth; elderly; minorities; social service organizations; environment; education; community development; Urban League (Fatherhood Responsibility Project); Opera for the Young (artist-in-residency program); Youth Basketball (program grant); Alzheimer's Association (program grant); African American Ethnic Academy (program for students in kindergarten through 8th grade); James C. Wright Middle School (Summer Inspiration Program)

Grants awarded to organizations located in the Madison vicinity.

808
Faye McBeath Foundation
1020 North Broadway
Milwaukee, WI 53202
(414) 272-2626

Program grants; Big Brothers/Big Sisters (mentoring program); S.E.T. Ministry, Inc. (program grant); Betty Brinn Children's Museum (Tot Time program); African American Children's Theatre (program grant); Wisconsin AIDS Fund (AIDS prevention program); Community Advocates (health project); Mental Health Association (mentor training program); Badger Association of the Blind (summer program); Notre Dame Middle School (after school program); Marva Collins Preparatory School of Wisconsin (program grant)

Grants awarded to organizations located in Wisconsin, with an emphasis in Milwaukee.

Typical grant range: $5,000 to $50,000

809
Milwaukee Foundation
1020 North Broadway
Milwaukee, WI 53202
(414) 272-5805

Program grants; Skylight Opera Theatre (education program); Ko-Thi Dance Company (education program); Milwaukee Public Theatre (youth project); Very Special Arts (program for children and adults who are disabled); Housing Resources, Inc. (home buyer counseling program); Wisconsin Humane Society (pet owner education program); YMCA (Milwaukee Mentors project); Project Equality of Wisconsin (Equal Employment Opportunity Program); Catholic Charities (day care program for adults); Family Service of Waukesha (education and counseling program); Our Next Generation, Inc. (after school and summer education program); Milwaukee Public Schools (recreation and education program); Medical College of Wisconsin (Reach Out and Read Program)

Grants awarded to organizations located in the Milwaukee vicinity.

Typical grant range: $1,000 to $40,000

810

The Northwestern Mutual Foundation, Inc.
720 E. Wisconsin Avenue
Milwaukee, WI 53202
(414) 299-2200

Program grants; Outreach for Women Program (program grant); Camp Heartland (program for children who have AIDS); The Milwaukee Council on Alcoholism and Drug Dependence (educational program); Milwaukee Art Museum (educational program); Wisconsin Lake Schooner's Maritime Education Center (educational program); Milwaukee Teacher Education Center (program grant); Notre Dame Middle School (after school tutoring program for Hispanic students)

Most grants awarded to organizations located in Milwaukee.

Typical grant range: $5,000 to $100,000

811

Jane B. Pettit Foundation, Inc.
660 E. Mason Street
Milwaukee, WI 53202
(414) 271-5900

Program grants; disabled; youth; women; social service organizations; health organizations; cultural organizations

Grants awarded to organizations located in Milwaukee.

Typical grant range: $1,000 to $150,000

812

A.O. Smith Foundation, Inc.
P.O. Box 23971
Milwaukee, WI 53223
(414) 359-4042

Program grants; Discovery World Museum (educational program); American Players Theater (educational program); YMCA (Black Achievers Program); Boy Scouts of America (leadership recognition program); Audubon Center (contribute to the preservation of wildlife programs); Zoological Society (science and environmental education program); American Cancer Society (Relay for Life program); American Lung Association (children's asthma research program); Children's Hospital Foundation (school-based health program); Center for the Deaf & Hard of Hearing (summer program); Impact-Alcohol & Other Drug Abuse Services (program grant); Salvation Army (program grant); Second Harvest (food program); Engineers & Scientists of Milwaukee (career guidance program); Literacy Services of Wisconsin (adult literacy program); Marquette High School (educational program)

Grants awarded to organizations located in areas of company operations (A.O. Smith Corporation).

813
Wausau Area Community Foundation, Inc.
500 Third Street, Suite 316
Wausau, WI 54403
(715) 845-9555

Program grants; Central Wisconsin Children's Theatre (All the World's a Stage project); Bridging the Gap Storytellers (storyteller program for preschoolers); 4-H Leaders Federation (Marathon County Horse Mentors Program); Marathon Youth Services (home improvement project for at-risk youth); Wausau and Marathon County Parks Foundation (playground program); Junior Achievement (program for elementary school students); Edgar Public School (environmental project); St. Paul School (Artist-in-Residence Program)

Grants awarded to organizations located in the Wausau vicinity.

814
Ruth St. John & John Dunham West Foundation, Inc.
980 Maritime Drive, Unit 5
Manitowoc, WI 54220
(920) 684-6110

Program grants; Wisconsin Association of Homes and Communities (First Book Program); Lutheran Social Services (program grant); Manitowoc Symphony Orchestra (program grant); Rahr-West Art Museum (program grant); Domestic Violence Center (transitional living program); Lakeland College (Hmong Teaching Project and Technology Program)

Grants awarded to organizations located in Manitowoc County.

Typical grant range: $1,000 to $100,000

WYOMING

815
Community Foundation of Jackson Hole
P.O. Box 574
Jackson, WY 83001
(307) 739-1026

Program grants; cultural organizations; social service organizations; environment; all levels of education; disabled; Cultural Council of Jackson Hole (project grant); Teton Literacy Program (Summer Remedial Reading Program); Jackson Hole Middle School (Focus on Success Program)

Grants awarded to organizations located in Teton County.

Typical grant range: $500 to $5,000

816
Willard H. Moyer Foundation
P.O. Box 801
Powell, WY 82435
(307) 754-2962

Program grants; youth; community development; cultural organizations

Grants awarded to organizations located in Powell.

817
Myra Fox Skelton Trust Foundation
c/o Wells Fargo Bank, Trust Department
P.O. Box 2799
Casper, WY 82602
(307) 235-7739

Program grants; secondary and higher education; social service organizations

Most grants awarded to organizations located in Casper.

Index to Foundations

(Alphabetical)

Citations are by entry number

G

Gage (Philip and Irene Toll) Foundation, 209

GAR Foundation, 607

Garland (John Jewett and H. Chandler) Fdn., 49

Gates Family Foundation, 131

Gazette Foundation, 281

Gebbie Foundation, Inc., 533

Gellert (Carl) and Celia Berta Gellert Foundation, 50

Gellert (Fred) Family Foundation, 51

General Mills Foundation, 409

General Motors Foundation, Inc., 373

GenRad Foundation, 339

George Foundation, 749

Georgia Health Foundation, 210

Gerber Foundation, 374

Gerbode (Wallace Alexander) Foundation, 52

German Protestant Orphan Asylum Association, 309

Gerson (Benjamin S.) Family Foundation, 608

Gheens Foundation, Inc., 300

Gifford (Rosamond) Charitable Corporation, 534

Gilmore (Irving S.) Foundation, 375

Gilmore (William G.) Foundation, 53

Glens Falls Foundation, 535

Goldman (Herman) Foundation, 536

Goldman (Lisa and Douglas) Fund, 54

Goldman (Richard and Rhoda) Fund, 55

Goldseker (Morris) Foundation of Maryland, 323

Gooding (Lucy) Charitable Foundation Trust, 190

Graco Foundation, 410

Graham (Philip L.) Fund, 171

Grand Haven Area Community Foundation, Inc., 376

Grand Rapids Community Foundation, 377

Greater Bridgeport Area Foundation, Inc., 147

Greater Cedar Rapids Community Foundation, 282

Greater Cincinnati Foundation, 609

Greater Harrisburg Foundation, 673

Greater Kanawha Valley Foundation, 800

Greater LaFayette Community Foundation, 266

Greater New Orleans Foundation, 310

Greater Wenatchee Community Foundation, 790

Greater Worcester Community Foundation, Inc., 340

Green (Allen P. and Josephine B.) Foundation, 439

Greenspun Family Foundation, 465

Greystone Foundation, 411

Grotto Foundation, Inc., 412

Gumbiner (Josephine S.) Foundation, 56

Gund (George) Foundation, 610

H

Haas, Jr. (Evelyn and Walter) Fund, 57

Haas (Paul and Mary) Foundation, 750

Haas (Walter and Elise) Fund, 58

Haigh-Scatena Foundation, 59

Hall Family Foundation, 440

Hamilton Community Foundation, Inc., 611

Hammill (Donald D.) Foundation, 751

Hansen (Dane G.) Foundation, 290

Harden Foundation, 60

Harland (John H. and Wilhelmina D.) Charitable Foundation, Inc., 211

Hartford Foundation for Public Giving, 148

Hasbro Charitable Trust, Inc., 708

Hasbro Children's Foundation, 537

Hawkins (Robert Z.) Foundation, 466

Hayswood Foundation, Inc., 301

Health Foundation of Central Massachusetts, 341

Health Foundation of Greater Indianapolis, 267

Hedrick (Frank and Betty) Foundation, 291

Heinz (Howard) Endowment, 674

Heinz (Vira I.) Endowment, 675

Heller (Clarence E.) Charitable Foundation, 61

Helmerich Foundation, 640

Heron (F.B.) Foundation, 538

Heuermann (Bernard K. & Norma F.) Foundation, 458

Hewlett (William and Flora) Foundation, 62

Hillman Foundation, Inc., 676

Hilton Head Island Foundation, Inc., 715

Hitchcock (Gilbert M. and Martha H.) Foundation, 459

Hobbs Foundation, Inc., 324

Hoblitzelle Foundation, 752

Hodges (Mary E.) Fund, 709

Hofmann Foundation, 63

Horizons Foundation, 791

Houston Endowment, Inc., 753

Hoyt (Stewart W. & Willma C.) Foundation, 539

HRK Foundation, 413

Hudson-Webber Foundation, 378

Humboldt Area Foundation, 64

Humphrey (George M. and Pamela S.) Fund, 612

Hunter (A.V.) Trust, Inc., 132

Huston (Stewart) Charitable Trust, 677

Hutchinson Community Foundation, 292

Hyams Foundation, Inc., 342

Hyde and Watson Foundation, 484

I

Idaho Community Foundation, 225

Inasmuch Foundation, 641

Independence Foundation, 678

Indianapolis Foundation, 268

International Multifoods Charitable Foundation, 414

Invacare Foundation, 613

Irvine (James) Foundation, 65

Irwin-Sweeney-Miller Foundation, 269

Island Foundation, Inc., 343

J

Jackson County Community Foundation, 379

Janirve Foundation, 581

Jennings (Martha Holden) Foundation, 614

Jennings (Mary Hillman) Foundation, 679

Jewett (George Frederick) Foundation, 66

Jewish Healthcare Foundation of Pittsburgh, 680

JJJ Foundation, Inc., 133

JM Foundation, 540

Joanna Foundation, 716

Johnson County Community Foundation, 270

Johnson (Helen K. and Arthur E.) Foundation, 134

Johnson (Samuel S.) Foundation, 651

Johnson (Walter S.) Foundation, 67

Jones (Cyrus W. & Amy F.) & Bessie D. Phelps Foundation, Inc., 149

Jones (Daisy Marquis) Foundation, 541

Jones (Fletcher) Foundation, 68

Joslyn (Carl W. and Carrie Mae) Charitable Trust, 135

Jovid Foundation, 172

Joyce Foundation, 243

K

Kalamazoo Community Foundation, 380

Kansas Health Foundation, 293

Kaplan (J.M.) Fund, Inc., 542

Kauffman (Ewing Marion) Foundation, 441

Kaul (Hugh) Foundation, 5

Kavanagh (T. James) Foundation, 681

Keck (W.M.) Foundation, 69

Kelley (Edward Bangs) and Elza Kelley Foundation, Inc., 344

Kelley (Margaret H. and James E.) Foundation, 415

Kellwood Foundation, 442

Kemper (James S.) Foundation, 244

Kempner (Harris and Eliza) Fund, 754

Kerney (James) Foundation, 485

Kerr (Grayce B.) Fund, Inc., 325

Kilworth (Florence B.) Charitable Foundation, 792

King (Kenneth Kendal) Foundation, 136

Kirchgessner (Karl) Foundation, 70

Kline (Josiah W. and Bessie H.) Foundation, Inc., 682

Knight (John S. and James L.) Foundation, 192

Knistrom (Fanny and Svante) Foundation, 486

Knott (Marion I. and Henry J.) Foundation, Inc., 326

Kopp Family Foundation, 416

Koret Foundation, 71

Kulas Foundation, 615

Kutz (Milton and Hattie) Foundation, 159

L

Laffey-McHugh Foundation, 160

Lamson-Howell Foundation, 773

Laurel Foundation, 683

Laurie (Blanche and Irving) Foundation, Inc., 487

Leach (Tom and Frances) Foundation, Inc., 588

Leake (John G.) Charitable Foundation, 19

Lee (Ray M. and Mary Elizabeth) Foundation, Inc., 212

Lee (Sara) Foundation, 245

Lehigh Valley Community Foundation, 684

Leigh (Charles N. & Eleanor Knight) Foundation, Inc., 193

Libra Foundation, 314

Lied Foundation Trust, 467

Lilly Endowment Inc., 271

Lincoln Community Foundation, Inc., 460

Lincoln Financial Group Foundation, Inc., 272

Lindsay (Agnes M.) Trust, 474

Lintilhac Foundation, 774

Long (R.A.) Foundation, 443

Longwood Foundation, Inc., 161

Lost Tree Village Charitable Foundation, Inc., 194

Lubrizol Foundation, 616

Lucas-Spindletop (Anthony Francis) Foundation, 173

Lupin Foundation, 311

Lurie (Louis R.) Foundation, 72

Lux (Miranda) Foundation, 73

Lyndhurst Foundation, 727

M

MacArthur (John D. and Catherine T.) Foundation, 246

Macy, Jr. (Josiah) Foundation, 543

Maddox (J.F.) Foundation, 496

Madison Community Foundation, 807

Madison County Community Foundation, 273

Maine Community Foundation, Inc., 315

Mandell (Samuel P.) Foundation, 685

Marbrook Foundation, 417

Mardag Foundation, 418

Margaret Hall Foundation, Inc., 302

Margoes Foundation, 74

Marin Community Foundation, 75

Marquette Community Foundation, 381

Mars Foundation, 779

Marshall Fund of Arizona, 14

Marshall (George Preston) Foundation, 327

Martin Foundation, Inc., 274

Martin (John G.) Foundation, 150

Mascoma Savings Bank Foundation, 475

Mathile Family Foundation, 617

Maytag (Fred) Family Foundation, 283

McBeath (Faye) Foundation, 808

McCann (James J.) Charitable Trust and McCann Foundation, Inc., 544

McCarthy Family Foundation, 76

McConnell Foundation, 77

McCune Charitable Foundation, 497

McCune Foundation, 686

McDermott (Eugene) Foundation, 755

McElroy (R.J.) Trust, 284

McFeely-Rogers Foundation, 687

McGregor Fund, 382

McIntosh (Alex & Agnes O.) Foundation, 195

McKay Family Foundation, 652

McKenna (Katherine Mabis) Foundation, Inc., 688

McKenna (Philip M.) Foundation, Inc., 689

McKesson Foundation, Inc., 78

Mead (Gilbert and Jaylee) Family Foundation, 174

Meadows Foundation, Inc., 756

Medina Foundation, 793

Medtronic Foundation, 419

Mellon (Richard King) Foundation, 690

Merchants Bank Foundation, Inc., 775

Mericos Foundation, 79

Merrick Foundation, 642

Meyer (Eugene and Agnes E.) Foundation, 175

Meyer Memorial Trust, 653

Michael (Herbert I. and Elsa B.) Foundation, 771

Mid-Iowa Health Foundation, 285

Midland Area Community Foundation, 383

Miller (Howard E. & Nell E.) Charitable Fdn., 691

Mills (Frances Goll) Fund, 384

Milwaukee Foundation, 809

Minneapolis Foundation, 420

Minnesota Mutual Foundation, 421

Mitsubishi Electric America Foundation, 780

Montana Community Foundation, 451

Monterey Peninsula Foundation, 80

Montgomery Foundation, 618

Moody Foundation, 757

Morgan (J.P.) Charitable Trust, 545

Morton-Kelly Charitable Trust, 316

Moss (Finis M.) Charitable Trust, 444

Moyer (Willard H.) Foundation, 816

Mt. Pleasant Area Community Foundation, 385

Mullen (J.K.) Foundation, 137

Murphy Family Foundation, 619

Musgrave Foundation, 445

N

Nagel (John F.) Foundation, Inc., 226

Nalco Foundation, 247

NEC Foundation of America, 546

New Britain Foundation for Public Giving, 151

New Hampshire Charitable Foundation, 476

New York Foundation, 547

New York Times Company Foundation, Inc., 548

Newland Family Foundation, Inc., 213

Nielsen (Aksel) Foundation, 138

Noble County Community Foundation, 275

Noble (Samuel Roberts) Foundation, Inc., 643

Nord Family Foundation, 620

Nordson Corporation Foundation, 621

Norfolk Foundation, 781

Norris (Kenneth T. and Eileen L.) Foundation, 81

North Carolina GlaxoSmithKline Foundation, 582

Northern New York Community Foundation, 549

Northern Trust Company Charitable Trust, 248

Northwest Fund for the Environment, 794

Northwestern Mutual Foundation, Inc., 810

Norton (Peter) Family Foundation, 82

Noyes, Jr. (Nicholas H.) Memorial Foundation, 276

O

O'Neill (William J. and Dorothy K.) Foundation, 622

Ohl, Jr. (George A.) Trust, 488

Oishei (John R.) Foundation, 550

Olin Corporation Charitable Trust, 152

Omaha Community Foundation, 461

Onan Family Foundation, 422

Orange County Community Foundation, 83

Ordean Foundation, 423

Oregon Community Foundation, 654

Outer Banks Community Foundation, Inc., 583

Owen (B.B.) Trust, 758

P

Pacific Life Foundation, 84

Packard (David and Lucile) Foundation, 85

Parker Foundation, 86

Parkersburg Area Community Foundation, 801

Parsons (Ralph M.) Foundation, 87

Peabody (Amelia) Charitable Fund, 345

Peabody (Amelia) Foundation, 346

Pella Rolscreen Foundation, 286

Peninsula Community Foundation, 88

Penn (William) Foundation, 692

Peoria Area Community Foundation, 249

Perpetual Trust for Charitable Giving, 347

Pettit (Jane B.) Foundation, Inc., 811

Pew Charitable Trusts, 693

Philadelphia Foundation, 694

Phillips (Dr. P.) Foundation, 196

Phillips (Jay and Rose) Family Foundation, 424

Pierce (Harold Whitworth) Charitable Trust, 349

Pillsbury Company Foundation, 425

Pinkerton Foundation, 551

Pittsburgh Foundation, 695

Plough Foundation, 728

PNC Charitable Trust, 696

PNM Foundation, Inc., 498

Polk Bros. Foundation, Inc., 250

Portland Foundation, 277

Portsmouth Community Trust, 782

PPG Industries Foundation, 697

Prentiss (Elisabeth Severance) Foundation, 623

Price (John E. & Aliese) Foundation, Inc., 197

Price (T. Rowe) Associates Foundation, Inc., 328

Princeton Area Community Foundation, Inc., 489

Principal Financial Group Foundation, Inc., 287

Prospect Hill Foundation, Inc., 552

Prudential Foundation, 490

Public Welfare Foundation, Inc., 176

Publix Super Markets Charities, 198

Puerto Rico Community Foundation, 706

Puterbaugh Foundation, 644

Putnam Foundation, 477

Q

Quaker Oats Foundation, 251

R

Rachofsky (Howard Earl) Foundation, 759

Ralphs-Food 4 Less Foundation, 89

Rapp (Robert Glenn) Foundation, 645

Raskob Foundation for Catholic Activities, Inc., 162

Rasmuson Foundation, 9

Ratshesky (A.C.) Foundation, 350

Rauch Family Foundation I, Inc., 252

Red Wing Shoe Company Foundation, 426

Redfield (Nell J.) Foundation, 468

Rehmeyer (Herbert M.) Trust, 698

Reinhold (Paul E. & Klare N.) Foundation, Inc., 199

Retirement Research Foundation, 253

Reynolds (Donald W.) Foundation, 469

Reynolds (Kate B.) Charitable Trust, 584

Reynolds (Z. Smith) Foundation, Inc., 585

Rhode Island Foundation, 710

Rice (Ethel and Raymond F.) Foundation, 294

Rice (Helen Steiner) Foundation, 624

Rich Foundation, Inc., 214

Richardson (C.E.) Benevolent Foundation, 783

Richardson (Sid W.) Foundation, 760

Richland County Foundation, 625

Riley (Mabel Louise) Foundation, 351

Riordan Foundation, 90

Rippel (Fannie E.) Foundation, 491

Roberts Foundation, 91

Robins Foundation, 784

Rochester Area Community Foundation, 553

Rockwell Fund, Inc., 761

Rosenberg Foundation, 92

Rosenberg (William J. and Tina) Foundation, 200

Ross (Dorothea Haus) Foundation, 554

Ross Foundation, 20

Rubinstein (Helena) Foundation, Inc., 555

Index to Foundations

(Subject Index)

Citations are by entry number

AIDS—2, 14, 28, 33, 37, 40, 42, 60, 75, 76, 87, 93, 95, 104, 116, 134, 143, 146, 165, 176, 221, 230, 241, 242, 248, 285, 340, 342, 363, 394, 401, 413, 437, 473, 475, 490, 523, 524, 542, 543, 555, 556, 567, 571, 579, 584, 595, 600, 606, 632, 636, 640, 653, 680, 692, 693, 706, 709, 736, 750, 752, 756, 776, 808, 810

ANIMAL WELFARE—7, 10, 14, 45, 47, 73, 91, 103, 107, 109, 115, 129, 140, 170, 180, 183, 190, 231, 270, 271, 294, 343, 369, 396, 397, 424, 451, 497, 499, 501, 507, 511, 521, 522, 540, 551, 552, 560, 572, 581, 651, 653, 659, 682, 692, 718, 733, 746, 753, 768, 779, 786, 794, 800, 809, 812

COMMUNITY DEVELOPMENT—1, 4, 5, 11, 20, 30, 32, 40, 48, 58, 64, 65, 67, 81, 84, 92, 93, 97, 99, 118, 119, 125, 126, 127, 129, 132, 134, 143, 144, 146, 147, 149, 156, 158, 167, 168, 169, 176, 177, 184, 188, 191, 208, 215, 217, 230, 234, 240, 242, 246, 248, 249, 251, 254, 255, 256, 257, 258, 261, 267, 268, 269, 270, 273, 275, 277, 282, 284, 286, 287, 292, 308, 315, 318, 319, 321, 322, 323, 326, 328, 329, 330, 335, 336, 351, 354, 357, 358, 367, 368, 370, 371, 373, 375, 376, 378, 379, 380, 383, 384, 385, 386, 388, 398, 399, 400, 402, 409, 410, 412, 418, 420, 424, 428, 435, 436, 440, 444, 445, 461, 463, 465, 466, 473, 481, 483, 485, 504, 507, 508, 513, 514, 515, 517, 518, 519, 524, 531, 542, 545, 547, 549, 556, 558, 559, 561, 564, 566, 568, 576, 577, 578, 587, 596, 597, 599, 601, 604, 606, 610, 613, 617, 619, 620, 622, 631, 633, 637, 644, 653, 657, 669, 672, 674, 676, 681, 684, 686, 688, 695, 696, 698, 699, 702, 704, 705, 706, 711, 713, 715, 716, 717, 718, 720, 723, 725, 726, 737, 738, 739, 754, 762, 767, 776, 777, 778, 783, 784, 790, 793, 796, 801, 802, 803, 805, 807, 809, 816

CULTURAL ORGANIZATIONS—1, 3, 4, 5, 6, 9, 11, 12, 13, 15, 23, 24, 25, 26, 27, 28, 29, 31, 32, 36, 38, 39, 40, 42, 43, 44, 45, 46, 47, 51, 52, 53, 56, 57, 58, 60, 61, 62, 63, 64, 65, 66, 67, 68, 69, 71, 72, 73, 74, 75, 78, 79, 81, 83, 84, 85, 86, 87, 88, 89, 90, 93, 94, 103, 105, 107, 108, 109, 111, 112, 113, 114, 115, 116, 117, 119, 120, 121, 122, 124, 125, 126, 128, 129, 130, 134, 136, 138, 139, 140, 141, 142, 143, 144, 145, 146, 148, 149, 150, 151, 153, 155, 156, 158, 161, 163, 165, 166, 167, 169, 170, 171, 172, 174, 175, 176, 177, 178, 179, 180, 182, 183, 184, 185, 186, 187, 188, 189, 191, 192, 193, 194, 195, 196, 198, 199, 200, 203, 205, 207, 208, 209, 211, 212, 214, 219, 221, 222, 223, 224, 225, 227, 228, 230, 233, 234, 235, 236, 238, 239, 240, 241, 242, 243, 244, 245, 246, 247, 248, 250, 253, 255, 256, 257, 258, 259, 260, 261, 262, 264, 265, 266, 268, 269, 271, 272, 273, 274, 275, 276, 277, 280, 281, 282, 283, 284, 286, 287, 288, 289, 294, 295, 296, 297, 298, 299, 300, 302, 303, 305, 306, 307, 308, 310, 311, 314, 315, 316, 317, 319, 322, 325, 326, 327, 328, 329, 330, 331, 332, 335, 336, 337, 338, 339, 340, 342, 343, 344, 345, 349, 350, 351, 355, 356, 358, 359, 362, 363, 364, 365, 366, 367, 368, 369, 370, 371, 372, 373, 375, 377, 378, 379, 382, 386, 387, 388, 391, 392, 393, 394, 395, 397, 398, 399, 401, 403, 404, 405, 406, 407, 408, 409, 411, 412, 414, 415, 417, 419, 420, 421, 422, 424, 428, 430, 431, 432, 433, 435, 437, 438, 440, 441, 443, 446, 447, 450, 451, 452, 453, 454, 455, 457, 459, 460, 463, 464, 465, 467, 470, 471, 476, 477, 482, 484, 485, 487, 489, 490, 492, 494, 495, 496, 497, 499, 500, 501, 502, 503, 504, 505, 507, 508, 509, 510, 511, 512, 513, 514, 515, 516, 517, 518, 519, 521, 522, 523, 525, 527, 528, 529, 530, 531, 533, 534, 536, 539, 541, 542, 544, 545, 548, 549, 550, 551, 552, 553, 555, 557, 558, 560, 561, 563, 565, 566, 568, 569, 570, 571, 572, 573, 575, 576, 577, 578, 580, 581, 583, 585, 586, 587, 588, 589, 590, 591, 593, 594, 595, 596, 597, 598,

599, 601, 602, 604, 605, 607, 608, 609, 610, 611, 612, 613, 614, 615, 616, 619, 620, 621, 622, 625, 628, 629, 630, 631, 632, 633, 634, 636, 638, 640, 641, 643, 646, 648, 649, 650, 651, 653, 654, 655, 656, 657, 658, 659, 660, 661, 663, 664, 665, 666, 667, 669, 670, 671, 672, 674, 675, 676, 677, 678, 679, 681, 682, 683, 684, 685, 686, 687, 688, 689, 690, 691, 692, 693, 694, 695, 696, 697, 698, 699, 703, 704, 705, 706, 710, 713, 715, 717, 718, 719, 720, 721, 722, 725, 728, 730, 731, 732, 733, 734, 735, 736, 737, 738, 739, 740, 742, 743, 744, 745, 746, 747, 748, 750, 752, 753, 755, 756, 757, 759, 760, 761, 762, 765, 766, 767, 768, 770, 772, 773, 774, 776, 777, 778, 779, 783, 784, 785, 787, 789, 790, 791, 792, 795, 796, 798, 799, 800, 801, 802, 803, 804, 806, 807, 808, 809, 810, 811, 812, 813, 814, 815, 816

DISABLED—1, 3, 5, 6, 10, 11, 12, 13, 16, 18, 19, 24, 27, 32, 33, 35, 39, 43, 44, 49, 50, 58, 60, 63, 64, 66, 70, 71, 74, 78, 81, 83, 84, 86, 88, 89, 93, 96, 97, 101, 104, 107, 109, 110, 111, 116, 117, 118, 119, 120, 121, 123, 125, 126, 130, 132, 133, 134, 135, 136, 137, 138, 140, 146, 148, 149, 151, 153, 157, 158, 160, 161, 163, 165, 167, 169, 170, 171, 176, 180, 181, 182, 184, 185, 187, 190, 191, 197, 198, 204, 205, 210, 216, 217, 219, 220, 222, 224, 228, 229, 230, 231, 234, 246, 247, 250, 253, 260, 264, 268, 271, 272, 283, 285, 287, 290, 292, 298, 300, 304, 306, 310, 311, 312, 318, 321, 324, 326, 327, 331, 332, 335, 336, 338, 340, 342, 345, 351, 352, 354, 364, 365, 369, 370, 373, 374, 375, 376, 379, 380, 382, 388, 392, 395, 398, 399, 402, 403, 406, 407, 408, 409, 410, 416, 423, 424, 428, 430, 433, 437, 439, 448, 450, 454, 458, 461, 464, 468, 474, 475, 476, 484, 486, 487, 489, 494, 495, 497, 499, 500, 505, 507, 513, 515, 518, 520, 521, 522, 523, 524, 525, 527, 529, 530, 535, 536, 539, 540, 546, 547, 548, 549, 550, 554, 556, 571, 577, 584, 590, 592, 596, 597, 598, 599, 601, 605, 607, 609, 612, 613, 614, 616, 620, 621, 622, 624, 627, 630, 632, 638, 641, 646, 647, 649, 650, 654, 655, 657, 659, 664, 666, 667, 673, 675, 676, 678, 679, 681, 682, 686, 688, 694, 695, 696, 697, 701, 702, 715, 717, 723, 726, 734, 737, 739, 741, 743, 744, 747, 748, 749, 751, 752, 753, 758, 760, 761, 765, 766, 768, 770, 777, 778, 780, 783, 785, 789, 793, 801, 802, 803, 804, 806, 808, 809, 811, 812, 815

EDUCATION (other than higher education)—1, 2, 3, 4, 5, 6, 7, 8, 9, 10, 11, 12, 14, 15, 19, 20, 21, 22, 24, 26, 27, 28, 29, 31, 32, 36, 37, 38, 39, 40, 41, 42, 43, 44, 45, 46, 49, 50, 53, 54, 56, 57, 58, 60, 61, 63, 64, 65, 66, 68, 69, 71, 72, 73, 74, 75, 76, 77, 78, 79, 80, 81, 82, 83, 84, 85, 86, 87, 88, 89, 90, 91, 93, 94, 97, 98, 99, 101, 102, 103, 105, 106, 107, 108, 109, 111, 112, 113, 114, 116, 117, 118, 120, 121, 122, 123, 125, 126, 127, 128, 129, 130, 132, 133, 134, 135, 137, 139, 140, 141, 142, 143, 144, 145, 146, 147, 148, 150, 151, 153, 154, 155, 156, 157, 158, 160, 161, 162, 163, 164, 167, 169, 170, 171, 172, 173, 174, 175, 176, 177, 178, 180, 182, 184, 185, 186, 187, 189, 190, 191, 192, 194, 195, 196, 197, 199, 200, 201, 202, 203, 204, 205, 206, 207, 208, 209, 210, 211, 212, 213, 215, 216, 217, 218, 219, 220, 221, 222, 223, 224, 225, 226, 227, 228, 229, 230, 231, 232, 234, 235, 237, 238, 239, 240, 241, 242, 243, 244, 246, 247, 248, 249, 250, 251, 253, 254, 255, 256, 257, 259, 260, 261, 262, 263, 264, 265, 267, 269, 270, 271, 272, 273, 275, 276, 279, 280, 282, 283, 284, 287, 289, 290, 291, 292, 294, 296, 297, 298, 299, 300, 301, 302, 303, 304, 305, 306, 307, 308, 309, 310, 312, 314, 315, 316, 319, 320, 321, 322, 323, 325, 326, 327, 328, 329, 330, 331, 332, 333, 334, 335, 336, 337, 338, 339, 340, 341, 342, 343, 345, 346, 347, 349, 350, 351, 353, 354, 355, 356, 357, 359, 360, 361, 362, 363, 364, 365, 366, 368, 369, 370, 372, 374, 375, 376, 377, 378, 379, 380, 381, 383, 384, 385, 387, 388, 389, 390, 392, 394, 395, 396, 397, 398, 399, 400, 401, 402, 403, 404, 405, 406, 408, 409, 412, 414, 416, 417, 418, 419, 420, 422, 424, 425, 426, 428, 429, 430, 431, 435, 436, 437, 438, 439, 441, 442, 443, 444, 445, 447, 448, 449, 450, 451, 452, 453, 454, 455, 456, 457, 458, 459, 460, 461, 462, 463, 464, 467, 468, 470, 471, 472, 473, 474, 475, 476, 477, 480, 482, 483, 484, 485, 487, 488, 489, 490, 493, 494, 495, 496, 497, 498, 499, 500, 501, 502, 503, 504, 505, 507, 508, 509, 510, 511, 512, 513, 514, 515, 516, 518, 520, 521, 522, 523, 524, 526, 527, 528, 529, 530, 532, 533, 535, 536, 537, 538, 540, 541, 542, 543, 545, 546, 548, 549, 550, 551, 552, 553, 554, 555, 556, 560, 562, 563, 564, 565, 567, 569, 570, 571, 572, 573, 574, 575, 576, 577, 578, 580, 581, 583, 584, 585, 586, 587, 588, 589, 590, 591, 592, 593, 594, 595, 596, 597, 598, 599, 600, 602, 603, 604, 605, 606, 607, 608, 610, 611, 612, 613, 614, 615, 616, 617, 618, 619, 620,

621, 623, 624, 625, 627, 628, 630, 631, 632, 633, 634, 635, 636, 637, 639, 640, 641, 643, 644, 645, 646, 648, 649, 650, 651, 653, 655, 656, 657, 658, 659, 660, 661, 663, 664, 665, 666, 667, 668, 669, 671, 672, 673, 674, 675, 676, 677, 678, 679, 681, 682, 683, 685, 686, 687, 689, 690, 691, 692, 693, 695, 697, 700, 701, 702, 704, 705, 706, 708, 710, 711, 712, 713, 717, 718, 719, 721, 722, 724, 726, 727, 728, 729, 730, 731, 732, 733, 734, 735, 736, 737, 738, 739, 740, 742, 743, 744, 745, 746, 747, 748, 749, 750, 751, 752, 753, 754, 755, 756, 757, 759, 760, 761, 762, 763, 764, 765, 766, 767, 768, 769, 771, 772, 773, 774, 775, 776, 777, 778, 779, 781, 782, 783, 784, 786, 787, 788, 789, 790, 792, 793, 795, 796, 797, 798, 799, 800, 801, 802, 803, 804, 805, 806, 807, 808, 809, 810, 812, 813, 815, 817

ELDERLY—9, 14, 16, 23, 28, 32, 33, 39, 41, 43, 44, 45, 49, 50, 51, 53, 55, 57, 60, 64, 66, 71, 72, 75, 77, 79, 86, 87, 88, 93, 95, 96, 99, 101, 110, 114, 116, 117, 120, 126, 127, 128, 129, 131, 132, 134, 135, 143, 146, 150, 151, 158, 160, 161, 163, 165, 172, 175, 177, 178, 181, 182, 184, 187, 191, 192, 193, 195, 200, 203, 204, 210, 213, 218, 229, 234, 238, 241, 242, 247, 248, 253, 264, 270, 273, 291, 301, 306, 320, 327, 331, 337, 339, 340, 349, 350, 354, 359, 363, 365, 369, 371, 397, 400, 407, 418, 419, 423, 424, 428, 430, 438, 448, 452, 457, 461, 463, 468, 469, 484, 488, 489, 491, 492, 495, 496, 497, 498, 501, 505, 506, 520, 521, 530, 534, 541, 547, 548, 550, 553, 556, 567, 569, 572, 581, 584, 588, 589, 590, 595, 597, 600, 609, 611, 614, 617, 619, 620, 621, 623, 625, 627, 628, 631, 635, 636, 638, 639, 647, 649, 651, 655, 656, 659, 667, 678, 680, 681, 693, 701, 711, 713, 718, 724, 737, 741, 751, 754, 756, 761, 766, 767, 768, 774, 776, 779, 781, 782, 789, 790, 793, 800, 803, 807, 809, 812

ENVIRONMENT—1, 3, 6, 8, 10, 11, 12, 21, 24, 26, 27, 30, 31, 32, 36, 37, 38, 39, 45, 47, 52, 54, 55, 61, 62, 63, 65, 66, 69, 73, 75, 76, 80, 84, 85, 94, 103, 106, 107, 111, 117, 119, 129, 133, 140, 141, 145, 146, 147, 152, 153, 154, 157, 163, 165, 170, 177, 178, 182, 185, 189, 193, 195, 200, 213, 215, 219, 220, 223, 226, 236, 239, 243, 258, 264, 274, 281, 282, 283, 284, 296, 315, 316, 321, 322, 329, 332, 334, 335, 340, 343, 344, 345, 355, 359, 361, 368, 372, 373, 380, 396, 397, 398, 399, 402, 404, 408, 412, 417, 426, 429, 460, 475, 476, 477, 482, 483, 489, 493, 495, 497, 499, 501, 504, 511, 512, 519, 521, 522, 525, 529, 533, 540, 542, 549, 551, 552, 553, 556, 561, 563, 566, 570, 572, 575, 578, 585, 606, 609, 610, 629, 640, 649, 663, 673, 676, 679, 681, 683, 688, 692, 716, 719, 727, 744, 745, 746, 753, 754, 756, 760, 766, 767, 768, 769, 770, 774, 776, 779, 786, 788, 791, 794, 807, 812, 813, 815

HEALTH ORGANIZATIONS—2, 9, 11, 12, 13, 14, 16, 17, 18, 23, 24, 27, 28, 32, 33, 34, 35, 36, 37, 39, 40, 42, 43, 44, 51, 53, 56, 57, 60, 61, 63, 65, 68, 69, 70, 72, 75, 76, 78, 80, 81, 84, 85, 86, 87, 88, 89, 91, 93, 95, 96, 98, 103, 104, 108, 109, 110, 111, 112, 113, 116, 119, 120, 121, 124, 125, 126, 127, 128, 129, 130, 134, 135, 139, 140, 143, 146, 147, 150, 151, 156, 157, 158, 162, 164, 165, 170, 171, 176, 178, 180, 181, 183, 184, 185, 186, 187, 194, 196, 197, 199, 200, 202, 208, 209, 210, 212, 214, 216, 217, 218, 219, 221, 222, 229, 230, 232, 234, 236, 241, 242, 247, 248, 250, 253, 254, 255, 257, 261, 263, 264, 265, 267, 274, 275, 276, 278, 280, 282, 283, 284, 285, 291, 292, 293, 294, 296, 299, 301, 303, 310, 312, 317, 319, 322, 324, 325, 327, 335, 336, 337, 339, 340, 341, 342, 344, 345, 346, 347, 351, 352, 356, 358, 361, 362, 363, 365, 369, 374, 375, 376, 379, 380, 382, 385, 388, 389, 391, 394, 400, 401, 411, 413, 420, 423, 424, 426, 437, 438, 439, 441, 447, 448, 449, 454, 460, 461, 462, 468, 469, 470, 471, 472, 473, 474, 475, 476, 480, 481, 484, 487, 488, 490, 491, 497, 498, 499, 501, 502, 505, 506, 507, 510, 513, 514, 520, 521, 523, 524, 526, 527, 530, 532, 534, 535, 536, 537, 539, 541, 542, 543, 545, 549, 550, 553, 554, 555, 562, 564, 565, 566, 567, 568, 569, 571, 574, 575, 579, 581, 582, 584, 586, 591, 592, 594, 597, 600, 601, 604, 606, 609, 612, 617, 620, 622, 623, 625, 627, 629, 630, 631, 632, 636, 639, 640, 643, 644, 646, 647, 651, 653, 654, 655, 656, 660, 670, 673, 678, 679, 680, 682, 683, 685, 686, 687, 692, 693, 694, 695, 702, 704, 706, 708, 709, 710, 711, 714, 717, 719, 720, 724, 728, 729, 730, 731, 732, 736, 737, 738, 740, 745, 746, 747, 748, 749, 750, 751, 752, 754, 756, 760, 761, 762, 763, 765, 766, 768, 775, 777, 779, 783, 785, 789, 790, 795, 796, 797, 799, 801, 802, 804, 806, 807, 808, 810, 811, 812

HIGHER EDUCATION—2, 6, 8, 14, 16, 18, 20, 21, 22, 24, 25, 27, 28, 29, 43, 45, 50, 52, 60, 61, 62, 65, 67, 68, 69, 74, 76, 77, 87, 98, 99, 100, 102, 118, 130, 131, 136, 141, 144, 146, 147, 148, 150, 154, 160, 170, 181, 189, 192, 198, 206, 207, 214, 222, 225, 226, 229, 231, 237, 239, 241, 242, 243, 244, 248, 251, 253, 257, 258, 260, 271, 278, 279, 280, 281, 284, 286, 300, 305, 309, 312, 316, 319, 323, 328, 333, 334, 341, 349, 360, 361, 363, 364, 365, 370, 372, 374, 375, 382, 393, 400, 401, 407, 408, 412, 415, 418, 419, 437, 438, 441, 449, 451, 452, 455, 458, 463, 467, 468, 469, 470, 477, 483, 496, 497, 508, 512, 521, 524, 528, 529, 531, 532, 536, 538, 539, 544, 548, 549, 550, 551, 553, 555, 562, 563, 567, 573, 582, 584, 585, 591, 595, 596, 607, 610, 614, 616, 617, 621, 630, 632, 639, 642, 643, 644, 646, 649, 650, 658, 661, 664, 666, 670, 674, 675, 676, 680, 681, 690, 692, 693, 702, 707, 714, 716, 729, 730, 731, 732, 738, 742, 747, 748, 752, 753, 754, 756, 757, 760, 761, 763, 767, 768, 769, 770, 773, 779, 780, 781, 783, 784, 786, 795, 798, 800, 802, 803, 809, 814, 815, 817

HOSPITALS—13, 17, 33, 35, 42, 44, 49, 68, 85, 93, 95, 100, 102, 110, 116, 126, 134, 147, 148, 149, 162, 171, 180, 189, 210, 228, 230, 231, 241, 242, 247, 253, 258, 284, 290, 312, 324, 332, 335, 336, 342, 347, 361, 363, 367, 375, 382, 400, 417, 419, 424, 449, 470, 491, 501, 502, 505, 521, 523, 526, 530, 531, 533, 536, 541, 551, 554, 567, 573, 579, 584, 591, 596, 600, 610, 622, 642, 647, 679, 685, 692, 693, 702, 707, 709, 711, 718, 719, 730, 739, 757, 760, 812

MINORITIES—11, 24, 27, 33, 34, 36, 55, 62, 65, 74, 83, 88, 89, 105, 112, 129, 131, 146, 152, 154, 162, 165, 168, 171, 174, 176, 177, 184, 188, 194, 205, 207, 215, 222, 235, 237, 239, 240, 242, 243, 245, 246, 250, 251, 256, 267, 271, 273, 288, 329, 335, 338, 346, 349, 350, 351, 355, 356, 363, 366, 368, 370, 373, 378, 382, 387, 398, 400, 401, 402, 404, 407, 409, 412, 417, 419, 420, 428, 430, 432, 436, 440, 451, 460, 463, 481, 482, 483, 497, 498, 499, 508, 510, 513, 514, 515, 518, 525, 528, 541, 542, 545, 547, 548, 556, 557, 570, 571, 575, 597, 600, 601, 610, 611, 616, 617, 636, 648, 655, 656, 664, 667, 672, 686, 694, 695, 697, 700, 702, 734, 736, 753, 755, 765, 768, 785, 803, 807, 808, 810, 812

RECREATION—1, 2, 3, 16, 18, 19, 22, 23, 28, 29, 32, 39, 41, 43, 45, 56, 57, 60, 64, 67, 68, 72, 73, 75, 77, 80, 83, 86, 93, 102, 106, 108, 109, 112, 113, 114, 116, 120, 121, 123, 125, 128, 130, 132, 133, 140, 142, 146, 147, 151, 158, 169, 175, 176, 177, 184, 189, 191, 192, 199, 203, 204, 206, 226, 229, 231, 237, 242, 248, 251, 252, 257, 261, 262, 263, 270, 271, 275, 279, 280, 284, 298, 299, 301, 304, 309, 312, 314, 319, 321, 325, 327, 330, 335, 336, 340, 343, 349, 350, 351, 359, 360, 363, 364, 365, 366, 369, 377, 390, 394, 397, 400, 403, 406, 418, 419, 424, 425, 430, 437, 438, 439, 441, 449, 454, 463, 464, 473, 475, 486, 488, 497, 500, 501, 502, 503, 505, 506, 507, 516, 521, 522, 523, 527, 529, 537, 549, 551, 555, 564, 584, 585, 586, 588, 590, 591, 594, 604, 605, 606, 617, 621, 622, 625, 631, 633, 634, 635, 643, 648, 650, 663, 665, 666, 669, 673, 675, 676, 677, 678, 681, 682, 683, 687, 690, 693, 698, 699, 702, 704, 707, 711, 715, 717, 718, 719, 721, 722, 724, 726, 732, 734, 739, 754, 756, 760, 766, 768, 779, 782, 783, 784, 785, 792, 797, 799, 800, 803, 805, 809, 812, 813

RELIGIOUS ORGANIZATIONS—2, 7, 16, 19, 21, 28, 29, 36, 41, 43, 50, 51, 54, 57, 58, 65, 71, 73, 74, 75, 85, 87, 98, 99, 101, 103, 108, 109, 113, 116, 118, 123, 129, 132, 134, 136, 137, 141, 142, 146, 147, 148, 149, 160, 162, 167, 168, 169, 171, 172, 174, 176, 180, 181, 184, 185, 189, 191, 192, 197, 199, 206, 209, 211, 216, 217, 218, 229, 230, 231, 236, 238, 242, 248, 250, 253, 254, 279, 291, 294, 302, 303, 304, 309, 316, 318, 319, 326, 327, 330, 331, 333, 335, 336, 340, 342, 343, 350, 359, 363, 364, 374, 376, 381, 394, 397, 398, 400, 401, 403, 412, 416, 418, 420, 424, 437, 438, 441, 446, 447, 453, 454, 456, 465, 470, 475, 487, 489, 497, 499, 500, 501, 505, 507, 511, 513, 514, 522, 524, 525, 526, 530, 533, 541, 544, 548, 551, 555, 562, 564, 566, 567, 572, 579, 581, 585, 586, 590, 595, 600, 605, 606, 617, 619, 622, 623, 624, 630, 631, 632, 635, 636, 643, 645, 649, 651, 653, 655, 664, 667, 674, 675, 676, 677, 678, 680, 681, 683, 687, 689, 690, 692, 693, 701, 702, 710, 714, 722, 724, 736, 752, 754, 756, 759, 760, 764, 765, 766, 767, 779, 784, 787, 800, 803, 805, 808, 809, 814

SOCIAL SERVICE ORGANIZATIONS—1, 2, 3, 4, 6, 7, 9, 11, 12, 14, 15, 16, 17, 18, 20, 23, 24, 25, 26, 28, 29, 32, 33, 35, 36, 38, 40, 42, 43, 44, 45, 48, 49, 50, 51, 53, 54, 55, 56, 57, 58, 59, 60, 61, 63, 64, 65, 66, 69, 71, 73, 75, 76, 78, 80, 81, 82, 83, 84, 85, 86, 87, 88, 89, 90, 91, 93, 95, 96, 97, 98, 99, 102, 103, 104, 105, 107, 108, 109, 110, 111, 112, 113, 115, 116, 117, 118, 119, 120, 121, 122, 123, 124, 126, 127, 128, 129, 131, 132, 133, 134, 136, 137, 138, 139, 140, 143, 144, 146, 147, 148, 149, 150, 151, 152, 155, 156, 158, 159, 160, 161, 162, 163, 164, 165, 166, 167, 168, 169, 171, 172, 173, 174, 175, 176, 178, 180, 181, 182, 183, 184, 185, 186, 187, 188, 189, 190, 191, 192, 193, 194, 195, 196, 198, 199, 200, 201, 202, 204, 205, 206, 208, 211, 212, 213, 214, 219, 220, 221, 222, 224, 228, 229, 230, 231, 232, 234, 235, 236, 237, 239, 240, 242, 244, 245, 247, 248, 249, 250, 253, 254, 255, 257, 258, 259, 260, 262, 265, 266, 267, 268, 271, 272, 273, 274, 275, 276, 277, 278, 279, 280, 281, 282, 283, 284, 285, 287, 288, 289, 292, 293, 294, 295, 296, 297, 298, 300, 301, 303, 304, 305, 306, 307, 308, 309, 310, 311, 313, 314, 317, 318, 319, 320, 321, 322, 324, 326, 328, 329, 331, 332, 335, 336, 337, 339, 340, 341, 342, 343, 344, 346, 347, 349, 350, 351, 352, 353, 354, 355, 356, 357, 358, 362, 363, 364, 365, 367, 368, 369, 371, 374, 375, 377, 382, 383, 384, 386, 387, 388, 389, 392, 393, 394, 395, 396, 397, 399, 400, 401, 402, 403, 404, 405, 407, 409, 410, 411, 413, 414, 415, 416, 417, 418, 420, 421, 422, 423, 424, 425, 426, 428, 429, 430, 431, 432, 433, 434, 435, 438, 439, 440, 442, 444, 445, 446, 447, 448, 449, 450, 451, 452, 453, 454, 456, 457, 459, 460, 461, 462, 463, 464, 466, 467, 469, 471, 472, 476, 480, 484, 486, 487, 488, 489, 492, 493, 495, 496, 497, 498, 499, 500, 501, 502, 505, 506, 507, 508, 511, 513, 514, 515, 516, 518, 520, 521, 522, 523, 524, 525, 527, 529, 531, 533, 534, 535, 536, 539, 540, 541, 542, 543, 544, 545, 549, 550, 551, 553, 554, 555, 556, 558, 559, 564, 565, 567, 568, 569, 571, 572, 573, 574, 576, 577, 578, 579, 580, 581, 583, 585, 587, 588, 589, 590, 591, 592, 593, 594, 595, 597, 599, 600, 601, 603, 606, 607, 608, 609, 610, 612, 615, 617, 618, 619, 620, 621, 622, 623, 624, 627, 629, 630, 631, 632, 633, 634, 635, 636, 637, 638, 639, 640, 641, 644, 645, 646, 647, 648, 649, 650, 651, 652, 653, 654, 655, 656, 660, 663, 665, 666, 667, 668, 669, 670, 671, 672, 673, 676, 677, 678, 680, 681, 682, 683, 684, 685, 686, 689, 690, 691, 692, 693, 694, 695, 696, 697, 698, 699, 700, 701, 702, 706, 708, 709, 710, 711, 712, 713, 715, 716, 717, 718, 719, 720, 721, 722, 724, 725, 726, 728, 729, 730, 732, 734, 735, 736, 737, 738, 739, 740, 741, 742, 743, 744, 745, 746, 747, 748, 749, 750, 751, 752, 753, 754, 756, 758, 759, 761, 762, 764, 765, 766, 767, 768, 770, 771, 772, 775, 776, 777, 778, 779, 783, 787, 789, 791, 792, 793, 795, 796, 797, 800, 801, 802, 803, 804, 805, 806, 807, 809, 810, 811, 812, 814, 815, 817

WOMEN/GIRLS—3, 5, 9, 11, 16, 18, 19, 22, 23, 24, 27, 28, 29, 30, 32, 33, 34, 36, 39, 40, 43, 45, 48, 49, 51, 54, 55, 56, 57, 60, 62, 65, 69, 73, 74, 75, 77, 81, 82, 83, 85, 86, 87, 88, 90, 93, 94, 95, 97, 98, 99, 101, 103, 106, 108, 109, 110, 112, 113, 116, 117, 118, 119, 120, 121, 125, 128, 129, 131, 132, 133, 137, 146, 147, 148, 151, 158, 165, 168, 169, 171, 172, 175, 176, 177, 180, 182, 184, 185, 189, 192, 194, 203, 204, 205, 218, 219, 221, 222, 223, 230, 231, 236, 238, 241, 242, 243, 244, 245, 246, 247, 248, 250, 251, 252, 260, 263, 264, 267, 270, 271, 274, 280, 288, 301, 303, 306, 309, 317, 318, 329, 332, 333, 334, 335, 336, 337, 340, 342, 343, 346, 347, 349, 350, 351, 356, 359, 361, 363, 364, 365, 367, 369, 377, 382, 387, 388, 397, 398, 399, 400, 402, 404, 406, 407, 409, 410, 412, 418, 419, 420, 423, 424, 425, 428, 430, 432, 433, 437, 438, 439, 440, 441, 447, 448, 449, 451, 452, 454, 461, 463, 464, 470, 473, 484, 489, 492, 496, 497, 500, 505, 506, 507, 508, 510, 511, 517, 519, 520, 521, 522, 523, 524, 527, 529, 533, 538, 540, 541, 542, 545, 546, 547, 551, 553, 555, 556, 559, 561, 564, 568, 571, 574, 577, 581, 584, 585, 586, 587, 589, 590, 591, 595, 599, 600, 601, 606, 607, 608, 609, 610, 614, 616, 617, 620, 621, 622, 623, 625, 630, 631, 632, 633, 634, 636, 638, 639, 644, 647, 648, 649, 653, 654, 655, 663, 666, 667, 668, 670, 672, 673, 675, 676, 678, 679, 680, 683, 684, 687, 690, 692, 693, 694, 696, 697, 698, 701, 702, 704, 709, 710, 718, 719, 720, 722, 724, 726, 730, 734, 736, 737, 738, 739, 742, 743, 744, 747, 749, 753, 754, 760, 761, 765, 766, 767, 768, 769, 776, 779, 782, 783, 784, 785, 790, 791, 793, 796, 799, 800, 806, 810, 811, 814